2008 Supplement

to

JUDITH AREEN & MILTON C. REGAN, JR., FAMILY LAW: CASES AND MATERIALS

FIFTH EDITION

by

MARC SPINDELMAN
Professor of Law
The Ohio State University
Moritz College of Law

and

MILTON C. REGAN, JR.
Professor of Law
Georgetown University Law Center

FOUNDATION PRESS
2008

© 2008 By THOMSON REUTERS/FOUNDATION PRESS
395 Hudson Street
New York, NY 10014
Phone Toll Free 1–877–888–1330
Fax (212) 367–6799
foundation–press.com
Printed in the United States of America

ISBN 978-1-59941-574-1

TEXT IS PRINTED ON 10% POST
CONSUMER RECYCLED PAPER

PREFACE TO THE 2008 SUPPLEMENT

This Supplement reflects a number of developments in Family Law since the Fifth Edition of the casebook. It is current through the middle of June, 2008.

We would like to thank Nat Birdsall (Michigan Law School, 2008), Brookes Hammock (Ohio State Moritz College of Law, 2010), and Catherine Perez (Georgetown University Law Center, 2009) for valuable research assistance; Kathy Hall, of the law library at Ohio State, for speedy and careful help collecting and staying on top of a sizeable range of materials, and also for organizing survey information on laws relating to same-sex marriage and same-sex relationships; Jocelyn Kennedy, of the Michigan Law Library, for help tracking down various sources; Ben McJunkin (Michigan Law School, 2009), Bluebooker extraordinaire, for backup; Ebony Mobley, of the Ohio State Moritz College of Law, for administrative support; and Dawn Parker, of the Ohio State Moritz College of Law, and Ashleigh Kenny, of The American Prospect, for help with copyright matters. We would also like to convey a special thanks to Anna Selden, of the Georgetown University Law Center, for flawless help with the detailed work of organizing the Supplement.

MARC SPINDELMAN
MILTON C. REGAN, JR.

Columbus, Ohio, and
Washington, DC

July, 2008

ACKNOWLEDGEMENT

We wish to thank *The American Prospect* for granting us permission to reprint an excerpt from Linda Hirshman, *Homeward Bound*, AM. PROSPECT, Dec. 2005, at 20.

TABLE OF CONTENTS

	Supplement Page	Casebook Page

PREFACE iii

ACKNOWLEDGMENTS v

TABLE OF CASES xi

PART I. HUSBANDS, WIVES, AND LOVERS

CHAPTER 2. Marrying 1

A. Restrictions on Who May Marry 1

  2. Traditional Restrictions 1

    c. Polygamy 1

      In re Steed 1 108

      Note 8

    d. Same-Sex Marriage 10

      In re Marriage Cases 10 119

      National Pride at Work, Inc. v. Governor

        of Michigan 30

      Note 41 119

      Note 41 120

      Note 42 121

CHAPTER 3. Marriage 43

C. Challenges to the Traditional Marriage Model 43

  2. Reallocation of Duties Within Marriage 43

    b. By Public Policy 43

    (2) . . . and the Nurturing Husband 43

      Note 43 232

      Linda Hirshman, *Homeward Bound* 43 237

      Note 49 237

	Supplement Page	Casebook Page
CHAPTER 3. Marriage (cont'd) 43		
D. Encroachments on the Doctrine of		
Family Privacy 50		
1. The Constitutional Right to Privacy 50		
Note..50		281
2. Domestic Violence..................................50		
c. Legal Responses to Violence 50		
(2) Mandatory Arrest Policy 50		
Note..50		345
CHAPTER 5. Custody of Children 51		
D. Applying the Best Interest Standard 51		
4. Religion..51		
Shepp v. Shepp 51		554
Note..62		
F. Modification 63		
2. Relocation 63		
Maynard v. McNett 63		609
G. Visitation..69		
LeClair v. Reed ex. rel. Reed 69		617
I. Unmarried Persons 74		
2. Couples 74		
A.H. v. M.P. 74		663
J. Jurisdiction 82		
2. International Custody Disputes 82		
Alonzo v. Claudino..................................82		682

	Supplement Page	Casebook Page
CHAPTER 6. Property, Alimony, and Child Support Awards **89**		
A. Property Division.............................89	89	
2. Distinguishing Marital from Separate Property. 89		
In re Marriage of Brown 89		709
4. Financial Misconduct 96		
Gershman v. Gershman 96		723
F. Child Support 102		
2. Modification 102		
Davis v. Knafel. 102		809
4. Unmarried Partners 110		
Dubay v. Wells...........................110		817
I. The Separation Agreement.................117		
Richardson v. Richardson................117		861
PART II. CHILDREN, PARENTS, AND THE STATE		
CHAPTER 7. Procreation...................123		
A. Voluntary Limits on Reproduction.......123		
3. Abortion..................................123		
Gonzalez v. Carhart......................123		916
Note..141		
C. Involuntary Limits on Reproduction.....142		
2. Indirect Restrictions....................142		
North Coast Women's Health Care Medical Group v. Superior Court...............142		954
Note..146		
D. Problems Posed by New Reproductive Techniques.......................................155		
Note..155		1016

	Supplement Page	Casebook Page
CHAPTER 8. Parents and Children 156		
B. Encroachments on the Doctrine of Family Privacy 156		
3. Criminal Law 156		
State v. Gewily 156		1047
CHAPTER 9. Growing up in the Law 164		
E. Age and Criminal Law 164		
State ex rel. Z.C. 164		1179
CHAPTER 10. Child Abuse and Neglect 171		
A. What Should the Standards Be for Intervening Between Parent and Child? 171		
2. Defining Child Neglect 171		
a. Standard 171		
In re Brittany T. 171		1222
Note 183		
C. Foster Care 184		
4. Liability 184		
Gomes v. Wood 184		1303
CHAPTER 11. Adoption 199		
C. Standards 199		
3. Sexual Orientation 199		
Finstuen v. Crutcher 199		1384
INDEX I-1		

TABLE OF CASES

Principal cases are in bold type. Non-principal cases are in ordinary roman type. References are to pages.

A.H. v. M.P., 857 N.E.2d 1061 (Mass. 2006), **74**

Alonzo v. Claudino, No. 1:06CV00800, 2007 WL 475340 (M.D.N.C. Feb. 9, 2007), **82**

Brittany T., *In re*, 835 N.Y.S.2d 829 (Fam. Ct. 2007), **171**

Brittany T., *In re*, 852 N.Y.S.2d 475 (App. Div. 2008), 183

Carswell, State v., 871 N.E.2d 547 (Ohio 2007), 41

Davis v. Knafel, 837 N.E.2d 585 (Ind. App. 2005), **102**

Dubay v. Wells, 506 F.3d 422 (6th Cir. 2007), **110**

Finstuen v. Crutcher, 496 F.3d 1139 (10th Cir. 2007), **199**

Gershman v. Gershman, 943 A.2d 1091 (Conn. 2008), **96**

Gewily, State v., 911 A.2d 293 (Conn. 2006), **156**

Gomes v. Wood, 451 F.3d 1122 (10th Cir. 2006), **184**

Gonzales v. Carhart, 550 U.S. ___, 127 S. Ct. 1610 (2007), 50, **123**, 141

Herring v. Richmond Med. Ctr. For Women, 550 U.S. ___, 127 S. Ct. 2094 (2007), 141

***In re* (see name of party)**

LeClair v. Reed *ex rel.* Reed, 939 A.2d 466 (Vt. 2007), **69**

Marriage Cases, *In re*, 183 P.3d 384 (Cal. 2008), **10**, 154 n.*

Marriage of Brown, *In re*, 183 P.3d 207 (Or. Ct. App. 2008), **89**

Maynard v. McNett, 710 N.W.2d 369 (N.D. 2006), **63**

Nat'l Pride at Work, Inc. v. Governor of Mich., 748 N.W.2d 524 (Mich. 2008), **30**

N. Coast Women's Care Med. Group v. Super. Ct., 40 Cal. Rptr. 3d 636 (Ct. App. 2006), **142**, 155

Richardson v. Richardson, 218 S.W.3d 426 (Mo. 2007), **117**

Richmond Med. Ctr. For Women v. Hicks, 409 F.3d 619 (4th Cir. 2005), 141

Richmond Med. Ctr. For Women v. Herring, 527 F.3d 128 (4th Cir. 2008), 142

Steed, *In re,* No. 03-08-00235-CV,
    2008 WL 2132014 (Tex. App.
    May 22, 2008), **1**

Shepp v. Shepp, 906 A.2d 1165
    (Pa. 2006), **51**

State *ex rel.* _____ v. _____ (see
    opposing party and relator)

State v. _____ (see opposing
    party)

Tex. Dep't of Family & Protective
    Servs., *In re,* No. 08-0391,
    2008 WL 2212383 (Tex. May
    29, 2008), 8, 8-10, 62

Tex. Dep't of Family & Protective
    Servs., *In re,* No. 08-0403,
    2008 WL 2212939 (Tex. May
    29, 2008), 8

Z.C., State *ex rel.,* 165 P.3d 1206
    (Utah 2007), **164**

CHAPTER 2: MARRYING

A. Restrictions on Who May Marry
2. Traditional Restrictions
c. Polygamy

Page 108. Add after *Sanderson v. Tryon*:

In re Steed

Texas Court of Appeals, 2008.
2008 WL 2132014.

■ PER CURIAM.

This original mandamus proceeding involves the temporary custody of a number of children who were removed from their homes on an emergency basis from the Yearning For Zion ranch outside of Eldorado, Texas.[1] The ranch is associated with the Fundamentalist Church of Jesus Christ of Latter-Day Saints (FLDS), and a number of families live there. Relators are thirty-eight women who were living at the ranch and had children taken into custody on an emergency basis by the Texas Department of Family and Protective Services based on allegations by the Department that there was immediate danger to the physical health or safety of the children.

Relators seek a writ of mandamus requiring the district court to vacate its temporary orders in which it named the Department the temporary sole managing conservator of their children. Relators complain that the Department failed to meet its burden under section 262.201 of the Texas Family Code to demonstrate (1) that there was a danger to the physical health or safety of their children, (2) that there was an urgent need for protection of the children that required the immediate removal of the children from their parents, or (3) that the Department made reasonable efforts to eliminate or prevent the children's removal from their parents.

---

[1] The Department removed over 450 children from their homes on the Yearning For Zion ranch over the course of three days. This proceeding does not involve parents of all of the children removed.

Tex. Fam. Code Ann. § 262.201 (West Supp. 2007). Without such proof, Relators argue, the district court was required to return the children to their parents and abused its discretion by failing to do so.

Removing children from their homes and parents on an emergency basis before fully litigating the issue of whether the parents should continue to have custody of the children is an extreme measure. It is, unfortunately, sometimes necessary for the protection of the children involved. However, it is a step that the legislature has provided may be taken only when the circumstances indicate a danger to the physical health and welfare of the children and the need for protection of the children is so urgent that immediate removal of the children from the home is necessary. *See id.*[4]

Section 262.201 further requires the Department, when it has taken children into custody on an emergency basis, to make a showing of specific circumstances that justify keeping the children in the Department's temporary custody pending full litigation of the question of permanent custody. Unless there is sufficient evidence to demonstrate the existence of each of the requirements of section 262.201(b), the court

---

[4] Section 262.201 provides, in relevant part, as follows: [] (a) Unless the child has already been returned to the parent, managing conservator, possessory conservator, guardian, caretaker, or custodian entitled to possession and the temporary order, if any, has been dissolved, a full adversary hearing shall be held not later than the 14th day after the date the child was taken into possession by the governmental entity. [] (b) At the conclusion of the full adversary hearing, the court shall order the return of the child to the parent, managing conservator, possessory conservator, guardian, caretaker, or custodian entitled to possession unless the court finds sufficient evidence to satisfy a person of ordinary prudence and caution that: [] (1) there was a danger to the physical health or safety of the child which was caused by an act or failure to act of the person entitled to possession and for the child to remain in the home is contrary to the welfare of the child; [] (2) the urgent need for protection required the immediate removal of the child and reasonable efforts, consistent with the circumstances and providing for the safety of the child, were made to eliminate or prevent the child's removal; and [] (3) reasonable efforts have been made to enable the child to return home, but there is a substantial risk of a continuing danger if the child is returned home. . . . . [] (d) In determining whether there is a continuing danger to the physical health or safety of the child, the court may consider whether the household to which the child would be returned includes a person who: [] (1) has abused or neglected another child in a manner that caused serious injury to or the death of the other child; or [] (2) has sexually abused another child. [] Tex. Fam. Code Ann. § 262.201 (West Supp. 2007).

is required to return the children to the custody of their parents. Tex. Fam. Code Ann. § 262.201(b).

In this case, the Department relied on the following evidence with respect to the children taken into custody from the Yearning For Zion ranch to satisfy the requirements of section 262.201:

- Interviews with investigators revealed a pattern of girls reporting that "there was no age too young for girls to be married";

- Twenty females living at the ranch had become pregnant between the ages of thirteen and seventeen;

- Five of the twenty females identified as having become pregnant between the ages of thirteen and seventeen are alleged to be minors, the other fifteen are now adults;

- Of the five minors who became pregnant, four are seventeen and one is sixteen, and all five are alleged to have become pregnant at the age of fifteen or sixteen;[5]

- The Department's lead investigator was of the opinion that due to the "pervasive belief system" of the FLDS, the male children are groomed to be perpetrators of sexual abuse and the girls are raised to be victims of sexual abuse;

- All 468 children[6] were removed from the ranch under the theory that the ranch community was "essentially one household comprised of extended family subgroups" with a single, common belief system and there was reason to believe that a child had been sexually abused in the ranch "household"; and

- Department witnesses expressed the opinion that there is a "pervasive belief system" among the residents of the ranch that it is acceptable for girls to marry, engage in sex, and bear children as soon as they reach

---

[5] One woman is alleged to have become pregnant at the age of thirteen. She is now twenty-two years old.

[6] This number has fluctuated. It will likely continue to fluctuate somewhat as disputes regarding the age of certain persons taken into custody are resolved.

puberty, and that this "pervasive belief system" poses a danger to the children.

In addition, the record demonstrates the following facts, which are undisputed by the Department:

• The only danger to the male children or the female children who had not reached puberty identified by the Department was the Department's assertion that the "pervasive belief system" of the FLDS community groomed the males to be perpetrators of sexual abuse later in life and taught the girls to submit to sexual abuse after reaching puberty;

• There was no evidence that the male children, or the female children who had not reached puberty, were victims of sexual or other physical abuse or in danger of being victims of sexual or other physical abuse;

• While there was evidence that twenty females had become pregnant between the ages of thirteen and seventeen, there was no evidence regarding the marital status of these girls when they became pregnant or the circumstances under which they became pregnant other than the general allegation that the girls were living in an FLDS community with a belief system that condoned underage marriage and sex;[7]

• There was no evidence that any of the female children other than the five identified as having become pregnant between the ages of fifteen and seventeen were victims or potential victims of sexual or other physical abuse;

• With the exception of the five female children identified as having become pregnant between the ages of fifteen and seventeen, there was no evidence of any physical abuse or harm to any other child;

• The Relators have identified their children among the 468 taken into custody by the Department, and none of the Relators' children are

---

[7] Under Texas law, it is not sexual assault to have consensual sexual intercourse with a minor spouse to whom one is legally married. Tex. Penal Code Ann. § 22.011(a), (c)(1), (2) (West Supp. 2007). Texas law allows minors to marry—as young as age sixteen with parental consent and younger than sixteen if pursuant to court order. Tex. Fam. Code Ann. § 2.101 (West 2006), §§ 2.102-.103 (West Supp. 2007). A person may not be legally married to more than one person. Tex. Penal Code Ann. § 25.01 (West Supp. 2007).

among the five the Department has identified as being pregnant minors; and

• The Department conceded at the hearing that teenage pregnancy, by itself, is not a reason to remove children from their home and parents, but took the position that immediate removal was necessary in this case because "there is a mindset that even the young girls report that they will marry at whatever age, and that it's the highest blessing they can have to have children."

The Department argues that the fact that there are five minor females living in the ranch community who became pregnant at ages fifteen and sixteen together with the FLDS belief system condoning underage marriage and pregnancy indicates that there is a danger to all of the children that warrants their immediate removal from their homes and parents, and that the need for protection of the children is urgent.[8] The Department also argues that the "household" to which the children would be returned includes persons who have sexually abused another child, because the entire Yearning For Zion ranch community is a "household." *See id.* § 262.201(d)(2).

The Department failed to carry its burden with respect to the requirements of section 262.201(b). Pursuant to section 262.201(b)(1), the danger must be to the *physical* health or safety of the child. The Department did not present any evidence of danger to the physical health or safety of any male children or any female children who had not reached puberty. Nor did the Department offer any evidence that any of Relators' pubescent female children were in physical danger other than that those children live at the ranch among a group of people who have a "pervasive system of belief" that condones polygamous marriage and underage females having children.[9] The existence of the FLDS belief

---

[8] The Department's position was stated succinctly by its lead investigator at the hearing. In response to an inquiry as to why the infants needed to be removed from their mothers, the investigator responded, "[W]hat I have found is that they're living under an umbrella of belief that having children at a young age is a blessing therefore any child in that environment would not be safe."

[9] The Department's witnesses conceded that there are differences of opinion among the FLDS community as to what is an appropriate age to marry, how many spouses to have,

system as described by the Department's witnesses, by itself, does not put children of FLDS parents in physical danger. It is the imposition of certain alleged tenets of that system on specific individuals that may put them in physical danger. The Department failed to offer any evidence that any of the pubescent female children of the Relators were in such physical danger. The record is silent as to whether the Relators or anyone in their households are likely to subject their pubescent female children to underage marriage or sex. The record is also silent as to how many of Relators' children are pubescent females and whether there is any risk to them other than that they live in a community where there is a "pervasive belief system" that condones marriage and child-rearing as soon as females reach puberty.

The Department also failed to establish that the need for protection of the Relators' children was urgent and required immediate removal of the children. As previously noted, none of the identified minors who are or have been pregnant are children of Relators. There is no evidence that any of the five pregnant minors live in the same household as the Relators' children.[10] There is no evidence that Relators have allowed or are going to allow any of their minor female children to be subjected to any sexual or physical abuse. There is simply no evidence specific to Relators' children at all except that they exist, they were taken into custody at the Yearning For Zion ranch, and they are living with people who share a "pervasive belief system" that condones underage marriage and underage pregnancy. Even if one views the FLDS belief system as creating a danger of sexual abuse by grooming boys to be perpetrators of sexual abuse and raising girls to be victims of sexual abuse as the Department contends, there is no evidence that this danger is "immediate" or "urgent" as contemplated by section 262.201 with

---

and when to start having children—much as there are differences of opinion regarding the details of religious doctrine among other religious groups.

[10] The notion that the entire ranch community constitutes a "household" as contemplated by section 262.201 and justifies removing all children from the ranch community if there even is one incident of suspected child sexual abuse is contrary to the evidence. The Department's witnesses acknowledged that the ranch community was divided into separate family groups and separate households. While there was evidence that the living arrangements on the ranch are more communal than most typical neighborhoods, the evidence was not legally or factually sufficient to support a theory that the entire ranch community was a "household" under section 262.201.

respect to every child in the community. The legislature has required that there be evidence to support a finding that there is a danger to the physical health or safety of the children in question and that the need for protection is *urgent* and warrants *immediate* removal. *Id.* § 262.201(b). Evidence that children raised in this particular environment may someday have their physical health and safety threatened is not evidence that the danger is imminent enough to warrant invoking the extreme measure of immediate removal prior to full litigation of the issue as required by section 262.201.

Finally, there was no evidence that the Department made reasonable efforts to eliminate or prevent the removal of any of Relators' children. The evidence is that the Department went to the Yearning For Zion ranch to investigate a distress call from a sixteen year-old girl.[12] After interviewing a number of children, they concluded that there were five minors who were or had been pregnant and that the belief system of the community allowed minor females to marry and bear children. They then removed all of the children in the community (including infants) from their homes and ultimately separated the children from their parents. This record does not reflect any reasonable effort on the part of the Department to ascertain if some measure short of removal and/or separation from parents would have eliminated the risk the Department perceived with respect to any of the children of Relators.

We find that the Department did not carry its burden of proof under section 262.201. The evidence adduced at the hearing held April 17-18, 2008, was legally and factually insufficient to support the findings required by section 262.201 to maintain custody of Relators' children with the Department. Consequently, the district court abused its discretion in failing to return the Relators' children to the Relators. The Relators' Petition for Writ of Mandamus is conditionally granted. The district court is directed to vacate its temporary orders granting sole managing conservatorship of the children of the Relators to the Department. The writ will issue only if the district court fails to comply with this opinion.

---

[12] The authenticity of this call is in doubt. Department investigators did not locate the caller on the ranch.

NOTE:

1. In an opinion dated May 29, 2008, the Texas Supreme Court refused "to disturb the court of appeals' decision." In re Texas Dep't of Family and Protective Servs., No. 08-0391, 2008 WL 2212383, at *2 (Tex. Sup. Ct. May 29, 2008) (per curiam); see also In re Texas Department of Family and Protective Servs., No. 08-0403, 2008 WL 2212939 (Tex. Sup. Ct. May 29, 2008) (per curiam). According to the concurring and dissenting opinion by Justice Harriett O'Neill:

> In this case, the Department of Family and Protective Services presented evidence that "there was a danger to the physical health or safety" of pubescent girls on the Yearning for Zion (YFZ) Ranch from a pattern or practice of sexual abuse, that "the urgent need for protection required the immediate removal" of those girls, and that the Department made reasonable efforts, considering the obstacles to information-gathering that were presented, to prevent removal and return those children home. Tex. Fam. Code § 262.201(b)(1)-(3). As to this endangered population, I do not agree with the Court that the trial court abused its discretion in allowing the Department to retain temporary conservatorship until such time as a permanency plan designed to ensure each girl's physical health and safety could be approved. *See id.* §§ 263.101-.102. On this record, however, I agree that there was no evidence of imminent "danger to the physical health or safety" of boys and pre-pubescent girls to justify their removal from the YFZ Ranch, and to this extent I join the Court's opinion. *Id.* § 262.201(b)(1).

> Evidence presented in the trial court indicated that the Department began its investigation of the YFZ Ranch on March 29th, when it received a report of sexual abuse of a sixteen-year-old girl on the property. On April 3rd, the Department entered the Ranch along with law-enforcement personnel and conducted nineteen interviews of girls aged seventeen or under, as well as fifteen to twenty interviews of adults. In the course of these interviews, the Department learned there were many polygamist families living on the Ranch; a number of girls under the age of eighteen living on the Ranch were pregnant or had given birth; both interviewed girls and adults considered no age too young for a girl to be "spiritually" married; and the Ranch's religious leader, "Uncle Merrill," had the unilateral power to decide when and to whom they would be married. Additionally, in the trial court, the Department presented "Bishop's Records"—documents seized from the Ranch—indicating the presence of several extremely young

mothers or pregnant "wives"[1] on the Ranch: a sixteen-year-old "wife" with a child, a sixteen-year-old pregnant "wife," two pregnant fifteen-year-old "wives," and a thirteen-year-old who had conceived a child. The testimony of Dr. William John Walsh, the families' expert witness, confirmed that the Fundamentalist Church of Jesus Christ of Latter Day Saints accepts the age of "physical development" (that is, first menstruation) as the age of eligibility for "marriage." Finally, child psychologist Dr. Bruce Duncan Perry testified that the pregnancy of the underage children on the Ranch was the result of sexual abuse because children of the age of fourteen, fifteen, or sixteen are not sufficiently emotionally mature to enter a healthy consensual sexual relationship or a "marriage."

Evidence presented thus indicated a pattern or practice of sexual abuse of pubescent girls, and the condoning of such sexual abuse, on the Ranch[2]—evidence sufficient to satisfy a "person of ordinary prudence and caution" that other such girls were at risk of sexual abuse as well. *Id.* § 262.201(b). This evidence supports the trial court's finding that "there was a danger to the physical health or safety" of pubescent girls on the Ranch. *Id.* § 262.201(b)(1)[.] Thus, [as to these girls,] the trial court did not abuse its discretion in finding that the Department met section 262.201(b)(1)'s requirements.

---

[1] Although referred to as "wives" in the Bishop's Records, these underage girls are not legally married; rather, the girls are "spiritually" married to their husbands, typically in polygamous households with multiple other "spiritual" wives. Subject to limited defenses, a person who "engages in sexual contact" with a child younger than seventeen who is not his *legal* spouse is guilty of a sexual offense under the Texas Penal Code. *See* Tex. Penal Code § 21.11(a)–(b). Those who promote or assist such sexual contact, *see id.* § 7.02(a)(2), or cause the child to engage in sexual contact, *see id.* § 21.11(a)(1), may also be criminally liable.

[2] The Family Code defines "abuse" to include "sexual conduct harmful to a child's mental, emotional, or physical welfare"—including offenses under section 21.11 of the Penal Code—as well as "failure to make a reasonable effort to prevent sexual conduct harmful to a child." Tex. Fam. Code § 261.001(1)(E)–(F). In determining whether there is a "continuing danger to the health or safety" of a child, the Family Code explicitly permits a court to consider "whether the household to which the child would be returned includes a person who . . . has sexually abused another child." Id. § 262.201(d).

In re Texas Dep't of Family and Protective Services, No. 08-0391, 2008 WL 2212383, at *2 (Tex. Sup. Ct., May 29, 2008) (O'Neill, J., concurring in part and dissenting in part).

d. Same-Sex Marriage

Page 119. Add after *Goodridge v. Department of Pub. Health*:

In re Marriage Cases

California Supreme Court, 2008.
183 P.3d 384.

■ GEORGE, C.J.

. . . The present proceeding . . . squarely presents the substantive constitutional question [of the validity of the California marriage statutes].

. . . The legal issue we must resolve is . . . whether our state Constitution prohibits the state from establishing a statutory scheme in which both opposite-sex and same-sex couples are granted the right to enter into an officially recognized family relationship that affords all of the significant legal rights and obligations traditionally associated under state law with the institution of marriage, but under which the union of an opposite-sex couple is officially designated a "marriage" whereas the union of a same-sex couple is officially designated a "domestic partnership." The question we must address is whether, under these circumstances, the failure to designate the official relationship of same-sex couples as marriage violates the California Constitution.

. . . Whatever our views as individuals with regard to this question as a matter of policy, we recognize as judges and as a court our responsibility to limit our consideration of the question to a determination of the constitutional validity of the current legislative provisions.

. . . .

III

We now turn to the significant substantive constitutional issues before us. We begin by examining the relevant California statutory provisions relating to marriage and domestic partnership that lie at the heart of this controversy.

[The court explains its view that the statutory limitations on marriage to man and woman, see Family Code 300 and Family Code 308.5,[*] as well as the statutory provisions recognizing domestic partnership benefits for same-sex couples, embodied in the California Domestic Partner Rights and Responsibilities Act of 2003, as amended, are relevant and "must be considered in determining whether the challenged provisions of the marriage statutes violate the constitutional rights of same-sex couples guaranteed by the California Constitution."]

IV

. . . .

A

Although our state Constitution does not contain any explicit reference to a "right to marry," past California cases establish beyond question that the right to marry is a fundamental right whose protection is guaranteed to all persons by the California Constitution. The United States Supreme Court initially discussed the constitutional right to marry as an aspect of the fundamental substantive "liberty" protected by the due process clause of the federal Constitution[,] see *Meyer v. Nebraska*, 262 U.S. 390, 399 (1923), but thereafter in *Griswold v. Connecticut*, 381 U.S. 479 (1965), the federal high court additionally identified the right to marry as a component of a "right of privacy" protected by the federal Constitution. *Griswold,* at p. 486. With California's adoption in 1972 of

---

[*] [Ed. Family Code section 300, subdivision (a), provides in relevant part: "Marriage is a personal relation arising out of a civil contract between a man and woman, to which the consent of the parties capable of making that contract is necessary." Family Code section 308.5, the result of a voter initiative known as "Proposition 22," provides in full: "Only marriage between a man and a woman is valid or recognized in California."]

a constitutional amendment explicitly adding "privacy" to the "inalienable rights" of all Californians protected by article I, section 1 of the California Constitution—an amendment whose history demonstrates that it was intended, among other purposes, to encompass the federal constitutional right of privacy, "particularly as it developed beginning with *Griswold v. Connecticut*[*, supra,*] 381 U.S. 479[,]" *Hill v. National Collegiate Athletic Assn.*, 7 Cal.4th 1, 28 (1994)—the state constitutional right to marry, while presumably still embodied as a component of the liberty protected by the state due process clause, now also clearly falls within the reach of the constitutional protection afforded to an individual's interest in personal autonomy by California's explicit state constitutional privacy clause.

Although all parties in this proceeding agree that the right to marry constitutes a fundamental right protected by the state Constitution, there is considerable disagreement as to the scope and content of this fundamental state constitutional right. . . .

Plaintiffs challenge the . . . characterization of the constitutional right they seek to invoke as the right to same-sex marriage, and on this point we agree[.] . . . In *Perez v. Sharp*, 32 Cal.2d 711 (1948)—this court's 1948 decision holding that the California statutory provisions prohibiting interracial marriage were unconstitutional—the court . . . focused on the *substance* of the constitutional right at issue—that is, the importance to an individual of the freedom "to join in marriage *with the person of one's choice*"—in determining whether the statute impinged upon the plaintiffs' fundamental constitutional right. . . .

       . . . .

In discussing the constitutional right to marry in *Perez v. Sharp*, *supra*, 32 Cal.2d 711, then[-]Justice Traynor in the lead opinion quoted the seminal passage from the United States Supreme Court's decision in *Meyer v. Nebraska*, *supra*. There the high court, in describing the scope of the "liberty" protected by the due process clause of the federal Constitution, stated that "'[w]ithout doubt, it denotes not merely freedom from bodily restraint, but also the right of the individual to contract, to engage in any of the common occupations of life, to acquire useful knowledge, *to marry, establish a home and bring up children*, to worship God according to the dictates of one's own conscience, *and, generally, to enjoy those privileges long recognized at common law as essential to the orderly pursuit of happiness by free men."* *Perez, supra,* 32 Cal.2d at p. 714 (italics added ["to marry" italicized by *Perez*], quoting *Meyer, supra,* 262 U.S. 390, 399). The *Perez* decision continued: *"Marriage is thus something more than a civil contract subject to regulation by the state; it is a fundamental right of free men."* *Perez, supra,* 32 Cal.2d at p. 714 (italics added).

Like *Perez,* subsequent California decisions discussing the nature of marriage and the right to marry have recognized repeatedly the linkage between marriage, establishing a home, and raising children in identifying civil marriage as the means available to an individual to establish, with a loved one of his or her choice, an officially recognized *family* relationship. . . .

. . . .

As . . . many . . . California decisions make clear, the right to marry represents the right of an individual to establish a legally recognized family with the person of one's choice, and, as such, is of fundamental significance both to society and to the individual.

. . . .

In light of the fundamental nature of the substantive rights embodied in the right to marry—and their central importance to an individual's opportunity to live a happy, meaningful, and satisfying life as a full member of society—the California Constitution properly must be interpreted to guarantee this basic civil right to *all* individuals and couples, without regard to their sexual orientation.

. . . .

. . . Thus, just as this court recognized in *Perez* that it was not constitutionally permissible to continue to treat racial or ethnic minorities as inferior[,] . . . we now similarly recognize that an individual's homosexual orientation is not a constitutionally legitimate basis for withholding or restricting the individual's legal rights.

In light of this recognition, sections 1 and 7 of article I of the California Constitution cannot properly be interpreted to withhold from gay individuals the same basic civil right of personal autonomy and liberty (including the right to establish, with the person of one's choice, an officially recognized and sanctioned family) that the California Constitution affords to heterosexual individuals. The privacy and due process provisions of our state Constitution—in declaring that "[a]ll people . . . have [the] inalienable right[] [of] privacy[,]" art. I, § 1[,] and that no person may be deprived of "liberty" without due process of law[,] art. I, § 7—do not purport to reserve to persons of a particular sexual orientation the substantive protection afforded by those provisions. In light of the evolution of our state's understanding concerning the equal dignity and respect to which all persons are entitled without regard to their sexual orientation, it is not appropriate to interpret these provisions in a way that, as a practical matter, excludes gay individuals from the protective reach of such basic civil rights.

. . . .

The Proposition 22 Legal Defense [and Education] Fund and the Campaign [for California Families] . . . contend that the only family that possibly can be encompassed by the constitutional right to marry is a family headed by a man and a woman. Pointing out that past cases often have linked marriage and procreation, these parties argue that because only a man and a woman can produce children biologically with one another, the constitutional right to marry necessarily is limited to opposite-sex couples.

This contention is fundamentally flawed for a number of reasons. To begin with, although the legal institution of civil marriage may well have originated in large part to promote a stable relationship for the procreation and raising of children, and although the right to marry and to procreate often are treated as closely related aspects of the privacy and liberty interests protected by the state and federal Constitutions, the constitutional right to marry never has been viewed as the sole preserve of individuals who are physically capable of having children. . . . Thus, although an important purpose underlying marriage may be to channel procreation into a stable family relationship, that purpose cannot be viewed as limiting the constitutional right to marry to couples who are capable of biologically producing a child together.

. . . .

Furthermore, although promoting and facilitating a stable environment for the procreation and raising of children is unquestionably one of the vitally important purposes underlying the institution of marriage and the constitutional right to marry, past cases make clear that this right is not confined to, or restrictively defined by, that purpose alone. . . . [O]ur past cases have recognized that the right to marry is the right to enter into a relationship that is "the center of the personal affections that ennoble and enrich human life"—a relationship that is "at once the most socially productive and individually fulfilling relationship that one can enjoy in the course of a lifetime." . . . Accordingly, this right cannot properly be defined by or limited to the state's interest in fostering a favorable environment for the procreation and raising of children.

. . . .

. . . [W]e conclude that the right to marry, as embodied in article I, sections 1 and 7 of the California Constitution, guarantees same-sex couples the same substantive constitutional rights as opposite-sex couples to choose one's life partner and enter with that person into a committed, officially recognized, and protected family relationship that enjoys all of the constitutionally based incidents of marriage.[52]

---

[52] We emphasize that our conclusion that the constitutional right to marry properly must be interpreted to apply to gay individuals and gay couples does not mean that this constitutional right similarly must be understood to extend to polygamous or incestuous relationships. Past judicial decisions explain why our nation's culture has considered the latter types of relationships inimical to the mutually supportive and healthy family relationships promoted by the constitutional right to marry. Although the historic disparagement of and discrimination against gay individuals and gay couples clearly is no longer constitutionally permissible, the state continues to have a strong and adequate justification for refusing to officially sanction polygamous or incestuous relationships because of their potentially detrimental effect on a sound family environment. Thus, our conclusion that it is improper to interpret the state constitutional right to marry as inapplicable to gay individuals or couples does not affect the constitutional validity of the existing legal prohibitions against polygamy and the marriage of close relatives.

B

The Attorney General, in briefing before this court, argues that even if, as we have concluded, the state constitutional right to marry extends to same-sex couples as well as to opposite-sex couples, the current California statutes do not violate the fundamental rights of same-sex couples, "because all of the personal and dignity interests that have traditionally informed the right to marry have been given to same-sex couples through the Domestic Partner Act." Maintaining that "under the domestic partnership system, the word 'marriage' is all that the state is denying to registered domestic partners," the Attorney General asserts that "[t]he fundamental right to marry can no more be the basis for same-sex couples to compel the state to denominate their committed relationships 'marriage' than it could be the basis for anyone to prevent the state legislature from changing the name of the marital institution itself to 'civil unions.'" Accordingly, the Attorney General argues that in light of the rights afforded to same-sex couples by the Domestic Partner Act, the current California statutes cannot be found to violate the right of same-sex couples to marry.

We have no occasion in this case to determine whether the state constitutional right to marry necessarily affords all couples the constitutional right to require the state to designate their official family relationship a "marriage," or whether, as the Attorney General suggests, the Legislature would not violate a couple's constitutional right to marry if—perhaps in order to emphasize and clarify that this civil institution is distinct from the religious institution of marriage—it were to assign a name other than marriage as the official designation of the family relationship for *all* couples. The current California statutes, of course, do not assign a name other than marriage for *all* couples, but instead reserve exclusively to opposite-sex couples the traditional designation of marriage, and assign a different designation—domestic partnership—to the only official family relationship available to same-sex couples.

Whether or not the name "marriage," in the abstract, is considered a core element of the state constitutional right to marry, one of the core elements of this fundamental right is the right of same-sex couples to have their official family relationship accorded the same dignity, respect, and stature as that accorded to all other officially recognized family relationships. The current statutes—by drawing a distinction between the name assigned to the family relationship available to opposite-sex couples and the name assigned to the family relationship available to same-sex couples, and by reserving the historic and highly respected designation of marriage exclusively to opposite-sex couples while offering same-sex couples only the new and unfamiliar designation of domestic partnership—pose a serious risk of denying the official family relationship of same-sex couples the equal dignity and respect that is a core element of the constitutional right to marry. As observed . . . at oral argument, this court's conclusion in *Perez, supra*, 32 Cal.2d 711, that the statutory provision barring interracial marriage was unconstitutional, undoubtedly would have been the same even if alternative nomenclature, such as "transracial union," had been made available to interracial couples.

Accordingly, . . . we conclude that the current statutory assignment of different designations to the official family relationship of opposite-sex couples and of same-sex couples properly must be viewed as potentially impinging upon the state constitutional right of same-sex couples to marry.

V

The current statutory assignment of different names for the official family relationships of opposite-sex couples on the one hand, and of same-sex couples on the other, raises constitutional concerns not only in the context of the state constitutional right to marry, but also under the state constitutional equal protection clause. Plaintiffs contend that by permitting only opposite-sex couples to enter into a relationship designated as a "marriage," and by designating as a "domestic partnership" the parallel relationship into which same-sex couples may enter, the statutory scheme impermissibly denies same-sex couples the equal protection of the laws, guaranteed by article I, section 7, of the California Constitution. The relevant California statutes clearly treat opposite-sex and same-sex couples differently in this respect, and the initial question we must consider in addressing the equal protection issue is the standard of review that should be applied in evaluating this distinction.

. . . .

Plaintiffs maintain, on three separate grounds, that strict scrutiny is the standard that should be applied in this case, contending the distinctions drawn by the statutes between opposite-sex and same-sex couples (1) discriminate on the basis of sex (that is, gender), (2) discriminate on the basis of sexual orientation, and (3) impinge upon a fundamental right. We discuss each of these three claims in turn.

A

Plaintiffs initially contend that the relevant California statutes, by drawing a distinction between couples consisting of a man and a woman and couples consisting of two persons of the same sex or gender, discriminate on the basis of sex and for that reason should be subjected to strict scrutiny under the state equal protection clause. Although the governing California cases long have established that statutes that discriminate on the basis of sex or gender are subject to strict scrutiny under the California Constitution[,] see, e.g., *Catholic Charities of Sacramento, Inc. v. Superior Court*, 32 Cal.4th 527, 564 [(2004)]; *Sail'er Inn* [*Inc. v. Kirby*], 5 Cal.3d 1, 17-20 [(1971)], we conclude that the challenged statutes cannot properly be viewed as discriminating on the basis of sex or gender for purposes of the California equal protection clause.

In drawing a distinction between opposite-sex couples and same-sex couples, the challenged marriage statutes do not treat men and women differently.   Persons of either gender are treated equally and are permitted to marry only a person of the opposite gender. In light of the equality of treatment between genders, the distinction prescribed by the relevant statutes plainly does not constitute discrimination on the basis of sex as that concept is commonly understood.

. . . .

. . . [P]ast judicial decisions, in California and elsewhere, virtually uniformly hold that a statute or policy that treats men and women equally but that accords differential treatment either to a couple based upon whether it consists of persons of the same sex rather than opposite sexes, or to an individual based upon whether he or she generally is sexually attracted to persons of the same gender rather than the opposite gender, is more accurately characterized as involving differential treatment on the basis of *sexual orientation* rather than an instance of *sex discrimination*, and properly should be analyzed on the *former* ground. These cases recognize that, in realistic terms, a statute or policy that treats same-sex couples differently from opposite-sex couples, or that treats individuals who are sexually attracted to persons of the same gender differently from individuals who are sexually attracted to persons of the opposite gender, does not treat an individual man or an individual woman differently *because of* his or her *gender* but rather accords differential treatment *because of* the individual's *sexual orientation*.

. . . .

For purposes of determining the applicable standard of judicial review under the California equal protection clause, we conclude that discrimination on the basis of sexual orientation cannot appropriately be viewed as a subset of, or subsumed within, discrimination on the basis of sex. . . .

↳ no discrimination based on gender

. . . .

B

Plaintiffs next maintain that . . . the applicable California statutes . . . discriminate on the basis of . . . sexual orientation, and that statutes that discriminate on the basis of sexual orientation should be subject to strict scrutiny under the California Constitution. . . .

↳ discrimination on sexual orientation

. . . .

In our view, the statutory provisions restricting marriage to a man and a woman cannot be understood as having merely a disparate impact on gay persons, but instead properly must be viewed as directly classifying and prescribing distinct treatment on the basis of sexual orientation. By limiting marriage to opposite-sex couples, the marriage statutes, realistically viewed, operate clearly and directly to impose different treatment on gay individuals because of their sexual orientation.

By definition, gay individuals are persons who are sexually attracted to persons of the same sex and thus, if inclined to enter into a marriage relationship, would choose to marry a person of their own sex or gender. A statute that limits marriage to a union of persons of opposite sexes, thereby placing marriage outside the reach of couples of the same sex, unquestionably imposes different treatment on the basis of sexual orientation. . . .

Having concluded that the California marriage statutes treat persons differently on the basis of sexual orientation, we must determine whether sexual orientation should be considered a "suspect classification" under the California equal protection clause, so that statutes drawing a distinction on this basis are subject to strict scrutiny. . . . The issue is one of first impression in California[.] . . .

. . . .

Past California cases fully support the . . . conclusion that sexual orientation is a characteristic (1) that bears no relation to a person's ability to perform or contribute to society, and (2) that is associated with a stigma of inferiority and second-class citizenship, manifested by the group's history of legal and social disabilities.

. . . [I]t is [not] appropriate to reject sexual orientation as a suspect classification, in applying the California Constitution's equal protection clause, on the ground that there is a question as to whether this characteristic is or is not "immutable." Although we noted in *Sail'er Inn*, *supra*, 5 Cal.3d 1, that generally a person's gender is viewed as an immutable trait, immutability is not invariably required in order for a characteristic to be considered a suspect classification for equal protection purposes. California cases establish that a person's religion is a suspect classification for equal protection purposes, and one's religion, of course, is not immutable but is a matter over which an individual has control. Because a person's sexual orientation is so integral an aspect of one's identity, it is not appropriate to require a person to repudiate or change his or her sexual orientation in order to avoid discriminatory treatment.

. . . [It has been suggested] that a *fourth* requirement should be imposed before a characteristic is considered a constitutionally suspect

What is a suspect class?

basis for classification for equal protection purposes—namely, that "a 'suspect' classification is appropriately recognized only for minorities who are unable to use the political process to address their needs." . . . [If so, the argument proceeds,] "[s]ince the gay and lesbian community in California is obviously able to wield political power in defense of its interests, this Court should not hold that sexual orientation constitutes a suspect classification."

Although some California decisions in discussing suspect classifications have referred to a group's "political powerlessness", our cases have not identified a group's *current* political powerlessness as a necessary *prerequisite* for treatment as a suspect class. Indeed, if a group's *current* political powerlessness were a prerequisite to a characteristic's being considered a constitutionally suspect basis for differential treatment, it would be impossible to justify the numerous decisions that continue to treat sex, race, and religion as suspect classifications. Instead, our decisions make clear that the most important factors in deciding whether a characteristic should be considered a constitutionally suspect basis for classification are whether the class of persons who exhibit a certain characteristic historically has been subjected to invidious and prejudicial treatment, and whether society now recognizes that the characteristic in question generally bears no relationship to the individual's ability to perform or contribute to society. . . . This rationale clearly applies to statutory classifications that mandate differential treatment on the basis of sexual orientation.

In sum, we conclude that statutes imposing differential treatment on the basis of sexual orientation should be viewed as constitutionally suspect under the California Constitution's equal protection clause.

. . . .

There is no persuasive basis for applying to statutes that classify persons on the basis of the suspect classification of sexual orientation a standard less rigorous than that applied to statutes that classify on the basis of the suspect classifications of gender, race, or religion. Because sexual orientation, like gender, race, or religion, is a characteristic that frequently has been the basis for biased and improperly stereotypical treatment and that generally bears no relation to an individual's ability to perform or contribute to society, it is appropriate for courts to evaluate with great care and with considerable skepticism any statute that embodies such a classification. The strict scrutiny standard therefore is applicable to statutes that impose differential treatment on the basis of sexual orientation.

C

Plaintiffs additionally contend that the strict scrutiny standard applies here not only because the statutes in question impose differential treatment between individuals on the basis of the suspect classification of sexual orientation, but also because the classification drawn by the statutes impinges upon a same-sex couple's fundamental, constitutionally protected privacy interest, creating unequal and detrimental consequences for same-sex couples and their children.

. . . [O]ne of the core elements embodied in the state constitutional right to marry is the right of an individual and a couple to have their own official family relationship accorded respect and dignity equal to that accorded the family relationship of other couples. Even when the state affords substantive legal rights and benefits to a couple's family relationship that are comparable to the rights and benefits afforded to other couples, the state's assignment of a different name to the couple's relationship poses a risk that the different name itself will have the effect of denying such couple's relationship the equal respect and dignity to which the couple is constitutionally entitled. Plaintiffs contend that in the present context, the different nomenclature prescribed by the current California statutes properly must be understood as having just such a constitutionally suspect effect.

We agree with plaintiffs' contention in this regard. Although in some contexts the establishment of separate institutions or structures to remedy the past denial of rights or benefits has been found to be constitutionally permissible, and although it may be possible to conceive of some circumstances in which assignment of the name "marriage" to one category of family relationship and of a name other than marriage to another category of family relationship would not likely be stigmatizing or raise special constitutional concerns, for a number of reasons we conclude that in the present context, affording same-sex couples access only to the separate institution of domestic partnership, and denying such couples access to the established institution of marriage, properly must be viewed as impinging upon the right of those couples to have their family relationship accorded respect and dignity equal to that accorded the family relationship of opposite-sex couples.

First, because of the long and celebrated history of the term "marriage" and the widespread understanding that this term describes a union unreservedly approved and favored by the community, there clearly is a considerable and undeniable symbolic importance to this designation. Thus, it is apparent that affording access to this designation exclusively to opposite-sex couples, while providing same-sex couples access to only a novel alternative designation, realistically must be viewed as constituting significantly unequal treatment to same-sex couples. . . .

Second, particularly in light of the historic disparagement of and discrimination against gay persons, there is a very significant risk that retaining a distinction in nomenclature with regard to this most fundamental of relationships whereby the term "marriage" is denied only to same-sex couples inevitably will cause the new parallel institution that has been made available to those couples to be viewed as of a lesser stature than marriage and, in effect, as a mark of second-class citizenship. . . .

Third, it also is significant that although the meaning of the term "marriage" is well understood by the public generally, the status of domestic partnership is not. While it is true that this circumstance may change over time, it is difficult to deny that the unfamiliarity of the term "domestic partnership" is likely, for a considerable period of time, to pose significant difficulties and complications for same-sex couples, and perhaps most poignantly for their children, that would not be presented if, like opposite-sex couples, same-sex couples were permitted access to the established and well-understood family relationship of marriage.

Under these circumstances, we conclude that the distinction drawn by the current California statutes between the designation of the family relationship available to opposite-sex couples and the designation available to same-sex couples impinges upon the fundamental interest of same-sex couples in having their official family relationship accorded dignity and respect equal to that conferred upon the family relationship of opposite-sex couples.

. . . .

. . . [W]e [thus] conclude that the classifications and differential treatment embodied in the relevant statutes significantly impinge upon the fundamental interests of same-sex couples, and accordingly provide a further reason requiring that the statutory provisions properly be evaluated under the strict scrutiny standard of review.

D

. . . [I]n circumstances, as here, in which the strict scrutiny standard of review applies, the state bears a heavy burden of justification. In order to satisfy that standard, the state must demonstrate not simply that there is a rational, constitutionally legitimate interest that supports the differential treatment at issue, but instead that the state interest is a *constitutionally compelling* one that justifies the disparate treatment prescribed by the statute in question. . . .

. . . .

. . . [T]he interest in retaining a tradition that excludes an historically disfavored minority group from a status that is extended to all others— even when the tradition is long-standing and widely shared—does not necessarily represent a compelling state interest for purposes of equal protection analysis.

After carefully evaluating the pertinent considerations in the present case, we conclude that the state interest in limiting the designation of marriage exclusively to opposite-sex couples, and in excluding same-sex couples from access to that designation, cannot properly be considered a compelling state interest for equal protection purposes. To begin with, the limitation clearly is not necessary to preserve the rights and benefits of marriage currently enjoyed by opposite-sex couples. Extending access to the designation of marriage to same-sex couples will not deprive any opposite-sex couple or their children of any of the rights and benefits conferred by the marriage statutes, but simply will make the benefit of the marriage designation available to same-sex couples and their children. . . . Further, permitting same-sex couples access to the designation of marriage will not alter the substantive nature of the legal institution of marriage; same-sex couples who choose to enter into the relationship with that designation will be subject to the same duties and obligations to each other, to their children, and to third parties that the law currently imposes upon opposite-sex couples who marry. Finally, affording same-sex couples the opportunity to obtain the designation of marriage will not impinge upon the religious freedom of any religious organization, official, or any other person; no religion will be required to change its religious policies or practices with regard to same-sex couples, and no religious officiant will be required to solemnize a marriage in contravention of his or her religious beliefs. Cal. Const., art. I, § 4.

While retention of the limitation of marriage to opposite-sex couples is not needed to preserve the rights and benefits of opposite-sex couples, the exclusion of same-sex couples from the designation of marriage works a real and appreciable harm upon same-sex couples and their children. . . . [B]ecause of the long and celebrated history of the term "marriage" and the widespread understanding that this word describes a family relationship unreservedly sanctioned by the community, the statutory provisions that continue to limit access to this designation exclusively to opposite-sex couples—while providing only a novel, alternative institution for same-sex couples—likely will be viewed as an official statement that the family relationship of same-sex couples is not of comparable stature or equal dignity to the family relationship of opposite-sex couples. Furthermore, because of the historic disparagement of gay persons, the retention of a distinction in nomenclature by which the term "marriage" is withheld only from the family relationship of same-sex couples is all the more likely to cause the new parallel institution that has been established for same-sex couples to be considered a mark of second-class citizenship. Finally, in addition to the potential harm flowing from the lesser stature that is likely to be afforded to the family relationships of same-sex couples by designating them domestic partnerships, there exists a substantial risk that a judicial decision upholding the differential treatment of opposite-sex and same-sex couples would be understood as *validating* a more general proposition that our state by now has repudiated: that it is permissible, under the law, for society to treat gay individuals and same-sex couples differently from, and less favorably than, heterosexual individuals and opposite-sex couples.

In light of all of these circumstances, we conclude that retention of the traditional definition of marriage does not constitute a state interest sufficiently compelling, under the strict scrutiny equal protection standard, to justify withholding that status from same-sex couples. Accordingly, insofar as the provisions of sections 300 and 308.5 draw a distinction between opposite-sex couples and same-sex couples and exclude the latter from access to the designation of marriage, we conclude these statutes are unconstitutional.[73]

VI

Having concluded that sections 300 and 308.5 are unconstitutional to the extent each statute reserves the designation of marriage exclusively to opposite-sex couples and denies same-sex couples access to that designation, we must determine the proper remedy.

When a statute's differential treatment of separate categories of individuals is found to violate equal protection principles, a court must determine whether the constitutional violation should be eliminated or cured by extending to the previously excluded class the treatment or benefit that the statute affords to the included class, or alternatively should be remedied by withholding the benefit equally from both the previously included class and the excluded class. . . .

In the present case, it is readily apparent that extending the designation of marriage to same-sex couples clearly is more consistent with the probable legislative intent than withholding that designation from both opposite-sex couples and same-sex couples in favor of some other, uniform designation. . . .

---

[73] We emphasize that in reaching this conclusion we do not suggest that the current marriage provisions were enacted with an invidious intent or purpose. . . .

Accordingly, in light of the conclusions we reach concerning the constitutional questions brought to us for resolution, we determine that the language of section 300 limiting the designation of marriage to a union "between a man and a woman" is unconstitutional and must be stricken from the statute, and that the remaining statutory language must be understood as making the designation of marriage available both to opposite-sex and same-sex couples. In addition, because the limitation of marriage to opposite-sex couples imposed by section 308.5 can have no constitutionally permissible effect in light of the constitutional conclusions set forth in this opinion, that provision cannot stand.

Plaintiffs are entitled to the issuance of a writ of mandate directing the appropriate state officials to take all actions necessary to effectuate our ruling in this case so as to ensure that county clerks and other local officials throughout the state, in performing their duty to enforce the marriage statutes in their jurisdictions, apply those provisions in a manner consistent with the decision of this court. Further, as the prevailing parties, plaintiffs are entitled to their costs.

The judgment of the Court of Appeal is reversed, and the matter is remanded to that court for further action consistent with this opinion.

■ BAXTER, J., concurring and dissenting.

The majority opinion reflects considerable research, thought, and effort on a significant and sensitive case, and I actually agree with several of the majority's conclusions. However, I cannot join the majority's holding that the California Constitution gives same-sex couples a right to marry. In reaching this decision, I believe, the majority violates the separation of powers, and thereby commits profound error.

. . . .

The People, directly or through their elected representatives, have every right to adopt laws abrogating the historic understanding that civil marriage is between a man and a woman. The rapid growth in California of statutory protections for the rights of gays and lesbians, as individuals, as parents, and as committed partners, suggests a quickening evolution of community attitudes on these issues. Recent years have seen the development of an intense debate about same-sex marriage. Advocates of this cause have had real success in the marketplace of ideas, gaining attention and considerable public support. Left to its own devices, the ordinary democratic process might well produce, ere long, a consensus among most Californians that the term "marriage" should, in civil parlance, include the legal unions of same-sex partners.

But a bare majority of this court, not satisfied with the pace of democratic change, now abruptly forestalls that process and substitutes, by judicial fiat, its own social policy views for those expressed by the People themselves. Undeterred by the strong weight of state and federal law and authority, the majority invents a new constitutional right, immune from the ordinary process of legislative consideration. The majority finds that our Constitution suddenly demands no less than a permanent redefinition of marriage, regardless of the popular will.

. . . .

History confirms the importance of the judiciary's constitutional role as a check against majoritarian abuse. Still, courts must use caution when exercising the potentially transformative authority to articulate constitutional rights. Otherwise, judges with limited accountability risk infringing upon our society's most basic shared premise—the People's general right, directly or through their chosen legislators, to decide fundamental issues of public policy for themselves. Judicial restraint is particularly appropriate where, as here, the claimed constitutional entitlement is of recent conception and challenges the most fundamental assumption about a basic social institution.

The majority has violated these principles. It simply does not have the right to erase, then recast, the age-old definition of marriage, as virtually all societies have understood it, in order to satisfy its own contemporary notions of equality and justice.

. . . .

. . . I would apply the normal rational basis test to determine whether, by granting same-sex couples all the substantive rights and benefits of marriage, but reserving the marriage label for opposite-sex unions,

California's laws violate the equal protection guarantee of the state Constitution. By that standard, I find ample grounds for the balance currently struck on this issue by both the Legislature and the People.

First, it is certainly reasonable for the Legislature, having granted same-sex couples all substantive marital rights within its power, to assign those rights a name other than marriage. After all, an initiative statute adopted by a 61.4 percent popular vote, and constitutionally immune from repeal by the Legislature, *defines marriage as a union of partners of the opposite sex.*

Moreover, in light of the provisions of federal law that, for purposes of federal benefits, limit the definition of marriage to opposite-sex couples[,] 1 U.S.C. § 7, California must distinguish same-sex from opposite-sex couples in administering the numerous federal-state programs that are governed by federal law. A separate nomenclature applicable to the family relationship of same-sex couples undoubtedly facilitates the administration of such programs.

Most fundamentally, the People themselves cannot be considered irrational in deciding, for the time being, that the fundamental definition of marriage, as it has universally existed until very recently, should be preserved. As the New Jersey Supreme Court observed, "We cannot escape the reality that the shared societal meaning of marriage—passed down through the common law into our statutory law—has always been the union of a man and a woman. To alter that meaning would render a profound change in the public consciousness of a social institution of ancient origin." *Lewis v. Harris*, 908 A.2d 196, [2]22 [(N.J. 2006)].

If such a profound change in this ancient social institution is to occur, the People and their representatives, who represent the public conscience, should have the right, and the responsibility, to control the pace of that change through the democratic process. Family Code sections 300 and 308.5 serve this salutary purpose. The majority's decision erroneously usurps it.

. . . .

National Pride at Work, Inc. v. Governor of Michigan

Michigan Supreme Court, 2008.
748 N.W.2d 524.

■ MARKMAN, J.

We granted leave to appeal to consider whether the marriage amendment, Const. 1963, art. 1, § 25, which states that "the union of one man and one woman in marriage shall be the only agreement recognized as a marriage or similar union for any purpose," prohibits public employers from providing health-insurance benefits to their employees' qualified same-sex domestic partners. Because we agree with the Court of Appeals that providing such benefits does violate the marriage amendment, we affirm its judgment.

I. FACTS AND HISTORY

The marriage amendment was approved by a majority of the voters on November 2, 2004, and took effect as a provision of the Michigan Constitution on December 18, 2004. At that time, several public employers, including state universities and various city and county governments, had policies or agreements in effect that extended health-insurance benefits to their employees' qualified same-sex domestic partners. In addition, the Office of the State Employer (OSE) and the United Auto Workers Local 6000 (UAW) had reached a tentative agreement to include same-sex domestic-partner health-insurance benefits in the benefit package for state employee members of the union. . . . .

. . . .

On March 21, 2005, plaintiffs[1] filed this declaratory judgment action

---

[1] Plaintiff National Pride at Work, Inc., is a nonprofit organization of the American Federation of Labor-Council of Industrial Organizations. The remaining plaintiffs are employees of the city of Kalamazoo, the University of Michigan, Michigan State University, Eastern Michigan University, Wayne State University, the Clinton/Eaton/Ingham County Community Mental Health Board, or the state of Michigan and those employees' same-sex partners. . . . Likewise, this opinion does not address whether private employers can provide health-insurance benefits to their employees' same-sex domestic partners.

against the Governor, seeking a declaration that the marriage amendment does not bar public employers from providing health-insurance benefits to their employees' qualified same-sex domestic partners. After the city of Kalamazoo announced its intention not to provide same-sex domestic-partner health-insurance benefits to its employees for contracts beginning in January 2006 absent a court ruling that such benefits do not violate the marriage amendment, plaintiffs added the city of Kalamazoo as a defendant. . . .

. . . .

III. ANALYSIS

A. DOMESTIC-PARTNERSHIP POLICIES

The tentative agreement reached by the OSE and the UAW would require domestic partners to meet the following criteria in order to receive health-insurance benefits:

1. Be at least 18 years of age.

2. Share a close personal relationship with the employee and be responsible for each other's common welfare.

3. Not have a similar relationship with any other person, and not have had a similar relationship with any other person for the prior six months.

4. Not be a member of the employee's immediate family as defined as employee's spouse, children, parents, grandparents or foster parents, grandchildren, parents-in-law, brothers, sisters, aunts, uncles or cousins.

5. Be of the same gender.

6. Have jointly shared the same regular and permanent residence for at least six months, and have an intent to continue doing so indefinitely.

7. Be jointly responsible for basic living expenses, including the cost of food, shelter and other common expenses of maintaining a

household. This joint responsibility need not mean that the persons contribute equally or in any particular ratio, but rather that the persons agree that they are jointly responsible.

The tentative agreement also provides: "In order to establish whether the criteria have been met, the employer may require the employee to sign an Affidavit setting forth the facts and circumstances which constitute compliance with those requirements."

The city of Kalamazoo's "Domestic Partner Benefits Policy," incorporated in its collective-bargaining agreements, provided health-insurance benefits to the domestic partners of the city's employees who met the following criteria:

> For the purposes of the City of Kalamazoo's program, the definition and use of the term *domestic partner* shall only include couples of the same sex. To be considered as domestic partners, the individuals must:
>
> A. Be at least 18 and mentally competent to enter into a contract;
>
> B. Share a common residence and have done so for at least six (6) months;
>
> C. Be unmarried and not related by blood closer than would prevent marriage;
>
> D. Share financial arrangements and daily living expenses related to their common welfare;
>
> E. File a statement of termination of previous domestic partnership at least six (6) months prior to signing another Certification of Domestic Partnership. [Emphasis in the original.]

The city also required the employee and his or her domestic partner to sign a notarized certification of domestic partnership that affirmed these criteria. In addition, they were required to provide evidence of "mutual economic dependence," such as a joint lease or mortgage, and evidence of a "common legal residence," such as driver's licenses or voter's registrations. Finally, the city's policy provided: "It is the intent of this program to provide insurance coverage and other benefits to domestic partners of the City of Kalamazoo identical to those provided to spouses of City employees."

For a domestic partner to be eligible for health-insurance benefits under the University of Michigan's "Same-Sex Domestic Partner Policy," the employee and his or her partner must:

• Be of the same sex; and

• Not be legally married to another individual; and

• Not be related to each other by blood in a manner that would bar marriage; and

• Have registered or declared the Domestic Partnership in the manner authorized by a municipality or other government entity;[2] and

• Have allowed at least six months to pass since the dissolution of a previous same-sex domestic partnership in the manner authorized by a municipality or other government entity.

Michigan State University provided health-insurance benefits to its employees' domestic partners if the employee and the domestic partner:

1. are [the] same-sex and for this reason are unable to marry each other under Michigan law,

2. are in a long-term committed relationship, have been in the relationship for at least 6 months, and intend to remain together indefinitely,

3. are not legally married to others and neither has another domestic partner,

4. are at least 18 years of age and have the capacity to enter into a

---

[2] The city of Ann Arbor's "Declaration of Domestic Partnership" requires the partners to "declare the following to be true": [] 1. We are in a relationship of mutual support, caring and commitment. [] 2. We share the common necessities of life. [] 3. We are not related by blood in a manner that would bar marriage in the State of Michigan. [] 4. We are not married or in any other domestic partnership. [] 5. We are at least 18 years of age and otherwise competent to enter into a contract.

contract,

5. are not related to one another closely enough to bar marriage in Michigan,

6. share a residence and have done so for more than 6 months,

7. are jointly responsible to each other for the necessities of life, and

8. provide a signed "partnership agreement" that obligates each of the parties to provide support for one another, and provides for substantially equal division, upon termination of the relationship, of earnings during the relationship and any property acquired with those earnings.[3]

B. MARRIAGE AMENDMENT

The marriage amendment, Const. 1963, art. 1, § 25, provides: "To secure and preserve the benefits of marriage for our society and for future generations of children, the union of one man and one woman in marriage shall be the only agreement recognized as a marriage or similar union for any purpose."

. . . [T]he primary objective of constitutional interpretation . . . is to faithfully give meaning to the intent of those who enacted the law. This court typically discerns the common understanding of constitutional text by applying each term's plain meaning at the time of ratification.

C. "SIMILAR UNION"

Plaintiffs argue that "the *only* thing that is prohibited by the [marriage] amendment is the recognition of a same-sex relationship *as a marriage*" and that the public employers here are not recognizing a domestic partnership "as a marriage." We respectfully disagree. First, the amendment prohibits the recognition of a domestic partnership "as a marriage *or similar union*. . . ." That is, it prohibits the recognition of a domestic partnership as a marriage or as a union that is similar to a

---

[3] When we use the term "domestic partnership" in this opinion, we refer to a partnership that satisfies the criteria contained in one of the domestic-partnership policies described in this opinion.

marriage. Second, just because a public employer does not refer to, or otherwise characterize, a domestic partnership as a marriage or a union similar to a marriage does not mean that the employer is not recognizing a domestic partnership as a marriage or a union similar to a marriage.

The pertinent question is not whether public employers are recognizing a domestic partnership as a marriage or whether they have declared a domestic partnership to be a marriage or something similar to marriage; rather, it is whether the public employers are recognizing a domestic partnership as a union similar to a marriage. A "union" is "something formed by uniting two or more things; combination; . . . a number of persons, states, etc., joined or associated together for some common purpose." *Random House Webster's College Dictionary* (1991). Certainly, when two people join together for a common purpose and legal consequences arise from that relationship, i.e., a public entity accords legal significance to this relationship, a union may be said to be formed. When two people enter a domestic partnership, they join or associate together for a common purpose, and, under the domestic-partnership policies at issue here, legal consequences arise from that relationship in the form of health-insurance benefits. Therefore, a domestic partnership is most certainly a union.

The next question is whether a domestic partnership is similar to a marriage. Plaintiffs and the dissent argue that because the public employers here do not bestow upon a domestic partnership *all* the legal rights and responsibilities associated with marriage, the partnership is not similar to a marriage. Again, we respectfully disagree. "Similar" means "having a likeness or resemblance, [especially] in a general way; having qualities in common[.]" *Random House Webster's College Dictionary* (1991)[.] A union does not have to possess *all* the same legal rights and responsibilities that result from a marriage in order to constitute a union "similar" to that of marriage. If the marriage amendment were construed to prohibit only the recognition of a union that possesses legal rights and responsibilities identical to those that result from a marriage, the language "or similar union" would be rendered meaningless, and an interpretation that renders language meaningless must be avoided. Further, the dissimilarities identified by plaintiffs are not dissimilarities pertaining to the *nature* of the marital and domestic-partnership unions themselves, but are merely dissimilarities pertaining to the *legal effects* that are accorded these relationships. However, given that the marriage amendment prohibits the recognition of unions similar to marriage "for any purpose," the pertinent question is not whether these unions give rise to all the same legal effects; rather, it is whether these unions are being recognized as unions similar to marriage "for any purpose."[6]

For these reasons, we . . . agree with the Court of Appeals that "a publicly recognized domestic partnership need not mirror a marriage in every respect in order to run afoul of article 1, § 25 because the amendment plainly precludes recognition of a 'similar union for any purpose.'"[7]

All the domestic-partnership policies at issue here require the partners to be of a certain sex, i.e., the same sex as the other partner.[8] Similarly, Michigan law requires married persons to be of a certain sex, i.e., a different sex from the other. MCL 551.1 ("Marriage is inherently a unique relationship between a man and a woman."). In addition, each of the domestic-partnership policies at issue in this case requires that the partners not be closely related by blood. Similarly, Michigan law requires that married persons not be closely related by blood. MCL 551.3[11] and MCL 551.4.[12] Although there are, of course, many different

---

[6] . . . Marriages give rise to many legal rights and responsibilities that domestic partnerships do not. However, we believe the pertinent question for purposes of the marriage amendment is not whether these relationships give rise to identical, or even similar, legal rights and responsibilities, but whether these relationships are similar in nature in the *context* of the marriage amendment. . . .

[7] Plaintiffs . . . contend that the amendment only prohibits the establishment of "civil unions" that confer the same rights and obligations as does a marriage. However, as explained earlier, a union does not have to confer all the same rights and obligations as does a marriage in order to be "similar" to a marriage. . . .

[8] Indeed, the Michigan State University policy specifically states that the partners must be of the "same-sex and for this reason are unable to *marry* each other under Michigan law[.]" [Emphasis added.]

[11] MCL 551.3 provides:

"A man shall not marry his mother, sister, grandmother, daughter, granddaughter, stepmother, grandfather's wife, son's wife, grandson's wife, wife's mother, wife's grandmother, wife's daughter, wife's granddaughter,

Michigan that are accorded legal significance—
parent-child, landlord-tenant, attorney-client,
arriages and domestic partnerships appear to be
ips that are defined in terms of *both* gender and
od connection. As discussed earlier, "similar"
ss or resemblance, [especially] in a general way;
mmon[.]" *Random House Webster's College*
rriages and domestic partnerships share two
d apparently unique (at least in combination),

Because marriages and domestic partnerships
alities, we believe that it can fairly be said that
another "in a general way." Therefore, although
partnerships are by no means identical, they are
ages and domestic partnerships are the only
an defined in terms of both gender and lack of a
n, and, thus, have these core "qualities in
that domestic partnerships are unions similar to

---

r's daughter, father's sister, mother's sister, or cousin
of the first degree, or another man."

[12] MCL 551.4 provides:

> "A woman shall not marry her father, brother, grandfather, son, grandson, stepfather, grandmother's husband, daughter's husband, granddaughter's husband, husband's father, husband's grandfather, husband's son, husband's grandson, brother's son, sister's son, father's brother, mother's brother, or cousin of the first degree, or another woman."

[14] Although we believe that these are the core qualities that make marriages and domestic partnerships similar, these relationships are similar in other respects as well. For instance, marriages and domestic partnerships are relationships that only two people may enter into. [] In addition, persons involved in either marital or domestic-partnership relationships must undertake obligations of mutual support. . . . [] Further, both marital and domestic-partnership relationships require agreements or contracts as a precondition. [] Additionally, both marital and domestic-partnership relationships have a minimum age requirement. . . . [] Further, both marriages and domestic partnerships are relationships of an indefinite duration. That is, they are both ongoing relationships that continue until one of the parties takes affirmative action to terminate the relationship. [] Finally, it seems relevant that all but one of the domestic-partnership policies at issue here require the partners to share a common residence, a circumstance typically defining the marital relationship as well.

marriage.

D. "RECOGNIZED"

The next question concerns whether public employers are truly recognizing a domestic partnership as a union similar to marriage when they provide health-insurance benefits to domestic partners on the *basis of* the partnership. "Recognize" is defined as "to perceive or acknowledge as existing, true, or valid[.]" *Random House Webster's College Dictionary* (1991). When a public employer attaches legal consequence to a relationship, that employer is clearly "recognizing" that relationship. . . . When public employers provide domestic partners health-insurance benefits on the basis of the domestic partnership, they are without a doubt recognizing the partnership.

E. "ONLY AGREEMENT"

The next question concerns whether public employers are recognizing an "agreement" when they provide health-insurance benefits to domestic partners. An "agreement" is "the act of agreeing or of coming to a mutual arrangement." *Id.* The city of Kalamazoo's, the University of Michigan's, and Michigan State University's policies require putative partners to sign a domestic-partnership agreement. The OSE's policy requires partners to "agree that they are jointly responsible" "for basic living expenses. . . ." Obviously, if two people have decided to sign a domestic-partnership agreement or have agreed to be jointly responsible for basic living expenses, they have come to a mutual arrangement. Therefore, public employers recognize an agreement when they provide health-insurance benefits to domestic partners on the basis of a domestic partnership.

[T]he marriage amendment specifically states that the "only" agreement that can be recognized as a marriage or similar union is the union of one man and one woman. "Only" means "the single one . . . of the kind; lone; sole[.]" *Random House Webster's College Dictionary* (1991). Therefore, a single agreement can be recognized within the state of Michigan as a marriage or similar union, and that single agreement is the union of one man and one woman. A domestic partnership does not constitute such a recognizable agreement.

F. "FOR ANY PURPOSE"

Furthermore, the marriage amendment specifically prohibits recognizing "for any purpose" a union that is similar to marriage but is not a marriage. "Any" means "every; all[.]" *Id.* Therefore, if there were any residual doubt regarding whether the marriage amendment prohibits the recognition of a domestic partnership for the purpose at issue here, this language makes it clear that such a recognition is indeed prohibited "for any purpose," which obviously includes for the purpose of providing health-insurance benefits. Whether the language "for any purpose" is essential to reach the conclusion that health-insurance benefits cannot be provided under the instant circumstances, or merely punctuates what is otherwise made clear in the amendment, the people of this state could hardly have made their intentions clearer.

G. "BENEFITS OF MARRIAGE"

The marriage amendment begins with a statement of its purpose that is effectively a preamble: "To secure and preserve the benefits of marriage for our society and for future generations of children. . . ." Plaintiffs argue that the marriage amendment does not prohibit public employers from providing health-insurance benefits to their employees' qualified same-sex domestic partners because health-insurance benefits do not constitute a benefit of marriage. However, the marriage amendment contains more than just a statement of purpose. In full, it states: "To secure and preserve the benefits of marriage for our society and for future generations of children, the union of one man and one woman in marriage shall be the only agreement recognized as a marriage or similar union for any purpose." The latter—the operative—part of this provision sets forth how the ratifiers intended to go about achieving the purposes set forth in the first part, "secur[ing] and preserv[ing] the benefits of marriage. . . ." This operative part specifies that public employers must not recognize domestic partnerships for any purpose. That is, the first part of the amendment states its purpose, and the second part states the means by which this purpose is to be achieved. Doubtless, there are those who would disagree about the efficacy of achieving the former purpose by the latter means. However, it is not for this Court to decide whether there are superior means for "secur[ing] and preserv[ing] the benefits of marriage," or indeed whether the means chosen in the amendment are ineffectual or even counterproductive. The people of this state have already spoken on this issue by adopting this amendment. They have decided to "secure and preserve the benefits of marriage" by ensuring that unions similar to marriage are not recognized in the same way as a marriage for any purpose.

H. EXTRINSIC EVIDENCE

Plaintiffs . . . argue that Citizens for the Protection of Marriage, an organization responsible for placing the marriage amendment on the 2004 ballot and a primary supporter of this initiative during the ensuing campaign, published a brochure that indicated that the proposal would not preclude public employers from offering health-insurance benefits to their employees' domestic partners. However, such extrinsic evidence can hardly be used to contradict the unambiguous language of the constitution. . . . When the language of a constitutional provision is unambiguous, resort to extrinsic evidence is prohibited, and, as discussed earlier, the language of the marriage amendment is unambiguous.

      . . . .

I. OTHER STATES

Finally, none of the decisions from other states on which plaintiffs rely is helpful because none involves the specific language contained in Michigan's marriage amendment. See, e.g., *State v. Carswell*, 114 Ohio St.3d 210, 871 N.E.2d 547 (2007) (constitutional provision, Ohio Const[.] art[.] 15 § 11, providing: "Only a union between one man and one woman may be a marriage valid in or recognized by this state and its political subdivisions.")[.] . . .

. . . [A]ll the cases cited by plaintiffs . . . [are] interpreting a provision of law that is simply too different from Michigan's marriage amendment to be of persuasive value in determining how this state's amendment should be interpreted.

IV. CONCLUSION

. . . [G]iven that the marriage amendment prohibits the recognition of unions similar to marriage "for any purpose," the pertinent question is not whether these unions give rise to all of the same legal effects; rather, it is whether these unions are being recognized as unions similar to marriage "for any purpose." . . . [W]e conclude that the marriage amendment, Const. 1963, art. 1, § 25, which states that "the union of one man and one woman in marriage shall be the only agreement recognized as a marriage or similar union for any purpose," prohibits public employers from providing health-insurance benefits to their employees' qualified same-sex domestic partners.

Page 119-120. Replace Note 1 with the following text:

1. The Ohio Supreme Court reached a dramatically different result when interpreting a similarly broad provision of the Ohio Constitution in *State v. Carswell*, 871 N.E.2d 547 (Ohio 2007). By its terms, Ohio's Marriage Amendment, enacted in 2004, provides: "Only a union between one man and one woman may be a marriage valid in or recognized by this state and its political subdivisions. This state and its political subdivisions shall not create or recognize a legal status for relationships of unmarried individuals that intends to approximate the design, qualities, significance or effect of marriage." OHIO CONST. art. XV, § 11. Interpreting the amendment's second sentence, the *Carswell* court declared it "means that the state cannot create or recognize a legal status for unmarried persons that bears *all* of the attributes of marriage—a marriage substitute." *Carswell*, 871 N.E.2d, at 551. The court's only stated example of "a marriage substitute": civil unions. See *id.* & n.1.

Pages 120-21. Replace Note 3 with the following text:

3. Massachusetts and California are the only states that recognize same-sex marriage. Connecticut, New Hampshire, New Jersey, and Vermont now recognize "civil unions" for same-sex couples. The District of Columbia, along with Hawaii, Maine, Oregon, and Washington recognize a substantial range of domestic partnership rights for same-sex couples.

Page 121. Replace Note 4 with the following text:

4. The constitutions of 26 states have been amended to prohibit same-sex marriage. They are: Alabama, Alaska, Arkansas, Colorado, Georgia, Idaho, Kansas, Kentucky, Louisiana, Michigan, Mississippi, Missouri, Montana, Nebraska, Nevada, North Dakota, Ohio, Oklahoma, Oregon, South Carolina, South Dakota, Tennessee, Texas, Utah, Virginia, and Wisconsin. The constitutional "marriage amendments" in Alaska, Colorado, Hawaii, Mississippi, Missouri, Montana, Nevada, Oregon, and Tennessee, only speak to same-sex marriage. Others contain language that sweeps farther than that. States in this category include: Alabama, Arkansas, Georgia, Idaho, Kansas, Kentucky, Louisiana, Michigan, Nebraska, North Dakota, Ohio, Oklahoma, South Carolina, South Dakota, Texas, Utah, Virginia, and Wisconsin. The following states also have statutory bans on same-sex marriage on their law books: Alabama, Alaska, Arkansas, Colorado, Georgia, Hawaii, Idaho, Kansas, Kentucky, Louisiana, Michigan, Missouri, Mississippi, Montana, North Dakota, Ohio, Oklahoma, South Carolina, South Dakota, Tennessee, Texas, Utah, Virginia, and Wisconsin. States that have only banned same-sex marriages by statute include Arizona, Connecticut, Delaware, Florida, Illinois, Indiana, Iowa, Maine, Maryland, Minnesota, New Hampshire, North Carolina, Pennsylvania, Vermont, Washington, West Virginia, and Wyoming. A current survey of related information can be found at http://moritzlaw.osu.edu/library/samesexmarriagelaws.php.

CHAPTER 3. MARRIAGE

C. Challenges to the Traditional Marriage Model
2. Reallocation of Duties within Marriage
b. By Public Policy
(2) . . . and the Nurturing Husband

Page 232. Add after *Knussman v. Maryland*:

NOTE:

Is *Knussman* a challenge to the traditional model of marriage or an affirmation of conservative "family values"? Both? See Eyal Press, *Family-Leave Values*, N.Y. TIMES MAG., July 29, 2007, at 36, *available at* http://www.nytimes.com/2007/07/29/magazine/29discrimination-t.html.

Page 237. Add after S.M. Miller, *The Making of a Confused Middle Class Husband*:

Linda Hirshman, Homeward Bound

The Am. Prospect, Dec. 2005, at 20.

Half the wealthiest, most-privileged, best-educated females in the country stay home with their babies rather than work in the market economy.

. . . .

Why did this happen? The answer I discovered—an answer neither feminist leaders nor women themselves want to face—is that while the public world has changed, albeit imperfectly, to accommodate women among the elite, private lives have hardly budged. The real glass ceiling is at home.

Looking back, it seems obvious that the unreconstructed family was destined to reemerge after the passage of feminism's storm of social change. Following the original impulse to address everything in the lives of women, feminism turned its focus to cracking open the doors of the public power structure. This was no small task. At the beginning, there were male juries and male Ivy League schools, sex-segregated want ads, discriminatory employers, harassing colleagues. As a result of feminist efforts—and larger economic trends—the percentage of women, even of mothers in full- or part-time employment, rose robustly through the 1980s and early '90s.

But then the pace slowed. The census numbers for all working mothers leveled off around 1990 and have fallen modestly since 1998. In interviews, women with enough money to quit work say they are "choosing" to opt out. Their words conceal a crucial reality: the belief that women are responsible for child-rearing and homemaking was largely untouched by decades of workplace feminism. Add to this the good evidence that the upper-class workplace has become more demanding and then mix in the successful conservative cultural campaign to reinforce traditional gender roles and you've got a perfect recipe for feminism's stall.

People who don't like the message attack the data. . . .

What evidence *is* good enough? Let's start with you. Educated and affluent reader, if you are a 30- or 40-something woman with children, what are you doing? Husbands, what are your wives doing? Older readers, what are your married daughters with children doing? I have asked this question of scores of women and men. Among the affluent-educated-married population, women are letting their careers slide to tend the home fires. If my interviewees are working, they work largely part time, and their part-time careers are not putting them in the executive suite.

Here's some more evidence: During the '90s, I taught a course in sexual bargaining at a very good college. Each year, after the class reviewed the low rewards for child-care work, I asked how the students anticipated combining work with child-rearing. At least half the female students described lives of part-time or home-based work. Guys expected their female partners to care for the children. When I asked the young men how they reconciled that prospect with the manifest low regard the market has for child care, they were mystified. Turning to the women who had spoken before, they said, uniformly, "But she chose it."

Even Ronald Coase . . . quotes the aphorism that "the plural of anecdote is data." . . . What better sample, I thought, than the brilliantly educated and accomplished brides of the "Sunday Styles" [section of *The New York Times*,] circa 1996? At marriage, they included a vice president of client communication, a gastroenterologist, a lawyer, an editor, and a marketing executive. In 2003 and 2004, I tracked them down and called them. I interviewed about 80 percent of the 41 women who announced their weddings over three Sundays in 1996. Around 40 years old, college graduates with careers: Who was more likely than they to be reaping feminism's promise of opportunity? Imagine my shock when I found almost all the brides from the first Sunday at home with their children. Statistical anomaly? Nope. Same result for the next Sunday. And the one after that.

Ninety percent of the brides I found had had babies. Of the 30 with babies, five were still working full time. Twenty-five, or 85 percent, were not working full time. Of those not working full time, 10 were working part time but often a long way from their prior career paths. And half the married women with children were not working at all.

And there is more. In 2000, Harvard Business School professor Myra Hart surveyed the women of the classes of 1981, 1986, and 1991 and found that only 38 percent of female Harvard MBAs were working full time. A 2004 survey by the center for Work-Life Policy of 2,443 women with a graduate degree or very prestigious bachelor's degree revealed that 43 percent of those women with children had taken a time out, primarily for family reasons. Richard Posner, federal appeals-court judge and occasional University of Chicago adjunct professor, reports that "the [*Times*] article confirms [] what everyone associated with such institutions [elite law schools] has long known: that a vastly higher percentage of female than of male students will drop out of the workforce to take care of their children."

How many anecdotes [does it take] to become data? The 2000 census showed a decline in the percentage of mothers of infants working full time, part time, or seeking employment. Starting at 31 percent in

1976, the percentage had gone up almost every year to 1992, hit a high
of 58.7 percent in 1998, and then began to drop—to 55.2 percent in
2000, to 54.6 percent in 2002, to 53.7 percent in 2003. Statistics just
released showed further decline to 52.9 percent in 2004. Even the
percentage of working mothers with children who were not infants
declined between 2000 and 2003, from 62.8 percent to 59.8 percent.

Although college-educated women work more than others, the 2002
census shows that graduate or professional degrees do not increase workforce participation much more than even one year of college. When their
children are infants (under a year), 54 percent of females with graduate
or professional degrees are not working full time (18 percent are working
part time and 36 percent are not working at all). Even among those who
have children who are not infants, 41 percent are not working full time
(18 percent are working part time and 23 percent are not working at all).

Economists argue about the meaning of the data, even going so far as
to contend that more mothers are working. They explain that the bureau
changed the definition of "work" slightly in 2000, the economy went into
recession, and the falloff in women without children was similar.
However, even if there wasn't a falloff but just a leveling off, this
represents not a loss of present value but a loss of hope for the future—a
loss of hope that the role of women in society will continue to increase.

The arguments still do not explain the absence of women in elite
workplaces. If these women were sticking it out in the business, law, and
academic worlds, now, 30 years after feminism started filling the
selective schools with women, the elite workplaces should be
proportionately female. They are not. Law schools have been graduating
classes around 40-percent female for decades—decades during which
both schools and firms experienced enormous growth. And, although the
legal population will not be 40-percent female until 2010, in 2003, the
major law firms had only 16-percent female partners, according to the
American Bar Association. It's important to note that elite workplaces
like law firms grew in size during the very years that the percentage of
female graduates was growing, leading you to expect a higher female
employment than the pure graduation rate would indicate. The Harvard
Business School has produced classes around 30-percent female. Yet
only 10.6 percent of Wall Street's corporate officers are women, and a

mere nine are Fortune 500 CEOs. Harvard Business School's dean, who extolled the virtues of interrupted careers on *60 Minutes*, has a 20-percent female academic faculty.

It is possible that the workplace is discriminatory and hostile to family life. If firms had hired every childless woman lawyer available, that alone would have been enough to raise the percentage of female law partners above 16 percent in 30 years. It is also possible that women are voluntarily taking themselves out of the elite job competition for lower status and lower-paying jobs. Women must take responsibility for the consequences of their decisions. It defies reason to claim that the falloff from 40 percent of the class at law school to 16 percent of the partners at all the big law firms is unrelated to half the mothers with graduate and professional degrees leaving full-time work at childbirth and staying away for several years after that, or possibly bidding down.

This isn't only about day care. Half my *Times* brides quit *before* the first baby came. In interviews, at least half of them expressed a hope never to work again. None had realistic plans to work. More importantly, when they quit, they were already alienated from their work or at least not committed to a life of work. One, a female MBA, said she could never figure out why the men at her workplace, which fired her, were so excited about making deals. "It's only money," she mused. Not surprisingly, even where employers offered them part-time work, they were not interested in taking it.

What is going on? Most women hope to marry and have babies. If they resist the traditional female responsibilities of child-rearing and householding, what Arlie Hochschild called "The Second Shift," they are fixing for a fight. But elite women aren't resisting tradition. None of the stay-at-home brides I interviewed saw the second shift as unjust; they agree that the household is women's work. As one lawyer-bride put it in explaining her decision to quit practicing law after four years, "I had a wedding to plan." Another, an Ivy Leaguer with a master's degree, described it in management terms: "He's the CEO and I'm the CFO. He sees to it that the money rolls in and I decide how to spend it." It's their work, and they must do it perfectly. "We're all in here making fresh apple pie," said one, explaining her reluctance to leave her daughters in order to be interviewed. The family CFO described her activities at home: "I take my [3-year-old] daughter to all the major museums. We go to little movement classes."

Conservatives contend that the dropouts prove that feminism "failed" because it was too radical, because women didn't want what feminism had to offer. In fact, if half or more of feminism's heirs (85 percent of the women in my *Times* sample), are not working seriously, it's because feminism wasn't radical enough: It changed the workplace but it didn't change men, and, more importantly, it didn't fundamentally change how women related to men.

. . . .

The privileged brides of the *Times*—and their husbands—seem happy. Why do we care what they do? After all, most people aren't rich and white and heterosexual, and they couldn't quit working if they wanted to.

We care because what they do is bad for them, is certainly bad for society, and is widely imitated, even by people who never get their weddings in the *Times*. This last is called the "regime effect," and it means that even if women don't quit their jobs for their families, they think they should and feel guilty about not doing it. . . .

As for society, elites supply the labor for the decision-making classes—the senators, the newspaper editors, the research scientists, the entrepreneurs, the policy-makers, and the policy wonks. If the ruling class is overwhelmingly male, the rulers will make mistakes that benefit males, whether from ignorance or from indifference. Media surveys reveal that if only one member of a television show's creative staff is female, the percentage of women on-screen goes up from 36 percent to 42 percent. A world of 84-percent male lawyers and 84-percent female assistants is a different place than one with women in positions of social authority. Think of a big American city with an 86-percent white police force. If role models don't matter, why care about Sandra Day O'Connor? Even if the falloff from peak numbers is small, the leveling off of women in power is a loss of hope for more change. Will there never again be more than one woman on the Supreme Court?

Worse, the behavior tarnishes every female with the knowledge that she is almost never going to be a ruler. Princeton President Shirley Tilghman described the elite colleges' self-image perfectly when she told her freshman last year that they would be the nation's leaders, and she clearly did not have trophy wives in mind. Why should society spend resources education women with only a 50-percent return rate on their stated goals? The American Conservative Union carried a column in 2004 recommending that employers stay away from such women or risk going out of business. Good psychological data show that the more women are treated with respect, the more ambition they have. And vice versa. The opt-out revolution is really a downward spiral.

Finally, these choices are bad for women individually. A good life for humans includes the classical standard of using one's capacities for speech and reason in a prudent way, the liberal requirement of having enough autonomy to direct one's own life, and the utilitarian test of doing more good than harm in the world. Measured against these time-tested standards, the expensively educated upper-class moms will be leading lesser lives. At feminism's dawning, two theorists compared gender ideology to a caste system. To borrow their insight, these daughters of the upper classes will be bearing most of the burden of the work always associated with the lowest caste: sweeping and cleaning bodily waste. . . . [These women are] voluntarily becom[ing] untouchables.

When she sounded the blast that revived the feminist movement 40 years after women received the vote, Betty Friedan spoke of lives of purpose and meaning, better lives and worse lives, and feminism went a long way toward shattering the glass ceilings that limited their prospects outside the home. Now the glass ceiling begins at home. Although it is harder to shatter a ceiling that is also the roof over your head, there is no other choice.

Page 237. Add at end of Note:

An even more recent discussion of some of these themes is in Lisa Belkin, *When Mom and Dad Share It All*, N.Y. TIMES MAG., June 15, 2008, at 44, *available at* http://www.nytimes.com/2008/06/15/magazine/15 parenting-t.html.

D. Encroachments on the Doctrine of Family Privacy
1. The Constitutional Right to Privacy

Page 281. Add after *Ayotte v. Planned Parenthood*:

NOTE:

In *Gonzalez v. Carhart*, 550 U.S. ___, 127 S. Ct. 1610 (2007), set forth in this Supplement, *infra*, Chapter 7, Section A, at pages 123-41, the Supreme Court affirmed a federal ban on "partial birth abortions."

2. Domestic Violence
c. Legal Responses to Violence

Page 345. Add at end of Note:

For a recent, insightful look at these—and other—issues, see also LISA A. GOODMAN & DEBORAH EPSTEIN, LISTENING TO BATTERED WOMEN: A SURVIVOR-CENTERED APPROACH TO ADVOCACY, MENTAL HEALTH, AND JUSTICE (2007).

CHAPTER 5: CUSTODY

D. Applying the Best Interest Standard
4. Religion

Page 554. Add after *Kendall v. Kendall*:

Shepp v. Shepp

Supreme Court of Pennsylvania, 2006.
906 A.2d 1165.

■ Justice NEWMAN.

We granted allocatur in this case to consider the extent to which courts can limit parents from advocating religious beliefs that, if acted upon, would constitute criminal conduct.

Facts and Procedural History

Stanley M. Shepp (Father) and Tracey L. Shepp, a/k/a Tracey L. Roberts (Mother) married in June of 1992. They converted to the Mormon faith prior to their marriage. Their child, Kaylynne Marie Shepp (Kaylynne), whose custody is at issue in this case, was born on February 3, 1993. The parties separated in April of 2000, and they divorced in February of 2001. Shortly after the divorce, the Mormon Church excommunicated Father because he is a fundamentalist who believes in polygamy.

Following the parties' separation, Kaylynne lived with Mother and her three other daughters from previous marriages. On January 2, 2002, Father filed a Petition seeking an order of shared legal and physical custody of Kaylynne. The trial court issued an Interim Order for Custody on January 30, 2002, which provided that the parties would share legal custody and that Mother would have primary physical custody. The Interim Order notes, "Father's position is that he requests primary physical custody, although the Petition does indicate shared physical custody." Order dated January 30, 2002, at 3.

The trial court held a hearing on May 6, 2002. Father testified that he practices Mormon fundamentalism and the teachings of Joseph Smith and Brigham Young. He further stated that fundamentalism "includes plural marriage." He testified that he has not set a limit on the number of wives he would like to have, but would have no problem with additional wives if they love his family and get along. With respect to discussing plural marriage with Kaylynne, Father stated that he has told the child of the possibility that she could have another mother who comes into the family through plural marriage. He indicated his belief that it is important for children to know, while they are young, about any lifestyle the family may practice, rather than to "all of a sudden pop something on them like that" when they are seventeen. When asked if he would try to marry Kaylynne into a polygamist relationship, he replied that he would not, but that in order for her to be happy, she has to have choices, and that as a father it is his job to help her learn about and understand alternatives. Father's current wife testified that she accepts the idea of plural marriage and that she is comfortable with the idea of participating in a family with more than one mother. She stated that there are no plans at the present time for her marriage to become a plural marriage.

Mother testified that Father's belief in polygamy was the reason for the parties' divorce. She stated that Father would like to have five wives, and expressed concerns that he would introduce Kaylynne to men so that she would be ready to engage in polygamy once she reaches the age of thirteen. She stated that she did not wish her daughter to interact with polygamist families or "to be taught polygamy in any way."

Manda Lee (Manda), Mother's daughter from a previous marriage, testified that when she was thirteen years old, Father (who is her stepfather) told her "that if you didn't practice polygamy or you didn't agree with it, but mostly if you didn't practice it, that you were going to hell." She further testified that Father told her that in Pennsylvania a fourteen-year old can get married with a parent's permission, and "since I was already living in the house and we were already related, that it would be a good idea for us to be married." On rebuttal, Father denied Manda's allegation that he suggested they participate in a polygamous relationship.

At the conclusion of the hearing, the trial court noted:

> Contact [between a parent and a child] can be limited only when the parent has been shown to suffer from severe mental or moral deficiencies that constitute a grave threat to the child.
>
> While we may have evidence of moral deficiency of [F]ather because of his belief in having multiple wives, there has been no evidence of a grave threat to the child in this case.

In its final Order, the court awarded joint legal custody to both parents, and primary physical custody to Mother. Noting that the parties had raised Kaylynne in the Mormon faith, the court directed, "the child will continue with that religious upbringing." However, the court ordered, "Father is specifically prohibited while the child is a minor from teaching her about polygamy, plural marriages or multiple wives."

Father filed a timely appeal to the Superior Court, which affirmed the decision of the trial court. However, the Superior Court disagreed with the conclusion of the trial court, stating, "[t]he court's factual findings as to the nature of the practice endorsed by [Father] and as to [Father's] own character render its conclusion that [Father] poses no grave threat to his daughter both erroneous and unreasonable." *Shepp v. Shepp*, 821 A.2d 635, 638 (Pa. Super. 2003). The Superior Court made this determination based on the following facts elicited during the testimony of Father's stepdaughter, which the trial court and the Superior Court deemed credible:

> [Father's] promotion of his beliefs to his stepdaughter involved not merely the superficial exposure of a child to the theoretical notion of criminal conduct, but constituted a vigorous attempt at moral suasion and recruitment by threats of future punishment. The child was, in fact, warned that only by committing an illicit act could she comply with the requirements of her religion.

The court further expressed concern that Father's intention to inculcate a belief in polygamy in his own daughter "may perhaps, as the child matures, even become insistence that she engage in such conduct." While recognizing the difference between discussion and coercion, the court held that the best interests of the child would be served by restricting Father from discussing polygamy with Kaylynne until she is eighteen years old.

Discussion

This case implicates two highly important values: the free exercise of religion as guaranteed by the First Amendment to the Constitution of the United States and the public policy of this Commonwealth, as set forth in Section 5301 of the Domestic Relations Code, "when in the best interest of the child, to assure a reasonable and continuing contact of the child with both parents after a separation or dissolution of the marriage and a sharing of the rights and responsibilities of child rearing by both parents." 23 Pa.C.S. § 5301.

The essence of Father's position is that he is simply a parent who wishes to share his sincere religious beliefs with his child. In support of his view that the courts may not interfere with this right, he relies on *Wisconsin v. Yoder*, 406 U.S. 205 (1972). In *Yoder*, the United States Supreme Court affirmed a decision of the Supreme Court of Wisconsin, which held that the convictions of Amish parents for violating the State's compulsory school attendance law were invalid pursuant to the First Amendment to the United States Constitution. Although the relevant statute required that all children between the ages of seven and sixteen attend school, Yoder and other parents refused to send their children to school beyond the eighth grade. The United States Supreme Court recognized the importance of the State's interest in universal education, but nevertheless concluded that such interest "is not totally free from a balancing process when it impinges on fundamental rights and interests, such as those specifically protected by the Free Exercise Clause of the First Amendment, and the traditional interest of parents with respect to the religious upbringing of their children." *Id.* at 214. Furthermore, "only those interests of the highest order and those not otherwise served can overbalance legitimate claims to the free exercise of religion." *Id.* at 215. Based on a review of the record, the United States Supreme Court noted that the Amish way of life, which the parents wished to maintain by prohibiting formal education beyond the eighth grade, was a matter of deep religious conviction.

Unchallenged expert testimony established that the "enforcement of the State's requirement of compulsory formal education after the eighth grade would gravely endanger if not destroy the free exercise of respondents' religious beliefs." *Id.* at 219.

. . . .

In the case *sub judice*, Father asserts that where the State interferes in matters of religious speech between parent and child, such action is subject to strict scrutiny, or a showing that a compelling governmental interest outweighs the fundamental right of a parent to make decisions concerning a child's upbringing.

Mother disagrees with Father's position that polygamy is a constitutionally protected practice within a religious context. In the nineteenth century, the United States Supreme Court issued four decisions in which it took a firm position against Mormon polygamy: *Reynolds v. United States*, 98 U.S. 145 (1878); *Murphy v. Ramsey*, 114 U.S. 15 (1885); *Davis v. Beason*, 133 U.S. 333 (1890); *Late Corp. of the Church of Latter Day Saints v. United States*, 136 U.S. 1 (1890). The Reynolds Court referred to polygamy as "odious among the northern and western nations of Europe." *Reynolds*, 98 U.S. at 164. The Late Corp. Court stated that Mormon polygamy is "a crime against the laws, and abhorrent to the sentiments and feelings of the civilized world." 136 U.S. at 48. In *Davis*, the Court upheld a law in the territory of Idaho that required an individual registering to vote to swear or affirm, *inter alia*, that he was not a bigamist or a polygamist, was not a member of an order that practices bigamy or polygamy, and that he did not and would not counsel or advise others to commit bigamy or polygamy. The Court stated:

> Bigamy and polygamy . . . are crimes by the laws of the United States, and they are crimes by the laws of Idaho. . . . If they are crimes, then to teach, advise, and counsel their practice is to aid in their commission, and such teaching and counseling are themselves criminal, and proper subjects of punishment, as aiding and abetting crime are in all other cases.

Davis, 133 U.S. at 341-42.

Plural marriage is a crime in Pennsylvania. Section 4301 of the Crimes Code, 18 Pa.C.S. § 4301 provides:

(a) Bigamy.—A married person is guilty of bigamy, a misdemeanor of the second degree, if he contracts or purports to contract another marriage, unless at the time of the subsequent marriage:

> (1) the actor believes that the prior spouse is dead;

> (2) the actor and the prior spouse have been living apart for two consecutive years throughout which the prior spouse was not known by the actor to be alive; or

> (3) a court has entered a judgment purporting to terminate or annul any prior disqualifying marriage, and the actor does not know that judgment to be invalid.

(b) Other party to bigamous marriage.—A person is guilty of bigamy if he contracts or purports to contract marriage with another knowing that the other is thereby committing bigamy.

In the instant matter, the illegal nature of polygamy becomes important when determining the appropriate level of scrutiny to apply to Father's free exercise claim. The decision of the United States Supreme Court in *Employment Division, Department of Human Resources of Oregon v. Smith*, 494 U.S. 872 (1990) (*Smith II*), is critical to this issue. Alfred Smith (Smith) and Galen Black (Black) were fired from their employment with a private drug rehabilitation organization because they ingested peyote while participating in a religious ceremony of the Native American Church. Pursuant to the relevant Oregon statute, persons in possession of peyote are guilty of a felony. Smith and Black applied for unemployment compensation benefits, which the Employment Division denied because their employer had discharged them for work-related misconduct. The Oregon Court of Appeals reversed based on its conclusion that the denial of benefits violated the free exercise rights of Smith and Black as protected by the First Amendment. The Oregon Supreme Court affirmed, holding that the criminality of the use of peyote was irrelevant because the purpose of the misconduct provision, pursuant to which the Employment Division denied relief, was not to enforce criminal laws, but to preserve the financial stability of the unemployment compensation fund. The Oregon Supreme Court held that this purpose did not justify the burden that denial of compensation placed on the religious practice of Smith and Black. On appeal, *Employment Division, Department of Human Resources of Oregon v. Smith*, 485 U.S. 660

(1988) (*Smith I*), the United States Supreme Court held, "if a State has prohibited through its criminal laws certain kinds of religiously motivated conduct without violating the First Amendment, it certainly follows that it may impose the lesser burden of denying unemployment compensation benefits to persons who engage in that conduct." *Id.* at 670. However, because the Oregon Supreme Court had not determined whether an exception to the controlled substance law existed for the sacramental use of peyote, the United States Supreme Court vacated the judgment and remanded to the Oregon Supreme Court for further proceedings. On remand, the Oregon Supreme Court held that there was no sacramental use exception to the criminal statute. It then determined that the prohibition was invalid pursuant to the Free Exercise Clause and, accordingly, reaffirmed its previous ruling.

The Employment Division again sought *certiorari*, which the United States Supreme Court granted. The Court, in an Opinion by Justice Scalia, reversed, determining that the *Sherbert* [*v. Verner*, 374 U.S. 398 (1963)] test, which requires a compelling government interest, does not apply where the challenged State action that is claimed to inhibit the free exercise of religion is a generally applicable criminal law. The Court noted:

> The government's ability to enforce generally applicable prohibitions of socially harmful conduct, like its ability to carry out other aspects of public policy, 'cannot depend on measuring the effects of a governmental action on a religious objector's spiritual development.' To make an individual's obligation to obey such a law contingent upon the law's coincidence with his religious beliefs, except where the State's interest is "compelling"—permitting him, by virtue of his beliefs, 'to become a law unto himself,' *Reynolds v. United States*, 98 U.S. at 167—contradicts both constitutional tradition and common sense.

Smith II, 494 U.S. at 885.

Like the Oregon law prohibiting the use of peyote, the Pennsylvania statute prohibiting bigamy is a law of general application. Therefore, pursuant to *Smith II*, a neutral law criminalizing polygamy overrides a claim that such law places an improper limitation on the free exercise of religion. Based on *Smith II*, Mother asserts, "[s]ince 18 Pa.C.S. § 4301 is a valid and otherwise neutral law, it follows that the Commonwealth of Pennsylvania has the right to enforce, regulate, and prohibit such conduct or speech that may be incidental to such conduct, whether it be the use of peyote, enforcement of social security taxes, or the practice of polygamy." Brief of Appellee at 14 (citation modified).

Smith II further recognized:

> The only decisions in which we have held that the First Amendment bars application of a neutral, generally applicable law to religiously motivated action have involved not the Free Exercise Clause alone, but the Free Exercise Clause in conjunction with other constitutional protections, such as freedom of speech and of the press . . . or the right of parents, acknowledged in *Pierce v. Society of Sisters*, 268 U.S. 510 (1925), to direct the education of their children, see *Wisconsin v. Yoder*, 406 U.S. 205 (1972) . . . .

494 U.S. at 881. Justice Scalia referred to such claims as presenting "a hybrid situation[,]" *id.* at 882, which is subject to strict scrutiny. The instant matter, combining free exercise claims with the fundamental right of parents to raise their children, is a hybrid case. As such, *Smith II*, which presents a "free exercise claim unconnected with any communicative activity or parental right," does not directly answer the question of whether a court may prohibit a parent from advocating religious beliefs, which, if acted upon, would constitute a crime.

In light of the fact that *Smith II* does not apply to hybrid cases, we must reject the position advanced by Mother that a court may prohibit a parent from discussing religious beliefs with a child solely because acting upon those beliefs would result in the commission of a crime. Instead, we believe that *Yoder* provides the appropriate standard by which to consider the issue before us. As previously noted, "only those interests of the highest order and those not otherwise served can overbalance legitimate claims to the free exercise of religion." *Yoder*, 406 U.S. at 215. Based on the record before us, it is clear that the Commonwealth's interest in promoting compliance with the statute criminalizing bigamy is not an interest of the "highest order" that would supersede the interest of a parent in speaking to a child about a deeply held aspect of his faith. However, this does not end our inquiry because *Yoder* also provides:

To be sure, the power of the parent, even when linked to a free exercise claim, may be subject to limitation under *Prince [v. Massachusetts*, 321 U.S. 158 (1944),] if it appears that parental decisions will jeopardize the health or safety of the child, or have a potential for significant social burdens.

Id. at 233-34. *Yoder* recognized that government has an interest in protecting "the physical or mental health of the child." *Id.* at 230. Applying strict scrutiny,

"The Government may . . . regulate the content of constitutionally protected speech in order to promote a compelling interest if it chooses the least restrictive means to further the articulated interest. We have recognized that there is a compelling interest in protecting the physical and psychological well-being of minors."

The state's compelling interest to protect a child in any given case, however, is not triggered unless a court finds that a parent's speech is causing or will cause harm to a child's welfare.

In the instant matter, the trial court determined that Father believed in polygamy, and that acting on that belief "would be not only illegal in Pennsylvania, but would also be immoral and illogical." The court noted that Father had approached his stepdaughter and "informed her that she would go to hell if she did not believe in polygamy," and that the stepdaughter recalled that Father "had suggested that when she became of age, that they would perhaps be married." Nevertheless, the trial court stated that there was, "no evidence of a grave threat to the child in this case." Engaging in speculation that Father's statements to his stepdaughter might lead to insistence that his own child engage in polygamy, the Superior Court improperly substituted its judgment for that of the trial court, and concluded that the teaching of plural marriage constituted a grave threat. In light of the fact that the trial court did not find a grave threat, it erred in restricting Father from teaching Kaylynne about polygamy.

By their very nature, decisions involving child custody must focus on the character and conduct of the individual parents and children involved. Accordingly, there may be instances where restricting a parent from teaching a child about a sincere religious belief involving illegal conduct is appropriate. However, we emphasize that the illegality of the proposed conduct on its own is not sufficient to warrant the restriction. Where, as in the instant matter, there is no finding that discussing such matters constitutes a grave threat of harm to the child, there is insufficient basis for the court to infringe on a parent's constitutionally protected right to speak to a child about religion as he or she sees fit.

Conclusion

For these reasons, we conclude that a court may prohibit a parent from advocating religious beliefs, which, if acted upon, would constitute a crime. However, pursuant to *Yoder*, it may do so only where it is established that advocating the prohibited conduct would jeopardize the physical or mental health or safety of the child, or have a potential for significant social burdens. Because such harm was not established in this case, there was no constitutional basis for the state's intrusion in the form of the trial court's Order placing a prohibition on Father's speech. That being the case, the second facet of the strict scrutiny test—whether the trial court's Order was narrowly tailored to achieve a compelling end—was not implicated. Accordingly, we reverse the Order of the Superior Court.

■ Justice BAER, dissents.

. . . .

. . . Manda Lee (Manda), one of Mother's daughters from a previous marriage and Child's half-sister, testified that when she was fourteen Father told her that if she failed to practice polygamy she would go to hell. He suggested that because he and Manda were already living under the same roof, it only made sense for them to marry. While Father denied that he had suggested marriage to Manda, he did not deny her other factual averments. . . . The trial court found Manda's version of what occurred credible.

. . . .

[R]elying on Manda's testimony and Father's statements toward Child, the trial court found, as a matter of fact—and in isolation from its restatement of what it took to be the governing standard—that Father had crossed the line between expression and conduct, finding that Father had every intention of "follow[ing] through" on his beliefs and, unchecked, would do whatever he could, in his position of considerable authority as Child's parent, to lead Child into a life of polygamy while still of tender years. In light of this factual finding, one entirely supported by the evidence of record, the trial court's remedy granting father partial custody and restricting him only from teaching his daughter about polygamy is not only constitutionally tolerable, but indeed laudably restrained. The trial court's order was narrowly tailored to hedge against Father's coercive conduct in seeking to induct Child into a repugnant and criminal activity in adolescence at a time when Child's lack of autonomy and worldly sophistication would make it difficult for her to protect herself and make an informed decision. On this basis alone, I would rule that the trial court's order was constitutionally permissible and appropriate to protect Child in light of the facts of record.

Moreover, even assuming *arguendo* that the trial court's order infringes Father's free expression or intrudes upon his fundamental right as a parent to direct the education and upbringing of Child, thus incurring constitutional protection, I would still find the trial court's order constitutional. The trial court, the Superior Court, and now a majority of this Court, adopted and applied the rule that only a "grave threat of harm" may justify such an intrusion, relying upon the United States Supreme Court's decision in *Wisconsin v. Yoder*, 406 U.S. 205 (1972). This is only half of the *Yoder* test. *Yoder* provided that "parental authority in matters of religious upbringing may be encroached upon only upon a showing of a 'substantial threat' of 'physical or mental harm to the child, *or to the public safety, peace, order, or welfare.*'" *Id.* at 230 (emphasis added).

. . . .

The first part of this limitation, concerning the health or safety of the child, suggests the "grave" or "substantial threat of harm" standard focused upon by the Majority and the courts below; the latter aspect, concerning the "potential for significant social burdens," suggests a broader inquiry assessing whether exercise of those prerogatives will conflict with the state's legitimate interests in preserving public welfare and mitigating significant social burdens. The Superior Court, as well as the Majority, have failed to address this distinct inquiry in the context of this case, which I believe is squarely presented and requires us to uphold the trial court's custody order narrowly limiting Father's right to inculcate Child into a practice long-since deemed immoral and criminal in every jurisdiction of the United States—not only because it presents a "grave threat of harm" to the child, but also because the practice of polygamy long has been identified as a "substantial threat" to public welfare, an unsustainable burden on society, and a crime.

We would in no way depart from settled caselaw, at the state or federal level, or act contrarily to Pennsylvania law, to identify the coercion by a parent of his child into the criminal practice of plural marriage as presenting "a potential for significant social burdens" sufficient to invoke the second aspect of the *Yoder* test. Indeed, that plural marriage has been criminalized in Pennsylvania and virtually everywhere else demonstrates an overwhelming consensus of moral opprobrium regarding the practice and refuting the notion that the burden on society of the practice can legitimately be claimed to be ephemeral or inchoate. Indeed, this Court specifically has observed that polygamy presents "a substantial threat to society," see *In re Green*, 338, 292 A.2d 387, 389 (Pa. 1972), echoing the language of *Yoder*.

Thus, I would adopt as part of Pennsylvania law the second half of the *Yoder* test recognizing government's need to protect society as a whole, and uphold the trial court's decision as affirmed by the Superior Court under either the first half of the *Yoder* test, which is already part of our law, or under the second half of *Yoder*, constraining individual action inimical to society as a whole.

NOTE:

In *In re Texas Dep't of Family and Protective Servs.*, No. 08-0391, 2008 WL 2212383, at *2 (Tex. Sup. Ct. May 29, 2008) (per curiam), the Texas Supreme Court upheld the appeals court's reversal of a trial court opinion granting emergency removal by the Texas Department of Family and Protective Services of a number of children from the "Yearning for Zion" ranch. The state had justified the removal, in part, on the ground that the religious community condones polygamous marriage and pregnancy and childbirth by minor females. See Chapter 2, Section A, in this Supplement, at pages 1-10.

F. Modification
2. Relocation

Page 609. Add after Note:

Maynard v. McNett

North Dakota Supreme Court, 2006.
710 N.W.2d 369.

■ SANDSTROM, JUSTICE.

Jeffery Maynard appeals an order allowing his former wife, Christa McNett, formerly known as Christa Maynard, to move from Fargo, North Dakota, to Branson, Missouri, with their nine-year-old daughter. The district court found that a move to Branson was in the best interests of the child. Because the parents have joint legal and physical custody, the district court erred in allowing one parent to move with the child. We hold that a parent with joint legal and physical custody may not be granted permission to move with the parties' child, unless the district court first determines the best interests of the child require a change in primary custody to that parent. There was no motion to change custody. We therefore reverse.

I

Maynard and McNett were married on June 26, 1993. The parties had one child born in 1996. On June 2, 1999, Maynard and McNett were divorced, and the parties stipulated to "joint legal and joint physical custody" of the child. The stipulation was incorporated into the judgment. Following the divorce, the child spent approximately twelve nights per month with Maynard and the remainder of each month with McNett.

In July 2004, McNett brought a motion to move her child out of state to Branson so she could pursue a job in her field of study, corporate community fitness. If McNett moved to Branson, she planned to take a position managing a "Why Weight? Women's Total Fitness" franchise. McNett's mother had agreed to pay for the start-up costs of the franchise and was planning to open two new "Why Weight?" stores on property she owned near Branson. Maynard, who lives in Fargo, opposed McNett's requested move to Branson, arguing that a move would infringe on his parental rights.

On August 30, 2004, a hearing was held before judicial referee Scott A. Griffeth. After hearing testimony, the judicial referee granted McNett's motion to move out of state. On September 28, 2004, Maynard requested a review of the judicial referee's decision. On October 21, 2004, after a de novo review of the record, Judge Wade L. Webb issued an order adopting the referee's findings and affirming the decision of the judicial referee. Maynard then moved to amend the findings of fact and judgment. The motion was denied. Maynard attempted to stay the judgment at the district court and this Court, but neither court granted a stay. This appeal followed.

On appeal, Maynard argues that McNett failed to show that the prospective move would be advantageous and in the best interests of the child, and that the court did not give sufficient weight to the joint physical custody arrangement. McNett argues the court properly weighed the evidence and concluded the move was in the best interests of the child.

The district court had jurisdiction under N.D. Const. art. VI, § 8, and N.D.C.C. § 27-05-06. The appeal was timely under N.D.R.App.P. 4(a). This Court has jurisdiction under N.D. Const. art. VI, §§ 2, 6, and N.D.C.C. § 27-02-04 and §§ 28-27-01 through 28-27-02.

II

Section 14-09-07, N.D.C.C., provides a custodial parent "may not change the residence of the child to another state except upon order of the court or with the consent of the noncustodial parent, if the noncustodial parent has been given visitation rights by the decree." "The purpose of N.D.C.C. § 14-09-07 is to protect the noncustodial parent's visitation rights if the custodial parent wants to move out of state." *State ex. rel Melling v. Ness,* 592 N.W.2d 565 (N.D. 1999). In determining whether a custodial parent should be allowed to relocate with a child to another state, the best interests of the child are the primary consideration. The custodial parent has the burden of proving, by a preponderance of the evidence, that a move is in the best interests of the child. The trial court's decision that a move is in the best interests of the child is a finding of fact that will not be reversed unless it is clearly erroneous.

III

McNett argues that because the child lived more days per month with her, as directed by the divorce judgment, the trial court properly determined she was the custodial parent. Whether the divorce judgment declared a primary custodian requires an interpretation of the judgment. Interpretation of a judgment is a question of law, and the interpretation of a judgment by a different trial judge than the one who ordered its entry is entitled to no deference. North Dakota law recognizes and permits joint legal and physical custody and does not require that the child reside equally with both parents in such an arrangement.

Under N.D.C.C. § 14-09-06.1:

> An order for custody of an unmarried minor child entered pursuant to this chapter must award the custody of the child to a person, agency, organization, or institution as will, in the opinion of the judge, promote the best interests and welfare of the child. Between the mother and father, whether natural or adoptive, there is no presumption as to who will better promote the best interests and welfare of the child.

[T]he designation of a single custodian is not required. Each parent can be declared a custodian and enjoy all the rights under the law designated to a custodial parent.

A custody arrangement stipulated to by the parties must be given a great deal of deference, and the parties must be bound by it to provide certainty in future disputes. Maynard and McNett stipulated to joint legal and physical custody and should be bound by it. Therefore, we hold that both Maynard and McNett are custodial parents with parenting rights to their child.

The district court failed to properly analyze the divorce judgment and decree, which established not *a* custodial parent but *joint legal and joint physical custody*. The district court wrote the grant of joint legal and joint physical custody out of the divorce judgment and decree and analyzed the case as though there were only one custodial parent.

IV

In *Stout v. Stout*, this Court discussed how the courts of North Dakota should decide whether allowing a custodial parent to relocate with a child under N.D.C.C. § 14-09-07 was in the best interests of the child. 560 N.W.2d 903 (N.D. 1997). The Court emphasized that when one parent has sole custody and the other parent has visitation rights, the child will look to the custodial parent for support, and when a custodial parent experiences a psychological adjustment, the child will also. Relying on *D'Onofrio v. D'Onofrio*, 365 A.2d 27 (N.J. Super. Ct. Ch. Div. 1976), this Court developed a four factor test for considering whether a move is in the best interest of a child:

   1.   The prospective advantages of the move in improving the custodial parent's and child's quality of life,

   2.   The integrity of the custodial parent's motive for relocation, considering whether it is to defeat or deter visitation by the noncustodial parent,

   3.   The integrity of the noncustodial parent's motives for opposing the move,

   4.   Whether there is a realistic opportunity for visitation which can provide an adequate basis for preserving and fostering the noncustodial parent's relationship with the child if relocation is allowed, and the likelihood that each parent will comply with such alternate visitation.

The fourth factor was altered in *Hawkinson v. Hawkinson* to address the negative effect a move can have on the noncustodial parent's relationship with the child:

   The potential negative impact on the relationship between the noncustodial parent and the child, including whether there is a realistic opportunity for visitation which can provide an adequate basis for preserving and fostering the noncustodial parent's relationship with the child if relocation is allowed, and the likelihood that each parent will comply with such alternate visitation.

591 N.W.2d 144 (N.D. 1999)

Stout recognized, however, the differences between a motion to relocate in a sole custody arrangement and a joint custody arrangement. In *Stout,* the majority said, "We emphasize that motions to relocate are *not* motions for change of custody. . . . In contrast, in a motion to relocate, the primary physical custody decision has already been made, and custody is *not* the issue." *Stout,* 560 N.W.2d at 903. The majority also said, however, "We recognize that there are cases in which the parents, pursuant to a final decree, share physical custody equally and an original determination of primary custody may be necessary in a motion to relocate by one parent." *Id.* at ¶ 54 n.7[.] . . .

This case presents a motion to relocate when there is true joint legal and joint physical custody. As acknowledged by the majority in *Stout*, this case requires a determination of primary custody before McNett may be granted to relocate with the child because primary custody has not been decided. To allow one parent to relocate without first deciding primary custody would completely undermine the joint custody rights the parties agreed to share.

The courts of other jurisdictions have recognized that before a motion to relocate can be granted in joint custody cases, there must be a declaration of primary custody. In *Voit v. Voit*, the father wanted to move from New Jersey to Arizona. 721 A.2d 317, 319 (N.J. Super. Ct. Ch. Div. 1998). He moved for change of custody and permission to relocate with the child. *Id.* at 326. The court said, "This case is first and foremost a request for modification of a joint legal and physical custody agreement." *Id.* The court held that because its analysis for relocation of a child in primary custody cases would be inappropriate, "to determine whether good cause exists for removal in this true joint-parenting case, this court must apply the standard appropriate to applications for a change in custody." *Id.* The moving parent had to prove there had been a substantial change in circumstances so that the best interests of the child demanded a transfer of custody. *Id.* The court ultimately concluded the father had made no showing why the best interests of the child would be better served in Arizona than in New Jersey. *Id.* at 327.

In *Brown v. Brown,* the mother wanted to move from Nebraska to New York. 621 N.W.2d 70, 75 (Neb. 2000). The mother moved for primary custody of the child and for permission to relocate. *Id.* The general standard in Nebraska for relocation of a child was that the move be for a legitimate purpose and be in the best interests of the child. *Id.* at 77. Because it was a joint custody case, however, the court held the moving party must first prove there had been a material change in circumstances for the court to declare a primary custodian. *Id.* at 78. Although relocation itself was not a *per se* change in circumstances, under the right fact situation, moving with the child could constitute a change in circumstances. *Id.* Therefore, to incorporate the material change in circumstances into its legitimate purpose and best-interests-of-the-child standard for relocation, the court held, "in cases of joint legal and physical custody, a legitimate reason for leaving the state, taken together with an expressed intent to do so, may constitute a material change in circumstances affecting the best interests of a child, sufficient to require examination of the best interests of the child." *Id.* The burden of proof is on the relocating party to show that relocation of the child with the parent is a legitimate and material change in circumstances in the best interests of the child. *Id.* at 80. The court applied its relocation best-interest-of-the-child factors, which were similar to *Stout-Hawkinson's.* *Brown*, at 80. The court noted that "[a]s a practical matter, the existence of a joint physical custody relationship is likely to make it more difficult for the relocating parent to meet these burdens," referring to the *Stout-Hawkinson*-like factors. *Brown,* at 78. "This fact, however, is not attributed to a heightened burden of proof, but simply to the unavoidable practical consequences of joint legal and physical custody, and it is considered in the context of whether a proposed move is in the best interests of the child." *Id.* at 80. Justice John Wright noted that, in his opinion, the party seeking to relocate should first prove a modification in custody is needed for the court to declare primary custody, thus wholly separating the issues of change of custody and relocation. *Id.* at 86 (Wright, J., concurring in result).

. . . .

A motion to relocate and the *Stout-Hawkinson* factors alone are inadequate in handling the case of a parent with joint custody of a child wishing to relocate with the child. We hold that a parent with joint legal and physical custody may not be granted permission to move with the parties' child, unless the district court first determines the best interests of the child require a change in primary custody to that parent. A parent with joint custody who wishes to relocate with the child must make two motions: one for a change of custody, governed by N.D.C.C. § 14-09-06.2, and one to relocate with the child, governed by N.D.C.C. § 14-09-07. The change-of-custody motion requires the party wishing to relocate to show there has been a significant change in circumstances and the best interests of the child would be served by the child's moving with the relocating parent.

. . . .

The district court may consider the intention of the parent making the motion to relocate with the child in judging the child's best interests under § 14-09-06.2. After assuming McNett will move to Missouri, the district court simply has to decide whether the child's best interest are better served with McNett in Missouri or with Maynard in North Dakota.

. . . .

V

There was no motion to change custody and therefore the motion to relocate could not have been properly granted. We reverse.

G. Visitation

Page 617. Add after Note:

LeClair v. Reed ex rel. Reed

Supreme Court of Vermont, 2007.
939 A.2d 466.

■ ENTRY ORDER

Appellant Robert LeClair appeals from a Windsor Family Court decision dismissing his action to establish parentage of, and rights and responsibilities for, a child conceived during a sexual assault he committed on appellee's daughter, a minor at the time.[1] We reverse and remand for a hearing.

---

[1] Appellee's daughter is no longer a minor.

The relevant facts and procedural history may be briefly summarized. In January 2005, appellant pleaded guilty to the sexual assault. At the time of the assault, appellant was thirty-seven and appellee's daughter was fifteen. See 13 V.S.A. § 3252(a)(3) (1998) (prohibiting sexual acts with persons under the age of sixteen). In February 2005, appellant filed a complaint seeking to establish parentage, parental rights and responsibilities, parent-child contact, and child support. Appellant dismissed the action voluntarily in early May 2005 in order to "get to a point in [his] treatment that [would] allow [him] to have visitation with [his] son." He then moved to reopen in July of that year. The motion to reopen was accompanied by appellant's affidavit stating that his treatment program would now allow him supervised visitation with the baby. Appellee opposed the motion and also moved to dismiss the action on the basis that appellant lacked standing to pursue the claim. In November 2005, the family court granted appellant's motion to reopen but simultaneously granted appellee's motion to dismiss. This appeal followed.

I. The Motion to Reopen

In granting the motion to reopen, the family court concluded from the plain language of 15 V.S.A. § 302 that the Legislature intended "[a]ny person alleging [themselves] to be the natural father" to have standing to pursue a parentage claim. The family court also concluded that appellant's pleading was sufficient to put appellee on notice of the claims against her. V.R.C.P. 7(b)(1). Appellee contends that the family court erred in granting the motion, because parentage proceedings should be entirely closed to putative parents who, like appellant here, father children by sexual assault. She also continues to argue that appellant's motion failed to set forth a concise statement of the relevant facts and the relief sought, and that the motion therefore ought to have been denied under V.R.C.P. 7. We disagree with appellee on both grounds.

. . . The family court noted that, although the Parentage Proceedings Act must be strictly construed because it is in derogation of the common law, it provides a cause of action for any "person alleged or alleging himself or herself to be the natural parent of a child." 15 V.S.A. § 302(a). As the family court noted, at least one state legislature has seen fit to deny standing to contest a termination of parental rights to "a biological father of [a child] conceived as a result of rape or incest." N.M. Stat.

Ann. § 32A-5-19 (1978). Our Legislature, however, made no such exception in the law it adopted, and instead provided broad standing, via § 302, for "any person" claiming to be the father of a child to pursue a parentage action. Our statutes do not expressly or implicitly limit the class of people with standing to bring parentage actions.

Accordingly, we must conclude that the family court did not abuse its discretion in granting the motion to reopen.

II. The Motion to Dismiss

We do find error, however, in the trial court's grant of appellee's motion to dismiss. Motions to dismiss for failure to state a claim are "not favored and rarely granted." *Ass'n of Haystack Prop. Owners v. Sprague*, 145 Vt. 443, 446-47, 494 A.2d 122, 125 (1985) (citation omitted). Motions to dismiss under V.R.C.P. 12(b)(6) should be granted only where it is "beyond doubt that there exist no facts or circumstances that would entitle . . . plaintiff to relief." *Richards v. Town of Norwich*, 726 A.2d 81, 85 (1999). "[C]ourts should be especially reluctant to dismiss [a cause of action] on the basis of pleadings when the asserted theory of liability is novel or extreme." In reviewing the family court's dismissal for failure to state a claim on which relief can be granted, we take all factual allegations in the complaint as true. We assume that "all contravening assertions in defendant's pleadings are false."

The Legislature has expressly stated a preference for contact between children and their natural parents, except where direct physical or emotional harm to the child or a parent is likely to result from such contact. 15 V.S.A. § 650. Parental rights and responsibilities are to be determined "for the benefit of all children, regardless of whether the child is born during marriage or out of wedlock." *Id.* § 301. It is abundantly clear, however, that neither public policy nor our statutes dictate that the parent-child relationship be maintained without regard to the emotional cost to the child. Indeed, termination or denial ab initio of parental rights is expressly envisioned; 33 V.S.A. § 5540, which defines the "best interests of the child," contemplates that a judicially mandated end to the relationship may be in the best interests of the child. With these standards in mind, we consider the family court's disposition of the motion to dismiss.

Here, for purposes of evaluating the motion, the family court was required to take as true appellant's assertions in his pleadings with the court. Appellant's pleadings uniformly stated that the mother of the child—as distinct from mother's mother, who was the named defendant in the family court and is the appellee here—did not necessarily oppose the establishment of parental rights and responsibilities, and wanted to become pregnant in the first instance. But, in its order, the family court characterized appellant's sexual contact with Reed as a "forcible" assault and stated that "the mother of the child opposes" the establishment of parentage, allegations which were not advanced by appellant.[4]

. . . The family court grant[ed] appellee's motion to dismiss on the basis that the court did "not endorse the establishment of paternal benefits as a result of conception resulting from a criminal sexual assault, at least where the mother of the child opposes it," citing the "public policy of denying the criminal the right to pursue parentage and re-victimize his crime victim." The court concluded that there was no set of facts under which a convicted perpetrator of sexual assault on a minor could ever be found to be a parent of the child resulting from that crime.

Our research, like the family court's, reveals no case squarely facing the question before us. There are two New York cases that are close. See *La Croix v. Deyo*, 437 N.Y.S.2d 517 (Fam. Ct. 1981); *Craig V. v. Mia W.*, 500 N.Y.S.2d 568 (App. Div. 1986). In *LaCroix*, the family court did not apply the shopworn rule that a wrongdoer should not benefit from his wrongful acts, noting that the rule had traditionally been applied only in cases involving property or money. *La Croix*, 437 N.Y.S.2d at 523. The *LaCroix* court noted, in this regard, that the rule failed to account for the "potential benefits to the child of an adjudication of [the statutory rapist's] paternity." *Id.* Similarly, in *Craig V.*, the appellate division held that "[t]he commission of the crime of statutory rape does not preclude [the rapist's] right to maintain the paternity and custody proceedings. That conduct is to be considered only as it relates to the child's best interest at the custody hearing." *Craig V.*, 500 N.Y.S.2d at 570.

---

[4] As a matter of law, of course, appellee's daughter could not have consented to the sexual act at issue here. *State v. Deyo*, 915 A.2d 249 (Vt. 2006). We have not similarly decided, however, that sexual acts committed with minors are "forcible" per se. We express no opinion on that question today.

Many courts have imposed parentage and its attendant liabilities (principally child support) on a minor parent when an adult woman conceived a child via unlawful sexual intercourse with a male minor. . . The[se] cases . . . , of course, do not cleanly answer the question before us. They do, however, give some guidance. The cases uniformly arise under schemes that, like ours, generally require the court to give foremost consideration to the welfare of the child to whose benefit a particular parental obligation might inure. And the courts in the above-cited cases all placed the welfare of the child above that of the parents, as should also be done where one of the parents was a minor victim of a sexual assault and the other the perpetrator. We conclude that the logic of the above-cited cases applies to the facts presented here, and that the family court erred in dismissing the action before a factual record was developed.

. . . A parentage determination made in a factual vacuum would not serve—or would serve only by happenstance—the explicit purpose of parentage proceedings, which is "that the legal rights, privileges, duties and obligations of parents be established *for the benefit of all children*, regardless of whether the child is born during marriage or out of wedlock." 15 V.S.A. § 301 (emphasis added).

We note also that the determination of parentage is distinct from determinations of parental rights and responsibilities, which in the context of benefit to the child may depend upon the age and consent of the custodial parent. In a matter involving a child conceived by rape, for instance, the unwillingness of the victim of the rape to consent to parent-child contact could be a factor in a court's review of a claim by the father of the child. 15 V.S.A. § 650. A person may be adjudicated a parent and yet be denied parent-child contact, rights or responsibilities, or be permitted minimal or no contact with either the child or the other parent, if such limitations are found to be in the best interests of the child. But an adjudication of paternity, unaccompanied by legal or physical rights and responsibilities, secures to the child many otherwise unavailable legal rights.[7] Our holding does not foreclose the possibility that appellant will

---

[7] Such rights include inheritance rights, 14 V.S.A. § 551; the right to bring certain causes of action, e.g., wrongful death, 14 V.S.A. § 1492(c); and rights to certain monies that may accrue to father at a later date, such as child-support offsets against wages and lottery winnings, 15 V.S.A. §§ 781, 792; workers' compensation death benefits, 21

not gain any parental rights or responsibilities on remand. We venture no opinion, on this bare record, as to how the family court should rule on rights of support, visitation, and custody once they are presented against a more complete factual backdrop.

For the foregoing reasons, the case is remanded for parentage—and, if necessary, parental rights and responsibilities—determinations to be made based on a more fully developed factual record.

Reversed and remanded.

I. Unmarried Persons
2. Couples

Page 663. Add after *ALI Topic 5: Allocations of Responsibility to Individuals Other Than Legal Parents*:

A.H. v. M.P.

Supreme Judicial Court of Massachusetts, 2006.
857 N.E.2d 1061.

■ MARSHALL, C.J.

This case raises two questions of first impression. First, whether an adult who is neither the biological nor the adoptive parent of a minor child may assert custody and support rights as a "de facto parent," see *E.N.O v. L.M.M.*, 429 Mass. 824, 711 N.E.2d 886, cert. denied, *528 U.S. 1005* (1999); *Youmans v. Ramos*, 711 N.E.2d 165 (Mass. 1999); and, second, whether and to what extent we should recognize estoppel principles as creating parental rights where the party claiming such rights is neither the biological nor adoptive parent of the child and does not meet the criteria of a de facto parent. See ALI Principles of the Law of Family Dissolution § 2.03 (1) (2002) (defining "parent" to include "de facto parent" and "parent by estoppel").

V.S.A. § 632; retirement benefits, 3 V.S.A. § 476a, 16 V.S.A. § 1946b, 24 V.S.A. § 5066a. A mere determination of parentage activates some of these rights; others require an earlier imposition of, for example, child-support obligations.

The plaintiff, A.H., appeals from the judgment of the Probate and Family Court dismissing her verified complaint in equity, see G. L. c. 215, § 6, against the defendant, M.P., her former same-sex partner, for parental rights to the child they agreed during their relationship to have and coparent. The parties separated when the child was eighteen months old. The plaintiff claims on appeal that the Probate and Family Court judge applied erroneously narrow standards for determining de facto parent status, that the defendant is estopped by her behavior during the relationship and her statements during the litigation from asserting that the plaintiff is not the child's de facto parent, that the plaintiff is entitled to "full parental rights" as the child's de facto parent, that the judge erred in not considering the child's best interests, and that the judge's legal conclusions and ultimate findings are not supported by the evidence. We affirm.

. . . .

1. *Background.* a. *Facts.* We summarize the judge's findings, supplemented as appropriate by uncontested evidence of record. We postpone the recitation of some facts to latter portions of this opinion.

The parties began their relationship in 1995, and jointly purchased a home in 1998. After investigating the options for gay and lesbian couples to become parents, they decided that each party should bear a child using the same anonymous sperm donor, with the defendant being the first to conceive. In 2000, the defendant began treatment at a Boston fertility clinic. The defendant and the plaintiff listed themselves as "parent 1" and "parent 2," respectively on clinic forms. The child was conceived through in vitro fertilization in January, 2001, and born in October of that year. The plaintiff attended prenatal appointments and parenting classes with the defendant, chose the child's pediatrician, was present at the child's birth, and was authorized by the defendant to make medical decisions on the child's behalf. The parties sent out a joint announcement of the child's birth and in all aspects were a family. The couple decided that the child would take the plaintiff's surname as his middle name, and would call the defendant "Mommy" and the plaintiff "Mama."

The parties contacted an attorney to discuss the plaintiff's adopting the child. The attorney explained the importance of adoption for securing the parental rights of lesbian and gay parents, and the plaintiff understood and appreciated these concerns. . . . Shortly after the child's birth, the attorney forwarded the documents for an expedited adoption process to the parties for their signatures and authorization to file. The defendant reviewed and made changes on several of the legal documents (a process that she testified took approximately forty-five minutes), and completed all the necessary steps she could to expedite the adoption process. The defendant then gave the adoption documents to the plaintiff for her review and action. On at least three separate occasions from November, 2001, to April, 2002, the defendant requested that the plaintiff take action on the adoption documents. At trial the plaintiff acknowledged that the defendant requested that she and her family complete the adoption papers but stated the defendant never set a deadline for the completion of the documents and that she (the plaintiff) viewed the adoption as a formality necessary only in the unlikely event of a "worst case scenario." At trial she likened the defendant's requests to being nagged to do yardwork or laundry and told the defendant to "get off her back." The plaintiff had not reviewed, revised, or signed the adoption papers at the time the parties separated. The judge found that, without impediment, the plaintiff's adoption of the child could have been completed within six months of filing the necessary legal documents.

After the child's birth, the defendant stopped working entirely to take full-time care of the child, an arrangement the parties expected to continue for about one year. The plaintiff took a three-month maternity leave from her job as the coexecutive director of a nonprofit agency, but returned to work after two months. During those two months the plaintiff's contributions to the child's caretaking were at their maximum. She soothed him in the evening when, as frequently happened, he awoke colicky, and she walked him, bathed him, diapered him, and otherwise attended to his well-being. Except for diapering, which was a special routine between the plaintiff and the child, the defendant also performed these caretaking tasks, as well as breast feeding and directing his daily routine and was, in the judge's words, the "final arbiter" in respect to the child's care.

During the first few months of the child's life, the plaintiff made efforts to reduce the hours of her work schedule and frequent travel that had caused friction between the parties even before the child's birth. However, the defendant reported to the guardians ad litem that, within six months of the child's birth, she became concerned that the plaintiff was not available to, or involved with, the family, and the defendant confided in a family friend that she felt that she was "going it alone." The plaintiff, despite her intentions, soon found herself resuming long hours working away from the home. Inevitably, the plaintiff's activities left the defendant to assume much of the caretaking responsibility for the child.

. . . .

b. *Procedural history*. On July 18, 2003, the plaintiff filed a verified complaint in equity for joint legal and physical custody and visitation, seeking to establish her status as a de facto parent, the establishment of custodial rights in accordance with the child's best interests, and an order that she, the plaintiff, pay child support. . . .

. . . .

On July 3, 2006, following [a] trial, the judge entered a judgment dismissing all of the plaintiff's claims and awarding sole legal and physical custody to the defendant, with any visitation between her and the child left to the defendant's discretion. The judge concluded that, among other things, the plaintiff had failed to meet her burden of proving de facto status. Specifically, she found that the plaintiff's efforts during the relationship toward the child's care were not equal either in quantity or quality to those of the defendant, that the plaintiff had failed to prove that continued contact between the plaintiff and the child was in his best interests, that visitation would not be in the child's best interests because the plaintiff, "in direct contravention of both the parties' previous practices and common sense . . . selectively ignored [the defendant's] directives regarding the child's care and custody," and that the child would not suffer irreparable harm from the severing of his contact with the plaintiff. She also concluded that the plaintiff had no standing to bring claims for either visitation or a support order under any other theory.

We turn now to our discussion of the legal claims.

2. *De facto parent.* We have recognized that, in certain limited circumstances, a child may, with the legal parent's assent, have developed a "significant preexisting relationship" with an adult who is

not the child's legal parent "that would allow an inference, when evaluating a child's best interests, that measurable harm would befall the child on the disruption of that relationship." *Care & Protection of Sharlene*, 840 N.E.2d 918 (2006), and cases cited. One such circumstance exists when the adult who is not the legal parent is found to meet the criteria of a "de facto parent." "A de facto parent is one who has no biological relation to the child, but has participated in the child's life as a member of the child's family. The de facto parent resides with the child and, with the consent and encouragement of the legal parent, performs a share of caretaking functions at least as great as the legal parent. . . . The de facto parent shapes the child's daily routine, addresses his developmental needs, disciplines the child, provides for his education and medical care, and serves as a moral guide." *E.N.O. v. L.M.M.*, 711 N.E.2d 886 (Mass. 1999). See ALI Principles, *supra* at § 2.03(1) (c) (defining de facto parent). Recognition of de facto parentage lies within the Probate and Family Court's general equity powers pursuant to G. L. c. 215, § 6, to protect the welfare of minors. It proceeds from the premise "that disruption of a child's preexisting relationship with a nonbiological parent can be potentially harmful to the child," thus warranting State intrusion into the private realm of the family. A judge has broad discretion to consider any factor that bears on the child's best interests.

The plaintiff maintains that, in assessing whether the plaintiff met her burden of proving that she was the child's de facto parent, the judge erred by failing to consider the plaintiff's financial contributions to the family, by adopting a quantitative rather than a qualitative analysis in assessing the parties' respective contributions to the child's care, and by ignoring the parent-by-estoppel principles set forth in the ALI Principles, *supra* at § 2.03(1)(b). We examine each claim in turn.

The judge found that the plaintiff was the primary "breadwinner" of the family, and that the defendant was the primary caretaker. The plaintiff ascribes error to the fact that the judge did not consider the plaintiff's financial contributions in considering the degree to which the plaintiff was involved in the child's caretaking during the relationship. There was no error.

We begin with the definition of a de facto parent found in ALI Principles, *supra* at § 2.03, from which our own de facto parent principles derive. The ALI Principles distinguish between general "[p]arenting functions," which are "tasks that serve the needs of the child or the child's residential family," ALI Principles, *supra* at § 2.03(6), and "[c]aretaking functions," the subset of parenting functions that focuses on "tasks that involve interaction with the child or that direct, arrange, and supervise the interaction and care provided by others." *Id.* at § 2.03(5). "Parenting functions" that are not "caretaking functions" include, for example, providing financial support and maintaining the home. See *id.* at § 2.03(6) & comment g, at 125. Caretaking functions "involve the direct delivery of day-to-day care and supervision of the child," including grooming, feeding, medical care, and physical supervision. *Id.* at § 2.03(5) & comment g.

The distinction between general parenting functions and caretaking is not meant to disparage or discount the role of breadwinners in providing for a child's welfare, as the plaintiff suggests. Rather, the distinction proceeds from the presumption that the parent-child bond grows from the myriad hands-on activities of an adult in tending to a child's needs. Unlike other parenting activities, such as serving on a committee at the child's school or remunerative employment—both of which benefit the child but are not performed directly for him or, usually, in his presence—caretaking tasks "are likely to have a special bearing on the strength and quality of the adult's relationship with the child." ALI Principles, *supra* at § 2.03 comment g. The focus on caretaking in the ALI Principles is one means by which to anchor the best interests of the child analysis in an objectively reasonable assessment of whether disruption of the adult-child relationship is potentially harmful to the child's best interests. And potential harm to the child is, of course, the criterion that tips the balance in favor of continuing contact with a de facto parent against the wishes of the fit legal parent, who has "fundamental liberty interests" in the child's care, custody, and control.

Our use of the term "caretaking" in cases concerning alleged de facto parent accords with the use of the term in the ALI Principles. The notion of "caretaking" as the particular subset of parenting tasks having most directly to do with interacting with and on behalf of the child serves as a valuable tool for assessing the adult's bond with the child. More than parental functions not aligned with "caretaking," it more directly and accurately furthers the principal goal of the de facto parent principle: to prevent trauma to the child, that may result from forced rupture of a parent-child bond forged in the "direct delivery of day-to-day care and supervision of the child." It does not denigrate the importance of an adult's financial contributions to a family, or the role of such contributions in securing the child's welfare, to require that one who is not a legal parent and who invokes the equity powers of the court to establish herself as a de facto parent demonstrate a history of substantial direct, loving, appropriate involvement in the child's supervision and care.

Moreover, a judge is free within her broad discretion to consider the impact of parental activity other than caretaking on forming the crucial parent-child bond at the heart of de facto parental status. Here, the judge specifically found that the plaintiff's financial contributions benefited the child. She also determined, however, that the child's "primary bond" was to his primary caretaker, the defendant, and that the relationship between the plaintiff and the child, however salutary to the child, did not "rise[] to that of a parental relationship."

Next, the plaintiff alleges that, "[r]ather than focusing on the quality of the relationship" between the plaintiff and the child, the judge "used a rudimentary quantitative analysis" to conclude that, because the plaintiff worked outside the home and provided financial support so that the defendant was able to stay home with the child, the plaintiff "could not" be a parent to the child. We are unpersuaded.

One of the factors that the ALI Principles set out for courts to consider when a nonlegal parent seeks to prove de facto parent status is that the individual "perform[s] a share of caretaking functions at least as great as that of the parent with whom the child primarily lives." ALI Principles, *supra* at § 2.03(1)(c)(ii)(B). The judge thus quite properly considered the amount of time that the child was in each party's care. To say that the judge then applied this information in a mechanistic fashion, however, is incorrect. In her rationale for the judgment, the judge noted that, in assessing the child's attachment to each party, she considered the "quantity [and] quality" of the parties' caretaking of the child during the relationship. Even a cursory review of the judge's findings reveals that she considered qualitative factors, such as which party deferred to the other in making major decisions concerning he child's care, and which party was able, when interacting with the child, to set the appropriate boundaries. In any event, the focus on the caretaking factor in determining de facto parent status does not preclude a judge from considering, within her broad discretion, any other factor of relevance to determining the child's best interests. There was no error.

3. *Parent by estoppel.* In addition to the arguments raised above, the plaintiff contends that the judge erred in not viewing the evidence through the lens of the parent by estoppel theory. While recognizing biological and adoptive legal parents and de facto parents within the definition of "parents," the ALI Principles also recognize "parent by estoppel." Into this category of parents falls an individual who, in relevant part, although not a legal parent, "(i) is obligated to pay child support . . . or . . . (iii) lived with the child since the child's birth, holding out and accepting full and permanent responsibilities as parent, as part of a prior co-parenting agreement with the child's legal parent . . . to raise a child together each with full parental rights and responsibilities, when the court finds that recognition of the individual as a parent is in the child's best interests." ALI Principles, *supra* at § 2.03(1)(b). There was no error.

The ALI Principles make clear that it is not the third party's reliance on the words or deeds of the legal parent but the best interests of the child that is the paramount consideration in the parent by estoppel analysis. *Id.* at § 2.03 & comment b(iii), at 115. Unlike a de facto parent, a parent by estoppel "is afforded all of the privileges of a legal parent." *Id.* at § 2.03 comment b. Thus, the parent by estoppel principle is a most dramatic intrusion into the rights of fit parents to care for their child as they see fit. It is perhaps for this reason that the ALI Principles contemplate that parent by estoppel status is most appropriate where "adoption is not legally available or possible." *Id.* at § 2.03 comment *b* (*iii*), at 114. In this jurisdiction, same-sex couples, like heterosexual couples, are free to adopt the children of their partners, and, as the evidence shows, adoption was available to the plaintiff virtually from the moment of the child's birth.

We decline in this case to accept the plaintiff's invitation to adopt the parent by estoppel theory. As noted above, a coparent agreement is the foundation of a parent by estoppel claim. Private agreement alone does not suffice to create parental rights in one who is not the child's biological or adoptive parent. . . . An express or implied agreement to have or raise a child may be relevant to the parties' intentions, help explain a course of conduct, or otherwise shed light on matters of material import to a custody or visitation determination. Here, the judge found that the parties entered into an agreement to have and raise a child together, and found that the parties' subsequent actions in respect to the agreement to parent jointly illuminate an important source of the couple's conflicts. But evidence of an agreement is not and cannot be dispositive on the issue whether the plaintiff is the child's legal parent. Contrary to the plaintiff's argument, the judge was not required to consider whether the plaintiff met the criteria of a parent by estoppel, and she appropriately did not elaborate at length on her conclusions.

In sum, we find no merit in the plaintiff's assertions that the judge took an erroneously narrow view of the criteria by which to assess the plaintiff's de facto parent claims.

. . . .

5. *Conclusion*. For the foregoing reasons, the judgment is affirmed.

So ordered.

J. Jurisdiction
2. International Custody Disputes

Page 682. Add after *Silverman v. Silverman*:

Alonzo v. Claudino

U.S. District Court, Middle District of North Carolina, 2007.
2007 WL 475340.

■ TILLEY, DISTRICT JUDGE.

This matter is before the Court on a petition filed pursuant to the Hague Convention on the Civil Aspects of International Child Abduction ("Hague Convention" or "Convention"), Oct. 25, 1980, T.I.A.S. 11,670, 19 I.L.M. 1501 (1980), and its implementing legislation, the International Child Abduction Remedies Act ("ICARA"), 42 U.S.C. §§ 11601-11610. Petitioner is seeking the return of his daughter to

Honduras on the ground that she was illegally abducted by her mother in violation of a valid Honduran custody order. For the reasons set forth below, the petition is GRANTED.

I.

Petitioner Ovidio Danilo Alonzo (Alonzo) and Respondent Yanira Ninoska Pineda Claudino (Ms[.] Pineda), both citizens of Honduras, were married in Tegucigalpa, Honduras on May 2, 1997. The couple has one child, Maria Jose Alonzo Claudino ("Maria Jose"), who was born in Tegucigalpa, Honduras on November 16, 1998. Mr. Alonzo and Ms. Pineda divorced on April 19, 2002. On May 8, 2002, Ms. Pineda was granted "guardianship and care" of Maria Jose by the Second Civil Court of the Family in Tegucigalpa, Honduras, with Mr. Alonzo retaining joint "parental authority." (Resp't Ex. 2.)

In 2003, following a failed business venture, Ms. Pineda left Honduras for the United States with the initial intention to remain for two years. For approximately the next year, Maria Jose remained in Honduras under the supervision of Ms. Pineda's parents. On August 10, 2004, Mr. Alonzo was granted "Provisional Guardianship and Care" of Maria Jose by the Second Civil Court of the Family in Tegucigalpa, Honduras. (Pet'r Exs. 1, 2.)

December 20, 2004, Mr. Alonzo and Maria Jose traveled to the States under a six-month tourist visa to visit Ms. Pineda, who was Durham, North Carolina. Ms. Pineda, admittedly, is residing in States as an illegal alien. Following Maria Jose and Mr. rival, Ms. Pineda took their passports to prevent them from to Honduras. During their stay in the United States, Maria Jose rolled in school and Mr. Alonzo worked for several months, opened a bank account, obtained a driver's license, and assisted Ms. Pineda with purchasing a car.

On June 14, 2005, one week before the expiration of the travel visa, Mr. Alonzo received a note from Ms. Pineda informing him that she had taken Maria Jose. Despite a diligent search, which included assistance from the Durham Police Department and the local Hispanic Center, Mr. Alonzo was unable to locate Maria Jose. Mr. Alonzo next sought counsel from the Honduran Embassy and was advised to return to Honduras to pursue Maria Jose's return through the proper international channels.

On September 19, 2006, Mr. Alonzo filed a petition for the return of Maria Jose under the Hague Convention. On November 9, 2006, Mr. Alonzo filed a petition requesting the government to take physical custody of Maria Jose pursuant to 42 U.S.C. § 11604(a) and N.C. Gen. Stat. § 50A-311. On January 24, 2007, following a hearing, the petition to take physical custody was granted and a warrant was issued for the United States Marshal's Service to take custody of Maria Jose. The warrant was executed on January 24, 2007[,] and a second hearing was held that day. Ms. Pineda was granted a continuance to retain counsel. Further, at the request of Ms. Pineda, Maria Jose remained in the custody of Mr. Alonzo pending the resolution of this matter. A hearing on the merits of the petition to return Maria Jose to Honduras was held on February 2, 2007, and this matter is ready for a ruling.

II.

Congress enacted ICARA in 1988 to "establish procedures for the implementation of the [Hague] Convention in the United States." 42 U.S.C. § 11601(b)(1); see 42 U.S.C. §§ 11601-11610. The Hague Convention seeks to protect children from the harmful effects of international parental child abduction by establishing civil procedures to ensure that abducted children are promptly returned to the country of their "habitual residence." Hague Convention, pmbl., art. 1, 19 I.L.M. at 1501. "[T]he primary purpose of the Hague Convention is 'to preserve the status quo and to deter parents from crossing international boundaries in search of a more sympathetic court.'" *Miller v. Miller*, 240 F.3d 392, 398 (4th Cir. 2001) (quoting *Friedrich v. Friedrich*, 983 F.2d 1396, 1400 (6th Cir. 1993) ("*Friedrich I*")).

Under the Hague Convention, "[t]he merits of any underlying custody case are *not* at issue." *Id.* (emphasis in original). The country of the child's "habitual residence" is the proper arbiter of the custody dispute. Instead, courts are tasked with securing "the prompt return of children wrongfully removed to or retained in any Contracting State" to the country of the child's "habitual residence." Hague Convention, art. 1, 19 I.L.M. at 1501.

A.

Mr. Alonzo bears the initial burden of proving by a preponderance of the evidence "that the child has been wrongfully removed or retained within the meaning of the Convention." 42 U.S.C. § 11603(e)(1)(A). Article 3 of the Hague Convention states that:

> The removal or retention of a child is to be considered wrongful where-
>
> a. it is in breach of rights of custody attributed to a person, an institution or any other body, either jointly or alone, under the law of the State in which the child was habitually resident immediately before the removal or retention; and
>
> b. at the time of removal or retention those rights were actually exercised, either jointly or alone, or would have been so exercised but for the removal or retention.
>
> The rights of custody mentioned in sub-paragraph a above, may arise in particular by operation of law or by reason of a judicial or administrative decision, or by reason of an agreement having legal effect under the law of that State.

Hague Convention, art. 3, 19 I.L.M. at 1501. Therefore, to establish a prima facie case of wrongful retention, Mr. Alonzo must establish: (1) that Maria Jose was a "habitual resident" of Honduras at the time of the retention; (2) that the retention was in breach of his custody rights under the law of Honduras; and (3) that he had been exercising those rights at the time of the retention. *Bader v. Kramer*, 445 F.3d 346, 349 (4th Cir. 2006).

To be deemed "wrongfully retained," the retention must be away from the child's country of "habitual residence." The interpretation of "habitual residence" is vitally important to the Convention because it will dictate both the child's ultimate destination and the arbiter of the custody dispute. However, neither the Hague Convention nor ICARA actually define the term "habitual residence."

. . . "[A] child's habitual residence is the place where he or she has been physically present for an amount of time sufficient for acclimatization and which has a 'degree of settled purpose' from the child's perspective." *Feder v. Evans-Feder*, 63 F.3d 217, 224 (3d Cir. 1995). This is a fact-specific inquiry that should be made on a case-by-case basis.

Because a young child does not usually have a "settled purpose" independent of that of his or her parents, a court should look to "the settled purpose and shared intent of the child's parents in choosing a particular habitual residence." *Whiting v. Krassner*, 391 F.3d 540, 550 (3d Cir. 2004). "The shared intentions of both parents for a child to establish a residence at a particular location, coupled with actions to establish the residence, may create a new habitual residence within a short time period." *Samholt v. Samholt*, 2006 U.S. Dist. LEXIS 51649, 2006 WL 2128061, at *2 (M.D.N.C. July, 26, 2006). Importantly, the emphasis is on the *shared intentions of both parents* rather than unilateral intentions of one parent. "[A] parent cannot create a new habitual residence by wrongfully removing [or retaining] and sequestering a child."

B.

If Mr. Alonzo is able to satisfy his initial burden of establishing wrongful retention, Maria Jose must be returned to Honduras unless Ms. Pineda can establish one of five available defenses. *See* 42 U.S.C. § 11603(e)(2)(A) (requiring proof by clear and convincing evidence that one of the exceptions set forth in article 13b or 20 of the Hague Convention applies); 42 U.S.C. § 11603(e)(2)(B) (requiring proof by a preponderance of the evidence that one of the exceptions set forth in article 12 or 13 of the Hague Convention applies).

The exceptions set forth in Articles 13b and 20 that must be established by clear and convincing evidence are: (1) that there was a grave risk that Maria Jose's return to Honduras would expose her to physical or psychological harm or otherwise place her in an intolerable situation, Hague Convention, art. 13b, 19 I.L.M. at 1502; or (2) that the return of Maria Jose to Honduras would not be permitted by the fundamental principles of the United States "relating to the protection of human rights and fundamental freedoms[,]" Hague Convention, art. 20, 19 I.L.M. at 1503.

The exceptions set forth in Articles 12 and 13 that must be established by a preponderance of the evidence are: (1) that this action was not commenced within one year of the abduction, and Maria Jose is now settled in the United States, Hague Convention, art. 12, 19 I.L.M. at 1502; (2) that Mr. Alonzo "was not actually exercising the custody rights at the time of . . . retention, or had consented to or subsequently acquiesced in the . . . retention[,]" Hague Convention, art. 13a, 19 I.L.M. at 1502; or (3) that Maria Jose "objects to being returned and has attained an age and degree of maturity at which it is appropriate to take account of [her] views[,]" Hague Convention, art. 13 ¶ 2, 19 I.L.M. at 1502-03.

These exceptions are to be narrowly interpreted and applied. . . .

III.

Mr. Alonzo has established by a preponderance of the evidence that he had lawful custody of Maria Jose under the most recent Honduran custody order and that he was exercising his custody rights at the time Maria Jose was taken by Ms. Pineda. The determinative issue is, therefore, whether or not Maria Jose was a "habitual resident" of Honduras when she was taken by Ms. Pineda on June 14, 2005. Mr. Alonzo argues that he came to the United States with Maria Jose in an effort to rekindle his relationship with Ms. Pineda and to persuade her to return home to Honduras. He insists that he and Maria Jose had no intention of remaining in the United States long term.

Ms. Pineda contends, on the other hand, that she and Mr. Alonzo had the mutually shared intention of remaining in the United States indefinitely. In support of this contention, Ms. Pineda points out that Maria Jose was enrolled in school and that Mr. Alonzo obtained employment in violation of his tourist visa, opened a bank account, obtained a driver's license, and helped her purchase a vehicle.

If there were truly a shared intent to remain in the United States, however, it would have been unnecessary for Ms. Pineda to take Maria Jose and Mr. Alonzo's passports to prevent them from returning to Honduras. Ms. Pineda simply cannot create a new habitual residence by preventing Mr. Alonzo from returning to Honduras with Maria Jose. Such action is tantamount to a constructive wrongful retention. Without the ability, or perceived ability, to leave the United States, it was necessary for Mr. Alonzo to earn a living and commendable for him to pursue educational opportunities for his daughter.

Further, considering Maria Jose and Ms. Pineda's illegal immigration status, there cannot be the "degree of settled purpose" required to establish habitual residency in the United States. It is impossible to be settled when you are subject to arrest and deportation at any time. *See Kijowska v. Haines*, 463 F.3d 583, 587 (7th Cir 2006) ("Indeed, as an illegal alien, she could be arrested and deported at any time; her link to this country was particularly tenuous."); *In re Ahumada Cabrera*, 323 F. Supp. 2d 1303, 1311 [(S.D. Fla. 2004)] ("[C]onsidering the child's current immigration status . . . it is difficult to find that the child has any settled purpose whatsoever."). Ms. Pineda has taken no steps to acquire legal status in the United States and, despite no family ties in the country, intends to remain as long as possible. Maria Jose was, therefore, a "habitual resident" of Honduras at the time Ms. Pineda took her on June 14, 2005.

Because Mr. Alonzo has established a prima facie case of wrongful retention, Maria Jose must be returned to Honduras unless Ms. Pineda can establish one of the five available defenses. [The court then concluded that Ms. Pineda was not able to establish any of these defenses.]

. . . .

IV.

For the reasons set forth above, Petitioner Ovidio Danilo Alonzo's Petition for Return of Child to Petitioner is GRANTED.

CHAPTER 6: PROPERTY, ALIMONY, AND CHILD SUPPORT AWARDS

A. Property Division
2. Distinguishing Marital from Separate Property

Page 709. Add after *Thomas v. Thomas*:

In re Marriage of Brown

Oregon Court of Appeals, 2008.
183 P.3d 207.

■ ARMSTRONG, J.

Husband appeals from a dissolution judgment awarding wife spousal support from husband's interests in two family trusts created by husband's father and grandmother. On *de novo* review, we reverse the award of spousal support, modify the property division by awarding wife, as part of the parties' property division, one-half of husband's interest in both trusts, and otherwise affirm.

Husband and wife were married for 24 years. They lived the majority of their married life in Montana, where they raised one daughter and where both practiced law: wife at Montana's water court, and husband in private practice, and in a county prosecutor's office. In this appeal, the dispute concerns the disposition of two family trusts of which husband is a beneficiary. Both trusts were created before husband's marriage, but husband received nothing from either trust until 1997.

The first trust, the Brown-Moore Trust, was created by husband's grandmother and grants to husband and his two sisters a monthly mandatory distribution of the trust's income. Husband's and his sisters' interests in the Brown-Moore Trust are for life only. Upon each sibling's death, that sibling's then-living children receive the deceased sibling's share of the trust. In husband's case, his daughter would be entitled to one-third of the trust upon his death.

The second trust, the Brown Trust, was created by husband's father and grants to husband and his two sisters a monthly mandatory distribution of the trust's income, until the youngest sibling turns 55, at which time each of the three siblings receives one-third of the trust corpus. At the time of the dissolution trial, which was just a year and a half before his youngest sibling's 55th birthday, the value of husband's interest in the Brown Trust corpus was $250,000.

Although husband argues that wife understood that he and wife would not depend on the trusts for their income, it is clear from the evidence that, not long after husband began receiving income from the trusts, the trusts became a significant financial asset for husband and wife. Less than a year after he began receiving income from the trusts, husband, concerned about his physical health after being diagnosed with type 2 diabetes, quit his full-time work at the prosecutor's office and began working on a part-time basis in various positions, including legal consulting, teaching at a university, and sitting in for judges at the city court. His earnings from those jobs totaled about half the earnings that he had received while at the prosecutor's office. Despite that, husband and wife decided to build a new home, which wife described as her "dream home," in Bozeman, Montana. Husband's sister, the trustee of both trusts, agreed to mortgage an asset of the Brown Trust corpus, a condominium in California, in order to provide husband and wife with sufficient funds to finance the construction of their new home. Husband and wife took the biggest portion of the mortgage proceeds, but husband's sisters also received some proceeds as well.

Even before the parties had built their new home, husband talked about leaving Montana and both husband and wife "retiring." After their daughter graduated from high school in 2000, husband's conversations with wife about retiring became more serious. Husband and wife, at this time, were in their mid-fifties, and wife did not want to leave her job, where she had achieved "quite a bit of success," nor did she wish to leave her home. Wife also expressed concern about whether they really had the income to retire. In particular, she was concerned about paying for their daughter's college education and still having sufficient funds to retire. Husband approached his sister about invading his portion of the Brown Trust in order for husband and wife to have more funds, but husband's sister refused. Eventually, husband's sister used part of the Brown-Moore Trust to pay some of their daughter's college expenses.

Husband continued to assure wife that they would have sufficient funds for them both to quit their employment in Bozeman. He testified that they discussed that, upon retiring, their monthly income would consist of an annuity from wife's stepfather, some monthly disbursements from deferred compensation plans, payments from wife's state retirement account, and his dispersals from the trusts, and that "if we were running low on cash, [we could get] part-time jobs or full-time jobs for awhile." Wife testified that husband was consistent in his statements to her that the trust income and the trust corpus "would be available to fund this retirement." By the time that wife agreed with husband to retire, husband was receiving $1,000 per month from the Brown Trust and $430 per month from the Brown-Moore Trust, all of which was deposited each month in the parties' joint checking account. Their other monthly income totaled $1,400 per month.

In 2002, husband and wife sold their home. According to husband, the parties then had approximately $120,000 in assets. They financed the purchase of a fifth-wheel trailer, traveled for a few months, and eventually settled in Gold Beach, Oregon, where they financed the purchase of a second recreational vehicle (RV). They maintained the RV as a stationary "home base" in an RV park, even constructing an addition to the RV and building decks around it. Sometime thereafter, it became clear that they did not have enough income to pay their monthly bills. Their $120,000 in assets had been spent, and their monthly fixed expenses by then included $670 per month for the fifth wheel, $690 per month for the mortgage on the RV, and $425 per month for the trailer park space rent. Husband began working as a private investigator, and wife worked in the trailer park office.

In 2004, wife and husband separated, and wife eventually moved back to Montana. At the time of trial, husband was still working part-time as a private investigator, and wife was working part-time in private legal practice, but they generated only modest incomes from their respective jobs. Moreover, their debt had grown, with wife, at the time of trial, having credit card and furniture store debt totaling $11,000, and husband having credit card debt totaling $25,500. Their fifth wheel was valued at $13,000 less than they owed on it, and the parties were having difficulty selling their RV, because although the RV, in its stationary setting and with the improvements husband and wife had made to it, was worth $130,000, no financial institution would finance its purchase.

The trial court concluded that husband's trust interests had been "completely integrated into the financial planning of the parties." The trial court, therefore, granted wife a judgment of $400 per month from husband's future trust income distributions until the RV was sold and, thereafter, a judgment of one-half of both trusts' monthly income distributions and one-half of any distribution of the Brown Trust corpus. The trial court furthermore ordered that these monies be treated as spousal support. The trial court awarded husband the fifth wheel and ordered the RV to be sold and the proceeds from that sale to be divided equally between husband and wife.

Husband appeals that portion of the judgment that awards wife monies from his trusts. He argues that he rebutted the presumption of equal contribution in acquiring his interests in the trusts, and that the trust interests should not have been included in the trial court's division of property. He further argues that the trial court erred in awarding spousal support, because the evidence does not support such an award. Husband also appeals the award of attorney fees to wife.

We start first with husband's second assignment of error, that the trial court erred in awarding spousal support. We conclude that the trial court did err in awarding spousal support, but on different grounds from those argued by husband. ORS 107.105(1) allows a trial court to include in a judgment of dissolution an award of spousal support and a division of real and personal property. It does not, however, authorize the court to award property as spousal support.[1] A trust interest is a property interest and is therefore to be treated as a divisible asset in a dissolution proceeding. *Jones and Jones,* 158 Or.App. 41, 49, *rev. den.,* 328 Or. 666 (1999)[.] The fact that the court awarded wife an interest that came in the form of monthly payments could not change the nature of the interest being divided. *Horesky and Horesky,* 30 Or.App. 941, 944 (1977), *rev. den.,* 281 Or. 1 (1978). Because husband's interests in the trusts are property interests, the court had no authority under ORS 107.105 to treat them as spousal support, and the trial court erred in doing so.

---

[1] ORS 107.105(1)(g) does allow the court to create a trust from the parties' property in order to allocate support to one or both of the parties. The trial court, in this case, did not establish a trust for that purpose. It simply ordered that husband's trust interests be treated as spousal support. Nothing in the statute allows the court to do that.

Husband's main contention, though, is that the trial court erred in awarding wife anything from his interests in the trusts. He argues that the trusts were his separate property, that wife was never an intended beneficiary of the trusts, and that wife made no contribution to the acquisition of his interests in those trusts. Consequently, husband argues, wife is not entitled to any portion of his interests in the trusts.

ORS 107.105(1)(f) guides the court's division of property in a dissolution proceeding. The overarching consideration is that the division be "just and proper in all the circumstances." *Id.; see also Kunze and Kunze,* 337 Or. 122, 132 (2004). In *Kunze,* the court explained that before the "just and proper" language is considered, the statute requires a court to "impose [] further considerations" when the property is a "marital asset"— that is, property acquired during the marriage. *Kunze,* 337 Or. at 133-34. Where the property is a marital asset, it is subject to a "rebuttable presumption that both spouses have contributed equally to the acquisition of property during the marriage[.]" ORS 107.105(1)(f). In other words, where the presumption applies, it is presumed to be "just and proper" to divide the property equally between the parties. *Kunze,* 337 Or. at 134.

Husband argues that, as to his interests in the trusts, he rebutted the presumption of equal contribution. We agree. The trusts were created by husband's father and grandmother, wife was not an intended beneficiary of either trust, and wife did nothing to contribute to husband's interests in the trusts. *Tsukamaki and Tsukamaki,* 199 Or.App. 577, 583 (2005) ("If one spouse can establish that the marital asset was acquired by gift and that the other spouse neither contributed to its acquisition nor was the object of the donative intent, then the statutory presumption is rebutted."). Were there no other considerations in this case, husband would be entitled to keep all of his interests in the trust. *Kunze,* 337 Or. at 135. We conclude, however, that it is "just and proper" to divide the interests in both trusts between husband and wife.

In *Kunze,* the court explained:

"Although the inquiry into the 'just and proper' division necessarily includes consideration of the statutory factors, including the court's determination under the presumption of equal contribution, that inquiry also takes into account the social and financial objectives of the dissolution, as well as any other considerations that bear upon the question of what division of the marital property is equitable. Although they will vary according to the individual circumstances of the parties, this court has identified some of the equitable considerations under ORS 107.105(1)(f) to include the preservation of assets; the achievement of economic self-sufficiency for both spouses; the particular needs of the parties and their children; and, * * * the extent to which a party has integrated a separately acquired asset into the common financial affairs of the marital partnership through commingling."

Id. at 135-36 (citations omitted). The court further stated:

"The trial court's ultimate determination as to what property division is 'just and proper in all the circumstances' is a matter of discretion. This court will not disturb that discretionary determination unless it concludes that the trial court misapplied the statutory and equitable considerations that ORS 107.105(1)(f) requires."

Id. at 136.

The trial court ordered the trust interests to be included in the property division because it concluded that husband's interests in the trusts had been "completely integrated into the financial planning of the parties." We agree with that determination. Husband used his interest in the Brown Trust corpus in order to finance the construction of their home. He convinced wife that they could retire based on income that included his interests in the trusts. In fact, the trust income made up half of the income that husband said the parties would rely on when they left their jobs and moved from Montana. The parties spent all of their assets within a short time of moving to Gold Beach, so that the only asset of significant value left was husband's interest in the Brown Trust corpus, valued at $250,000. Although it is true that the money from the trusts was not a consideration for a good portion of their marriage, it became key to the decisions that the couple made for their early retirement. At that point, husband's financial decisions and his assurances to wife all indicated his intention to integrate his trust interests into "the common financial affairs of the marital partnership." *Id.* at 136.

Husband's assurances and his financial planning with regard to the trusts caused wife to change her circumstances dramatically, leaving a new home and a satisfying, stable job to begin a retirement that was more husband's desire than hers. That change of position, in reliance on husband's actions, cannot be ignored in making an equitable division of the property.

Moreover, this marriage was of long duration, and in such cases, "we are less concerned with identifying the relative contributions of the parties than we are with ensuring that the parties separate on as equal a basis as possible under the circumstances." *Bentson and Bentson,* 61 Or.App. 282, 285, *rev. den.*, 294 Or. 613 (1983). In this case, the most valuable asset the parties have is husband's interest in the Brown Trust corpus, valued at $250,000. There is no other asset of the parties that is comparable. Were we to ignore that asset in dividing the marital property, we would not leave the parties "on as equal a basis as possible." *Id.* It is therefore just and proper to give wife a portion of husband's interests in the trusts.

Husband argues that the trust income is too speculative for the court to award any monies from it. While it is true that the exact amount of monthly trust income is unknown, husband's right to a mandatory monthly distribution and his right to one-third of the Brown Trust corpus *are* known, and the court may, therefore, "order the division or distribution of [the] party's trust benefits effective as of the time they are received or are reachable by the party." *Jones,* 158 Or.App. at 49. Moreover, there is no evidence in the record to suggest that the value of husband's interest in the Brown Trust corpus, worth $250,000, would change dramatically before the time at which husband became entitled to his share of the corpus.

We therefore agree with the trial court's division of the property, including its division of the trust interests. The trial court's only error was in designating the division of the trust interests as spousal support. In light of our holding on the division of property, we need not address husband's third assignment of error relating to wife's award of attorney fees.

Judgment reversed as to award of spousal support and modified as to the property division to award wife one-half of husband's interest in the trusts; otherwise affirmed.

4. Financial Misconduct

Page 723. Add after *Siegel v. Siegel*:

Gershman v. Gershman

Connecticut Supreme Court, 2008.
943 A.2d 1091.

■ VERTEFEUILLE, J.

The dispositive issue in this appeal is whether the trial court properly concluded that the defendant had dissipated marital assets where there was no evidence that the defendant had engaged in financial misconduct for a nonmarital purpose. We conclude that the trial court improperly determined that the defendant had dissipated marital assets, and, accordingly, we reverse the judgment of the trial court.

The trial court reasonably found the following facts. The plaintiff, Debra S. Gershman, and the defendant, Donald Gershman, were married in 1987. Three children were born during the parties' eighteen year marriage: a son in 1989, and twin daughters in 1996. The plaintiff was employed as an attorney from 1986 to 1992, but stopped working outside the home in 1993 so that she could remain at home to care for her son on a full-time basis. In 1999, the plaintiff began working part-time as an art teacher at a private school, earning an annual salary of $14,000. At the time of trial, the plaintiff was still employed part-time as an art teacher. The plaintiff was forty-six years old and in good health.

The defendant, who is also a licensed attorney, served as the couple's primary income earner during the marriage. From 1986 to 2005, the defendant was employed first as an attorney, and then worked in real estate development for Konover Properties Corporation (Konover), rising to the position of vice president of that organization. At Konover, the defendant's salary increased from $75,000 in 1986 to $196,000 in 2005.[3] The defendant was forty-nine years old and in good health. The defendant's employment with Konover was to terminate in January,

---

[3] The defendant also received a bonus of $25,000 from Konover in 2005.

2006, at which time he was to receive a severance package that included one year's salary in addition to one year of health insurance coverage.

In 2002, the defendant invested in a business development opportunity (Alkon partnerships) with one of the principals of Konover. The defendant initially had asked the plaintiff to invest some of her separately owned funds in these partnerships, but the plaintiff declined to do so. The defendant thereafter opted to use his own funds to make an initial investment of $105,000.[4] At the time of the dissolution of the marriage, the Alkon partnerships were valued at $31,074.

The parties purchased their first home, in West Hartford, in 1987. They lived together in this house for several years, but thereafter decided to construct a larger home to accommodate their growing family. The parties moved into their new home on Arlen Way in the West Hartford in 2002 (Arlen Way residence). Although they originally had set a budget of $500,000 to $600,000 for the Arlen Way residence, the construction of the house, which was overseen primarily by the defendant, ultimately cost $994,000, including $50,000 for a construction manager hired by the defendant. The trial court found that the defendant had been primarily responsible for the allegedly excessive cost of the house, and that the plaintiff had not been aware of the magnitude of the cost until she filed for divorce in 2004. The house ultimately was sold pendente lite for $787,500.

The parties both had substantial, separate financial assets before they were married and at the time of dissolution. The plaintiff's premarital assets, family gifts and inherited assets totaled $1,171,900.87. The total cash value of her assets on her amended financial affidavit at the time of the dissolution trial was approximately $1,796,144. By contrast, the defendant's assets declined over the course of the marriage. Although he entered the marriage with premarital assets, inheritances and family gifts totaling $795,737, his financial affidavit at trial listed total assets of $782,304.72, including a 401(k) account of $193,275.72, which had accrued during the marriage.

---

[4] The cost of investing in the Alkon partnerships was $105,000 plus a note for an additional $105,000 to be paid from the profits of the partnerships. The defendant also had an interest in another partnership, known as Alkon Livonia, LLC, and Franklin Commercial Associates, L.P. The trial court found that the defendant paid a total of "approximately $123,000" for his interest in the two groups of Alkon partnerships.

When the trial court rendered judgment dissolving the marriage, it entered orders regarding child support, property distribution, alimony and other matters. In issuing its award, the trial court concluded: "[The defendant] made a bad investment in the Alkon partnerships, paying approximately $123,000 for an asset he now values at $31,074. The court finds that he was primarily responsible for the cost overruns for the home on Arlen Way and [the parties] lost $200,000 on the sale of the home. The matter of the dissipation of family assets has been taken into consideration in the overall asset division." This appeal followed.

On appeal, the defendant claims that the trial court improperly . . . determined that he had dissipated marital assets despite the absence of any evidence of financial misconduct for a nonmarital purpose[.] . . .

The defendant . . . asserts that his conduct did not constitute dissipation as a matter of law, because dissipation requires a finding that one spouse engaged in financial misconduct, such as intentional waste or selfish financial impropriety, and a further finding that such conduct was motivated by a purpose unrelated to the marriage. . . . We agree . . . and, accordingly, we reverse the judgment of the trial court.

. . . Although we generally apply the well settled abuse of discretion standard in domestic relations matters, our review in the present case is plenary because we address the question of what, as a matter of law, constitutes dissipation in the context of a marital dissolution proceeding.

Generally, dissipation is intended to address the situation in which one spouse conceals, conveys or wastes marital assets in anticipation of a divorce. See 2 B. Turner, Equitable Distribution of Property (3d Ed. 2005) § 6:102, p. 539. Most courts have concluded that some type of improper conduct is required before a finding of dissipation can be made. Thus, courts have traditionally recognized dissipation in the following paradigmatic contexts: gambling,[6] support of a paramour,[7] or the transfer

---

[6] *Wilner v. Wilner,* 192 App.Div.2d 524, 525, 595 N.Y.S.2d 978 (1993) (where husband incurred gambling losses depleting substantial marital funds, proper to award wife 75 percent of remaining assets).

[7] *In re Marriage of Osborn,* 206 Ill.App.3d 588, 600-601, 151 Ill.Dec. 663, 564 N.E.2d 1325 (1990) (funds spent by husband on trips to Brazil, Argentina, Aruba and

of an asset to a third party for little or no consideration.[8] Well-defined contours of the doctrine are somewhat elusive, however, particularly in more factually ambiguous situations.

A review of the case law in other jurisdictions[9] reveals that findings of financial misconduct are fact specific, and frequently turn on the motivation of the party charged with misconduct. A representative case is *McDavid v. McDavid*, 333 S.C. 490 (1999). In *McDavid*, the South Carolina Supreme Court interpreted a statute that allowed a family court to consider in the equitable division of property the "marital misconduct or fault of either or both parties." (Internal quotation marks omitted.) Id., at 493. The trial court had found that, in the context of a marital dissolution proceeding, the husband's expenditure of $24,143.50, without his wife's knowledge, to support his failing business constituted "misconduct" under the statute, and warranted a downward adjustment in his share of the marital assets at the time of dissolution. Id. The Maryland Court of Appeals reversed the trial court and the state Supreme Court affirmed, holding that one spouse may be chargeable with a downward modification of his or her share of equitable distribution "only where he/she acts in bad faith with an intent to deprive the other spouse of marital assets." Id., at 495. More specifically, the court concluded that "poor business decisions, in and of themselves, do not warrant a finding of marital misconduct" and "there must be some evidence of willful misconduct, bad faith, intention to dissipate marital assets, or the like, before a court may alter the equitable distribution award for such misconduct." (Internal quotation marks omitted.) Id., at 496; see also *In re Marriage of Fennelly*, 737 N.W.2d 97, 106 (Iowa 2007) (husband dissipated marital assets through unexplained cash advances on his credit cards at end of marriage).

Minnesota with another woman were dissipation), appeal denied, 137 Ill.2d 666, 156 Ill.Dec. 563, 571 N.E.2d 150 (1991).

[8] *Hollander v. Hollander*, 89 Md.App. 156, 163, 597 A.2d 1012 (1991) (dissipation found where husband gave dental practice to daughter to deceive court).

[9] Connecticut appellate cases involving dissipation provide little or no explication of the elements of dissipation in the marital dissolution context.

Many courts require that a marital asset be used for a nonmarital purpose before there can be any finding of dissipation. For example, in *Harris v. Harris,* 261 Neb. 75, 621 N.W.2d 491 (2001), the Nebraska Supreme Court considered whether a husband who had withdrawn more than $48,000 from a marital savings account in anticipation of a marriage dissolution could be charged with having dissipated those assets and consequently penalized in the dissolution asset distribution. The Supreme Court ruled that the trial court improperly had concluded that the husband had dissipated the entire sum because the trial court had failed to account for the fact that the husband had spent a substantial portion of the funds on marital expenses, including, for example, car payments, utilities for the home, and grocery purchases. Id., at 86. On remand, the trial court was instructed to subtract the expenses incurred for a valid marital purpose from the aggregate amount of the withdrawal, and to consider only the difference as having been dissipated. Id.

Poor investment decisions, without more, generally do not give rise to a finding of dissipation. The North Dakota Supreme Court reversed a trial court that had found that the husband committed economic misconduct by transferring joint marital assets to a potato farming investment. *Hoverson v. Hoverson,* 629 N.W.2d 573 (N.D.2001). "A majority of this court has never agreed that financial mismanagement, without more, constitutes economic fault. Spouses who are in business may have to make business decisions. We also recognize business decisions may result in losses." Id., at 581. Mere mismanagement, the court concluded, did not constitute dissipation. Id. [S]ee also 2 B. Turner, supra, at p. 586 ("Investment is a valid marital purpose if the investor has a good faith intent to make a profit for the marital estate. . . . [I]f a party makes good faith investments which lose money through no fault of his or her own, there is no dissipation.").

Similarly, the weight of authority holds that the use of marital assets to purchase marital property generally does not constitute dissipation. The rationale, according to Turner, is that in such a situation, the funds are not actually dissipated but "have merely been changed into another form." 2 B. Turner, supra, p. at 591; but see *Reynolds v. Reynolds,* 109 S.W.3d 258, 276-77 (Mo.App.2003) (dissipation found where wife sold marital property at garage sales and other informal settings, obtaining unreasonably low price and failing to determine fair value of assets sold); *Syslo v. Syslo,* Ohio Court of Appeals, Docket No. L-01-1273,

2002 WL 31166937, 2002 Ohio App. Lexis 5280 (September 30, 2002) (dissipation where husband sold approximately $86,500 in marital property at garage sale, netting only $7400), appeal denied, 98 Ohio St.3d 1477, 784 N.E.2d 711, cert. denied, 540 U.S. 983, 124 S.Ct. 468, 157 L.Ed.2d 373 (2003).

The conclusion in these cases comports with the view expressed in leading treatises on domestic relations law, which generally provide that a harmful or selfish expenditure of marital assets undertaken for a nonmarital purpose is required before one spouse can be found to have dissipated marital assets. See, e.g., 2 B. Turner, supra, §§ 6:102 and 6:107; 24 Am.Jur.2d, Divorce and Separation §§ 560 through 562 (1998).[10] We conclude that, at a minimum, dissipation in the marital dissolution context requires financial misconduct involving marital assets, such as intentional waste or a selfish financial impropriety, coupled with a purpose unrelated to the marriage.

We now turn to the trial court's findings in the present case. As we have noted previously herein, the trial court considered the defendant's "dissipation of family assets" in ordering the overall asset division between the parties. The trial court specifically referred to two acts of dissipation. The first was the defendant's "bad investment" in the various Alkon partnerships.[11] The second was the $200,000 loss on the sale of the excessively expensive marital home. The trial court, however, did not

---

[10] Many authorities also have found a temporal element to be an essential component of dissipation. Specifically, many courts have found dissipation only where the financial misconduct occurred at a time when the marriage was in jeopardy or in anticipation of divorce. See, e.g., *Herron v. Johnson,* 714 A.2d 783, 785 (D.C.1998) (dissipation occurs "where one spouse uses marital property for his own benefit and for a purpose unrelated to the marriage at a time when the marriage is undergoing an irreconcilable breakdown"); *In re Marriage of Charles,* 284 Ill.App.3d 339, 343, 219 Ill.Dec. 742, 672 N.E.2d 57 (1996) (noting that dissipation occurs "at a time that the marriage is undergoing an irreconcilable breakdown" [internal quotation marks omitted]). Neither party in the present case has raised or addressed a temporal element and we therefore do not address it.

[11] The trial court found that the defendant had made the investments in the various partnerships from "his own funds. . . ." Given that he did not use marital assets for the investments, we question whether the investments could be determined to be dissipation regardless of the purpose.

find either financial misconduct, e.g., intentional waste or a selfish financial transaction, or that the defendant had used marital assets for a nonmarital purpose with regard to either of these transactions. In the absence of such findings, we must reverse the judgment of the trial court and remand the case for a new trial.

. . . .

In this opinion the other justices concurred.

F. Child Support
2. Modification

Page 809. Add after *Bender v. Bender*:

Davis v. Knafel

Indiana Court of Appeals, 2005.
837 N.E.2d 585.

■ BAKER, JUDGE.

Appellant-respondent Elliott Lydell Davis[1] appeals the trial court's order granting appellee-petitioner Karla Kay Knafel's motion to modify child support. Specifically, Davis contends that the trial court erred in increasing child support for T.D., the parties' minor child, from $760 per week to $2,308 per week. Finding that there have not been changed circumstances so substantial and continuing as to make the terms of the original child support order unreasonable, we reverse the judgment of the trial court and remand for proceedings consistent with this opinion.

FACTS

T.D. was born to Knafel and Davis, who were never married, on February 22, 2000. However, the name of Knafel's current husband was

---

[1] Basketball fans will know the Appellant better as Dale Davis, who played with the Indiana Pacers for ten seasons. Davis is currently playing for the Detroit Pistons. *See* *NBA.com* at http://www.nba.com/playerfile/dale_davis/bio.html.

placed on T.D.'s birth certificate as the father. On July 2, 2001, an agreed paternity decree resulted in the determination that Davis was the biological and legal father of T.D. Knafel was given custody of T.D. Davis's weekly income at the time as an NBA player was $121,327, and Knafel's weekly income was $450. The Indiana Child Support Guidelines yielded the sum of $758 per week in child support payments, and the parties agreed that Davis would pay $760 per week.

On March 21, 2003, Knafel filed a petition to modify child support. The petition alleged a substantial change in circumstances since the entry of the decree that made its continued operation unreasonable, namely, Davis's income had increased substantially—from $6,309,004 annually to $9,061,875 for the 2003-04 season and $10,068,750 for the 2004-05 season. Ten percent of Davis's income is withheld from him and paid to the NBA.

The trial court held a hearing on the petition on November 29, 2004. Knafel submitted worksheets that indicated that her income was $206 per week. On January 6, 2005, the second day of the hearing, Knafel testified on cross-examination that her income was approximately $750 per week. Knafel further testified that she and her husband own one 6,000 square foot house in Greenwood, which they purchased for $403,000. Knafel described her residence as "a normal house" rather than the "million dollar home" that "Dale's son should be living in."

From testimony elicited at the deposition and at the hearing, Davis acknowledged having a daughter for whom he voluntarily pays child support of $855 per week. Davis's financial declaration shows monthly expenses of approximately $80,000, excluding monthly taxes in the approximate amount of $293,747.25. Davis owns three homes, one of which he purchased during the pendency of this petition that is valued at $1,700,000.

Davis has no set parenting time schedule with T.D., and he exercises overnight parenting time with T.D. approximately four or five times each year. It was undisputed that Davis was current on his previously-ordered child support payments and that T.D.'s needs were being met. But Knafel testified that she wanted T.D. to have the kind of lifestyle that he would have if he lived with Davis, for example, by attending private school, going on more vacations, and wearing nicer clothes.

On March 4, 2005, the trial court entered its findings of fact, conclusions of law, and judgment in favor of Knafel. The trial court ordered that Davis's child support obligation should be increased from $760 per week to $2,308 per week, retroactive to March 21, 2003[.] In its findings, the trial court acknowledged that the application of the Child Support Guidelines would increase Davis's child support payment by only $7.15 per week, but deviation from the Child Support Guidelines was necessary in order to "achieve the goal of providing [T.D.] with a standard of living that he would have enjoyed had his parents been married and the marriage remained in tact [sic]." Davis now appeals.

DISCUSSION AND DECISION

Davis contends that the trial court erred in increasing his child support obligation from $760 per week to $2,308 per week. Specifically, he argues that there was no substantial and continuing change of circumstances that warranted the increase in child support.

Generally, decisions regarding child support are left to the sound discretion of the trial court. On appeal, we will not disturb a trial court's order modifying child support unless the trial court abused its discretion or erred as a matter of law. . . .

Where, as here, the trial court enters findings of fact and conclusions thereon, we consider whether the evidence supports the findings and whether the findings support the judgment. Findings are clearly erroneous only when the record contains no facts to support them either directly or by inference. A judgment is clearly erroneous if it applies the wrong legal standard to properly found facts. In order to determine that a finding or conclusion is clearly erroneous, our review of the evidence must leave us with the firm conviction that a mistake has been made.

Initially, we address Knafel's contention that Davis's argument is waived for failing to present it to the trial court. Knafel asserts that Davis did not advance the argument that his increase in income did not amount to a substantial and continuing change in circumstances and that "this case was tried on the issue of whether or not, in determining the amount of support that [Davis] should pay, the Trial Court should deviate from the formula set forth in paragraph 2 of the Commentary to Child.Supp. G.3(D)."

The petitioner has the burden of proof in child support modification cases, *MacLafferty v. MacLafferty,* 829 N.E.2d 938, 940 (Ind. 2005), and the record reveals that Knafel directed her arguments to the issue of whether the trial court should deviate from the Child Support Guidelines. Davis defended against this argument. He was not required to respond to arguments that Knafel did not make.

Modification of child support orders is controlled by Indiana Code section 31-14-11-8, and it states:

> A support order may be modified or revoked upon a showing:
>
> (1) of a substantial change in circumstances that makes the terms unreasonable; or
>
> (2) that:
>
>> (A) a person has been ordered to pay an amount in child support that differs by more than twenty percent (20%) from the amount that would be ordered by applying the child support guidelines; and
>>
>> (B) the support order requested to be modified or revoked was issued at least twelve (12) months before the petition requesting modification was filed.

As the trial court found in its order, the difference in child support under the Guidelines is only $7.15—a one percent increase. Thus, the only way that the trial court had legal authority to modify Davis's support obligation is by finding a change of circumstances so substantial and continuing as to make the terms unreasonable. This is a mixed question of law and fact, and to the extent that it is a question of law, it is our duty to give it de novo review, promoting the values of consistency, predictability, and enunciation of standards that curb arbitrariness. *MacLafferty,* 829 N.E.2d at 941.

In *MacLafferty,* Father, the non-custodial parent, petitioned for a reduction in his support obligation based solely on an increase in Mother's income, which would have produced only a fourteen percent decrease in child support payments. Our Supreme Court found that, generally, a change in income that changes support payments by less than twenty percent standing alone would not constitute a substantial and continuing change in circumstances. *Id.* at 942. But our Supreme Court stopped short of holding that a modification could "never be made under subsection (1) where the changed circumstance alleged is a change in one parent's income that only changes one parent's payment by less than 20%." *Id.* The *MacLafferty* Court found that there might be situations where a variety of factors converge to make such a modification permissible under the terms of the statute. *Id.*

The only changed circumstance alleged by Knafel was Davis's increased income. Our review of the transcript shows that the only changed circumstance that Knafel argued before the trial court was Davis's increased income. Knafel asserts that the trial court found several other factors, but none of them appear to be applicable here. First, Knafel contends that T.D.'s standard of living would be different "if the parents were married and the marriage had remained intact." This argument is derivative of Indiana Code section 31-14-11-2, which state in relevant part:

> (a) The court may order either or both parents to pay any reasonable amount for child support after considering all relevant factors, including the following:
>
> . . .
>
> (2) The standard of living the child would have enjoyed had the parents been married and remained married to each other.

But Knafel has made no showing that anything has changed in the relationship of the parties between the date of the original order and the date of the modification that would make the consideration of this factor different now than in 2001. Thus, we cannot say that this constitutes a change of circumstances.

Knafel also asserts that Davis had a change in lifestyle. As evidence, she points to the lone fact that Davis purchased a $1,700,000 residence. But she fails to show how this is a change in lifestyle for a man who already owned two homes in two different states and who earns several million dollars per year.

Knafel further contends that Davis's voluntary support of his daughter and his lack of contact with T.D. are changed circumstances. But Davis's daughter is older than T.D., and he has been voluntarily paying her support all along. And Knafel introduced no evidence that Davis previously had more contact with T.D. than he has now. In sum, the record does not demonstrate that either of these factors has changed since the original order was issued.

Finally, Knafel asserts that T.D.'s age and developing educational needs are changed circumstances. We note that Indiana Code section 31-16-6-1 takes the child's education needs into consideration in making the initial child support order, and there is no evidence that, at the age of five, T.D.'s educational needs have changed substantially since the original child support order was made. Nor do we find in the record any evidence that T.D.'s needs have changed substantially with his age. In short, we cannot see that there have been any substantial changes in circumstances apart from Davis's income.

At this point, the argument seems like a slam dunk for Davis. But Knafel attempts a block by pointing out that *MacLafferty* is distinguishable on its facts. While we acknowledge that *MacLafferty* involved a noncustodial parent requesting a reduction in child support and the present case involves a custodial parent requesting an increase in child support, the reasoning of the *MacLafferty* Court applies equally here. It would vitiate Subsection (2) of Indiana Code section 31-16-8-1 to hold that a change in income that results in less than a twenty percent difference in child support without other converging factors is sufficient to modify a parent's obligation. *See MacLafferty,* 829 N.E.2d at 942. It is of no moment who requests the modification. Based on our reading of binding Supreme Court precedent, we therefore find that the trial court erred in modifying Davis's child support obligation when the only changed circumstance was his increased income that resulted in less than a twenty percent increase in his child support obligation under the Child Support Guidelines.

. . . .

The judgment of the trial court is reversed and remanded for proceedings consistent with this opinion.

■ MATHIAS, JUDGE, dissenting.

I respectfully dissent from the majority's conclusion that the trial court erred in modifying Davis's child support obligation. I agree with the majority's recognition of the importance of *MacLafferty*. However, I disagree with the majority's interpretation of that case.

In *MacLafferty,* the trial court granted Father's request to decrease his weekly child support obligation because Mother obtained full-time employment and her income more than doubled. However, Mother's income increased from only $16,848 to $36,868 per year, while Father's income, minus any bonus compensation, increased from $118,924 to $125,164. *Id.* at 939. Our supreme court reversed the trial court's order and noted that even with the increase in her income, "Mother's income was quite modest compared to Father's: Father's income (excluding bonuses) was approximately 3-1/4 times that of Mother. We hold that the change alleged here was not so substantial as to render the terms of the prior order unreasonable." *Id.* at 942.

Concerning the issues presented in this appeal, the *MacLafferty* court indicated that in most cases, a change in income will generally not justify a modification of child support under Indiana Code section 31-16-8-1(1), which requires a showing of "changed circumstances so substantial and continuing as to make the terms unreasonable." However, and most importantly regarding the case before us, the court also stated, "we do not hold that a modification may never be made under subsection (1) where the changed circumstances alleged is a change in one parent's income that only changes one parent's payment by less than 20%. There may be situations where a variety of factors converge to make such a modification permissible under the terms of the statute. While we do not find this case to be such a situation, we do not foreclose such a possibility." *Id.*

The focus of child support, whether pertaining to a child born within a marriage or out of wedlock, has always been to assure the child of a standard of living approaching the lifestyle the child would have enjoyed had his or her parents been and remained married through his or her minority. *See* Ind. Code § 31-14-11-2 (1998 & Supp.2005) (The paternity child support standard clearly focuses on "the standard of living the child would have enjoyed had the parents been married and remained married to each other.").

Davis was a well-paid professional athlete when T.D. was born and the lifestyle T.D. would have enjoyed had Davis and Knafel been and remained married throughout T.D.'s minority is beyond even the imagination of most Hoosiers. Yet that standard of living, along with Knafel's financial resources, T.D.'s physical and mental condition, T.D.'s educational needs, and Davis's financial resources and needs are the criteria the General Assembly has established for calculating child support. *See* Ind.Code § 31-14-11-2.

Since the original agreed order in paternity and agreed child support order, Davis's income has increased by 43.5 percent. His current annual income is $10,068,750. Due to the majority's reversal of the child support modification, Davis's child support obligation will return to $760 per week, or $39,520 per year, which is substantially less than one-half of one percent (.39 percent) of Davis's current annual income.[3] Mother earns less than $40,000 per year.

In light of the statutory criteria established in Indiana Code section 31-14-11-2, the vast disparity in the parties' incomes, and the more than forty percent increase in Davis's income since the entry of the original support order, I believe that the circumstances presented here create precisely the situation contemplated in *MacLafferty*, where a change in income is sufficient to support a modification under subsections one of Indiana Code sections 31-16-8-1 or 31-14-11-8. Moreover, as the trial court noted, given Davis's considerable income and the substantial increase in his income over the last few years, his standard of living is well above that which is enjoyed by his child, T.D. Accordingly, I agree with the trial court's conclusion that "an increase in [Davis's] income in the amount of $2,752,870.60 per year is a substantial change in circumstances . . . [and] the existing support order of $760 per week is clearly unreasonable." I believe to conclude otherwise betrays the underlying equitable intent of child support in Indiana and sends the wrong message to parents like Mr. Davis about the ongoing obligations they should expect regarding their children.

---

[3] The modified support obligation of $2[,]308 per week, or $120,016 per year, amounts to just 1.19 percent of Davis's current annual income.

4. Unmarried Partners

Page 817. Add after *Johnson v. Louis*:

Dubay v. Wells

U.S. Court of Appeals for the Sixth Circuit, 2007.
506 F.3d 422.

■ CLAY, CIRCUIT JUDGE.

Plaintiff Matthew Dubay ("Dubay") appeals from the district court's dismissal of his case pursuant to Federal Rule of Civil Procedure 12(b)(6)[.] . . . After Wells told Dubay she was infertile and using birth control, she became pregnant with Dubay's child, had the baby, and sued for child support. A Michigan court awarded child support and Dubay brought this action challenging the constitutionality of the Michigan Paternity Act, Mich. Comp. Laws § 722.711 *et seq.* (2002), and related statutes under the Equal Protection Clause of the Fourteenth Amendment.

. . . [W]e AFFIRM the judgment of the district court.

I. BACKGROUND

This case is before us on an appeal from a dismissal for failure to state a claim upon which relief can be granted pursuant to Rule 12(b)(6) of the Federal Rules of Civil Procedure. In reviewing such a dismissal, we "must accept all well-pleaded factual allegations of the complaint as true and construe the complaint in the light most favorable to the plaintiff." In the instant case, the facts alleged in Dubay's amended complaint are not in dispute.

In the fall of 2004, Dubay and Wells became involved in a romantic relationship. At that time, Dubay informed Wells that he had no interest in becoming a father. In response, Wells told Dubay that she was infertile and that, as an extra layer of protection, she was using contraception. Dubay, in reliance on these assurances, participated in a consensual sexual relationship with Wells.

The parties' relationship later deteriorated. Shortly thereafter, and much to Dubay's surprise, Wells informed Dubay that she was pregnant, allegedly with Dubay's child. Wells chose to carry the child to term and the child, EGW, was born on an unspecified date in 2005. During the pregnancy and birth of the child, Dubay was consistently clear about his desire not to be a father.

A few weeks after EGW's birth, the County brought a paternity complaint against Dubay in the Saginaw County Circuit Court under the Michigan Paternity Act. Wells and the County sought a judgment of filiation, child support, reimbursement for delivery of the child, and other statutory and equitable relief. Dubay requested a stay so that the constitutional issues presented by the litigation could be resolved, but the trial court denied that request. Dubay thereafter brought this action against Wells and the County in federal district court, seeking relief under 42 U.S.C. § 1983.

In his amended complaint, filed on March 29, 2006, Dubay alleged that the application of the Michigan Paternity Act to his case violated the Equal Protection Clause of the Fourteenth Amendment, as well as Article 1, Section 2 of the Michigan Constitution, which loosely parallels the Equal Protection Clause. . . .

. . . .

On appeal, Dubay challenges . . . the district court's dismissal of his § 1983 claim under Rule 12(b)(6)[.] . . .

II. DISCUSSION

We review de novo the district court's grant of a defendant's motion to dismiss pursuant to Federal Rule of Civil Procedure 12(b)(6). *Directv, Inc. v. Treesh,* 487 F.3d 471, 476 (6th Cir. 2007). . . .

. . . .

Dubay seeks relief under 42 U.S.C. § 1983, which provides a remedy against "[e]very person who, under color of any statute, ordinance, regulation, custom, or usage, of any State . . . subjects, or causes to be subjected, any citizen of the United States . . . to the deprivation of any rights, privileges, or immunities secured by the Constitution." In support of his § 1983 claim, Dubay alleges that the Michigan Paternity Act violates the Equal Protection Clause of the Fourteenth Amendment, which guarantees that "[n]o state shall . . . deny to any person within its jurisdiction the equal protection of the laws." U.S. Const. amend. XIV, § 1.

Though Dubay does not specify which sections of the Michigan Paternity Act he challenges, a review of the statute reveals two primary contenders. First, § 2 establishes the duty of unmarried parents to support their children. This section states, in relevant part, that "[t]he parents of a child born out of wedlock are liable for the necessary support and education of the child." Mich. Comp. Laws § 722.712(1). Second, § 7 requires the court to "enter an order of filiation declaring paternity and providing for the support of the child" if the court determines that the defendant is the father of the child, if the defendant acknowledges paternity, or if the defendant has a default judgment entered against him on the issue. Mich. Comp. Laws § 722.717(1). The statute directs the court to "specify the sum to be paid weekly or otherwise" in the order of filiation. Mich. Comp. Laws § 722.717(2). The amount of support is determined according to a formula established by the state friend of the court bureau, but can be modified by the court upon a showing that the amount calculated by the formula would be "unjust or inappropriate." Mich. Comp. Laws §§ 722.717(2), 552.605. A defendant who fails to comply with an order to pay child support faces serious consequences, including wage garnishment, suspension of drivers or professional licenses, or jail.

Dubay argues that the enforcement of the Michigan Paternity Act against him denies him the equal protection of the law in two ways.[2]

---

[2] Dubay has repeatedly asserted . . . that his § 1983 claim is not a substantive due process challenge but rather is based upon a violation of the Equal Protection Clause. Despite these assertions, his "equal protection" arguments rely heavily upon Supreme Court cases addressing substantive due process claims. To the extent that Dubay seeks to establish a substantive due process right to disclaim fatherhood and thereby avoid paying child support, we find this argument to be foreclosed by our decision in *N.E. v. Hedges,* 391 F.3d 832, 836 (6th Cir. 2004) (holding that Kentucky statutes which

First and foremost, Dubay argues that the Michigan statutes deny him the equal protection of the law by affording mothers a right to disclaim parenthood after engaging in consensual sex (*i.e.*, through abortion) while denying that right to fathers. Second, Dubay contends that Michigan law denies men equal protection by making it easier for a woman to place a child in adoption or drop the newborn off at a hospital or other social service agency. An examination of these claims under our equal protection jurisprudence, however, reveals that they lack merit.

The Equal Protection Clause of the Fourteenth Amendment "is essentially a direction that all persons similarly situated should be treated alike." However, "the Fourteenth Amendment does not deny to [the] State the power to treat different classes of persons in different ways." In reviewing state legislation for an equal protection violation, "we apply different levels of scrutiny to different types of classifications." In general, we start with the presumption that the statute is valid. To overcome this presumption, the party challenging the statute must demonstrate that the statute is not rationally related to a legitimate government purpose. If the legislation's official classification is based on gender, however, the justification must be "exceedingly persuasive." *United States v. Virginia*, 518 U.S. 515, 532-33 (1996) (citing *Mississippi Univ. for Women v. Hogan*, 458 U.S. 718 (1982)). For such classifications, the burden is on the state to demonstrate that the legislation serves "important governmental objectives and that the discriminatory means employed are substantially related to the achievement of those objectives." *Id.* (internal quotation marks removed)[.] Finally, classifications affecting fundamental rights "are given the most exacting scrutiny." Under strict scrutiny, a regulation infringing upon a fundamental right will only be upheld if it is narrowly tailored to serve a compelling state interest.

Dubay cannot prevail under any of these equal protection theories. First, strict scrutiny does not apply because the Michigan Paternity Act does not affect any of Dubay's fundamental rights. In *N.E. v. Hedges*, we found that the right to privacy, articulated in the Supreme Court's substantive due process jurisprudence, does not encompass a right to

---

require biological fathers to pay child support for biological children do not violate the substantive due process guarantees of the Fourteenth Amendment).

decide not to become a parent after conception and birth. 391 F.3d 832, 835 (6th Cir. 2004). *See also Rivera v. Minnich,* 483 U.S. 574, 580 (1987) (finding that a "putative father has no legitimate right and certainly no liberty interest in avoiding financial obligations to his natural child that are validly imposed by state law"). In doing so, we explicitly rejected the argument, which Dubay raises in his brief, that "fairness" dictates that men should receive a right to disclaim fatherhood in exchange for a woman's right to abortion.[3] *Hedges,* 391 F.3d at 835. Our discussion clarified that it is not a fundamental right of any parent, male or female, to sever his or her financial responsibilities to the child after the child is born. *See id.* Thus, to the extent that Dubay claims that Michigan is not affording him equal protection of the law by denying men, but not women, "the right to initiate consensual sexual activity while choosing to not be a parent," his argument must fail.

Second, we do not need to apply intermediate scrutiny because the Michigan Paternity Act does not discriminate on the basis of gender. The statutory provisions that impose the obligation of support upon Dubay, and similarly situated fathers, are gender neutral. See Mich. Comp. Laws § 722.712(1) ("The *parents* of a child born out of wedlock are liable for

---

[3] Despite Dubay's protestations to the contrary, our holding in Hedges is consistent with the right to abortion articulated by the Supreme Court in *Roe v. Wade,* 410 U.S. 113, 153 (1973). The woman's right to abortion is not solely, or even primarily, based upon her right to choose not to be a mother after engaging in consensual sexual intercourse. Rather, the right to abortion, as articulated in *Roe,* derives from the woman's right to bodily integrity and her privacy interest in protecting her own physical and mental health. *See id.* (focusing on the negative mental and physical health effects that would follow from denying a woman's choice to terminate her pregnancy).

Moreover, Dubay's claim that a man's right to disclaim fatherhood would be analogous to a woman's right to abortion rests upon a false analogy. In the case of a father seeking to opt out of fatherhood and thereby avoid child support obligations, the child is already in existence and the state therefore has an important interest in providing for his or her support. *See Kulko v. Superior Court of California,* 436 U.S. 84, 98 (1978)[.] When a woman exercises her right to abortion, the pregnancy does not result in a live birth and there remains no child for the state to have an interest in supporting. If the state allowed a mother to unilaterally disclaim the legal rights and obligations incident to motherhood after the child was born, then the law would be extending a right to mothers which it does not afford to fathers. However, the Michigan Paternity Act is clear that both "parents" of a child must provide support to the child once it is born. Mich. Comp. Laws § 722.712(1).

the necessary support and education of the child." (emphasis added)). Likewise, while the provision allowing for a judgment of filiation is technically based upon gender as it only provides for an order establishing that a man is the legal *father* of the child,[4] *see* Mich. Comp. Laws § 722.717(1), this provision must be read in light of Michigan's entire statutory scheme which also requires the identification of a *mother* at the child's birth, *see* Mich. Comp. Laws § 333.2822, and establishes a judicial remedy to ensure that this mother is providing adequate support to the child. Mich. Comp. Laws § 722.721(1). By requiring the identification of a mother and a father for the child and by demanding that both these parents provide support to the child, the Michigan statutes do not discriminate against either sex in imposing parenting obligations and, thus, do not need to be reviewed under intermediate scrutiny.

Finally, the Michigan Paternity Act withstands rational basis review because it is rationally related to a legitimate government purpose. "The underlying purpose of the Paternity Act is to ensure that the minor children born outside a marriage are provided with support and education." *Crego v. Coleman*, 615 N.W.2d 218, 228 (Mich. 2000). This is undoubtedly a legitimate, and an important, governmental interest. *Kulko v. Superior Court of California*, 436 U.S. 84, 98 (1978) (recognizing that a state's interest in "protecting the welfare of its minor residents" is "unquestionably important"). Moreover, the means that the statute uses to achieve this end—requiring support from the legal parents, and determining legal fatherhood based on the biological fatherhood—is substantially, let alone rationally, related to this legitimate, and probably

---

[4] The district court argued that "[a] judgment of filiation under the Paternity Act itself does not make Dubay a father, it merely confirms a biological fact—that the man has sired the child—upon presentation of proper proof." This is a flawed reading of the statute. Liability for support does not attach to being a biological parent, but rather to being the legal parent of the child. Section 722.712 thus does more than simply "confirm a biological fact"—it establishes that the putative father is the legal father, which gives rise to legal consequences. *See Sinicropi v. Mazurek*, 729 N.W. 2d 256, 166 (Mich. App. 2006) ("[T]he Legislature astutely envisioned cases in which it is discovered that the biological father is not the same individual who executed [a document acknowledging parenthood]. . . . If an acknowledgment of parentage has been properly executed, subsequent recognition of a person as the father in an order of filiation by way of a paternity action cannot occur unless the acknowledgment has been revoked.").

important, government purpose.[5] Accordingly, we find that Dubay has raised no viable equal protection challenge to the Michigan Paternity Act.

However, undeterred by this lack of legal authority, and failing to cite the specific statutes that he challenges, Dubay further argues that "[u]nder Michigan's safe haven and abandonment laws, a mother can also unilaterally drop off a newborn at the hospital, police department, or clinic without any legal or financial recourse whatsoever, something not afforded men. It is also easier for a woman to place a child for adoption, and again avoid being forced into unwanted parenthood." As with his challenge to the Paternity Act, this argument lacks legal foundation.

By failing to cite a single challenged statute, Dubay has essentially waived the argument. In any event, the laws that Dubay appears to be challenging are gender neutral and are rationally related to a legitimate government interest. *See, e.g.*, Safe Delivery of Newborns Act, Mich. Comp. Laws §§ 712.1-712.20 (2002). Dubay has produced no evidence that any of these acts were motivated by a discriminatory intent or for a discriminatory purpose. *See Bennett v. City of Eastpointe,* 410 F.3d 810, 818 (6th Cir. 2005). Accordingly, we again find that Dubay cannot demonstrate that the challenged Michigan laws violate the Equal Protection Clause.

Because Dubay has no legal basis for his claim that the Michigan Paternity Act and other unspecified statutes violate the Equal Protection Clause, he cannot show that the County's application of these laws to his case has deprived him of his constitutional rights as required for this § 1983 action. Therefore, we hold that the district court properly dismissed Dubay's case for "failure to state a claim upon which relief can be granted." Fed.R.Civ.P. 12(b)(6).

. . . .

---

[5] As our analysis indicates, while we do not apply intermediate scrutiny to the Michigan Paternity Act because it does not discriminate on the basis of gender, we believe that the law would withstand such review.

I. The Separation Agreement

Page 861. Add after *Kelley v. Kelley*:

Richardson v. Richardson

Supreme Court of Missouri, 2007.
218 S.W.3d 426.

■ WILLIAM RAY PRICE, JR., JUDGE.

INTRODUCTION

Joseph A. Richardson (Joseph) appeals the Judgment of the St. Louis Circuit Court dismissing Count II of his Motion to Modify Judgment and Decree of Dissolution. This Court affirms.

A. BACKGROUND

Joseph and Ida Richardson (Ida) divorced in December 1997. They executed a separation agreement (Agreement) which contained the terms of the divorce, and which they agreed would be incorporated into the decree of dissolution. The Agreement provided that Joseph would pay maintenance to Ida in the amount of $2,425.00 per month. The obligation was to terminate upon Ida's remarriage or the death of either party. The Agreement stated that "[t]he terms of this Agreement shall not be subject to modification or change, regardless of the relative circumstances of the parties[.] . . ." The trial court found that the Agreement was not unconscionable, and incorporated it into the Judgment and Decree of Dissolution. The court's decree also specifically stated that maintenance was non-modifiable.

Joseph filed a motion to modify in 2004. In Count II of this motion, Joseph sought to terminate his maintenance obligation, alleging, *inter alia,* that Ida "sought out a person(s) for the purpose of burglarizing [Joseph's] home," "sought out a person(s) for the purposes of murdering [Joseph]," and "attempted to hire a person or otherwise engage services to murder [Joseph]." Joseph further alleged that Ida thus "breached the separation agreement, violated public policy, committed criminal acts and waived any claim to maintenance payable by [Joseph][.] . . ."

The trial court dismissed Count II of Joseph's Motion with prejudice for failure to state a claim upon which relief can be granted. The trial court's order dismissing Count II was certified as a final order and judgment in accordance with Rule 74.01(b). Joseph appealed the dismissal. The matter was transferred to this Court post-opinion by the Eastern District Court of Appeals.

B. POINT ON APPEAL

In his only point on appeal, Joseph asserts that "[t]he trial court erred in granting [Ida's] 'Motion to Dismiss for Failure to State a Claim upon which Relief could be Granted', because the trial court misinterpreted Section 452.325 RSMo,[1] in that, consistent with tenants (sic) of Missouri contract law, Missouri public policy and the doctrine of waiver, the trial court has discretion under the statute to terminate or modify an otherwise 'non-modifiable' separation agreement post-dissolution, upon a finding that terms of the agreement are unconscionable due to immoral criminal acts on the part of the payee spouse."

C. STANDARD OF REVIEW

"A motion to dismiss for failure to state a cause of action is solely a test of the adequacy of the plaintiff's petition." *Bosch v. St. Louis Healthcare Network*, 41 S.W.3d 462, 464 (Mo. banc 2001). "It assumes that all of plaintiff's averments are true, and liberally grants to plaintiff all reasonable inferences therefrom." *Id.* "No attempt is made to weigh any facts alleged as to whether they are credible or persuasive." *Id.* "Instead, the petition is reviewed in an almost academic manner, to determine if the facts alleged meet the elements of a recognized cause of action, or of a cause that might be adopted in that case." *Id.* In other words, no court has determined that Joseph's allegations are true. At this point, we simply ask whether-assuming the allegations are true-Joseph would have a right to have his maintenance obligation modified.

---

[1] All statutory references are to RSMo 2000, unless otherwise stated.

D. ANALYSIS

I.

"Dissolution of marriage is a statutory action, unknown to the common law." *Cates v. Cates*, 819 S.W.2d 731, 734 (Mo. banc 1991). This Court is generally bound by the statutory pronouncements of the General Assembly regarding dissolution law. *Id.*

Section 452.335 RSMo allows a court to order one spouse to pay maintenance to the other and provides the guidelines which a court must follow in determining whether to award maintenance and in what amount. Section 452.325 provides that "the parties may enter into a written separation agreement containing provisions for the maintenance of either of them[.]" [Section 452.325(1).] That section also provides that "[i]n a proceeding for dissolution of marriage or for legal separation, the terms of the separation agreement, except terms providing for the custody, support, and visitation of children, are binding upon the court unless it finds, after considering the economic circumstances and any other relevant evidence produced by the parties, on their own motion or on request of the court, that the separation agreement is unconscionable." [Section 452.325(2).] "If the court finds that the separation agreement is not unconscionable as to support, maintenance or property . . . , [u]nless the separation agreement provides to the contrary, its terms shall be set forth in the decree of dissolution[.]" [Section 452.325(4).] Subsection 6 states that "[t]he decree may expressly preclude or limit modification of terms set forth in the decree if the separation agreement so provides."

II.

This case is controlled by section 452.325. The statute authorizes parties to resolve the various property issues which arise during the dissolution of their marriage by entering into a separation agreement. The statute further provides that "[t]he decree may expressly preclude or limit modification of terms set forth in the decree if the separation agreement so provides." [Section 452.325(6).]

Joseph and Ida's separation agreement, incorporated into the dissolution decree, provided that "[t]he terms of this Agreement shall not be subject to modification or change, regardless of the relative circumstances of the parties[.] . . ." Neither the Agreement, nor the decree, nor the statute authorizes a court to modify the terms of the agreement or the decree on account of subsequent circumstances. *See, e.g., Thomas v. Thomas,* 171 S.W.3d 130 (Mo.App. 2005); *Mason v. Mason,* 873 S.W.2d 631 (Mo.App. 1994) ("A non-modifiable agreement which the court found conscionable at the time of its execution does not suddenly become unenforceable due to changed circumstances.").

A non-modification provision can cut both ways. No one can know which party will need more or deserve less as time passes. As with all contract terms, a non-modification provision is an agreed allocation of future risk, bargained for and for which consideration is exchanged.

The Missouri legislature has seen fit to allow such a clause to be elevated from contractual to judicial status by incorporation into the dissolution decree. We are bound to respect the statute and to enforce these documents as agreed to and ordered.

III.

Joseph nonetheless argues against application of section 452.325(6) on four grounds: (1) unconscionability; (2) Missouri contract law; (3) the doctrine of waiver and (4) public policy. None of these grounds justif[ies] a departure from the statute.

a.

Joseph contends that a trial court may modify or refuse to enforce a non-modifiable maintenance agreement incorporated into a dissolution decree upon a finding that subsequent events have rendered it unconscionable. However, there is no authority in the dissolution statutes for the court to revisit the issue of conscionability at any time after the decree is entered. Section 452.325(4) makes clear that the court may only incorporate the terms of a separation agreement into the divorce decree *if* it determines that the terms are not unconscionable. The determination is made before entry of the decree, not after.

b.

Joseph also asserts that under Missouri contract law, Ida's alleged acts constitute a change in circumstances that renders the separation agreement "unconscionable." In support, Joseph cites *Werner v. Ashcraft Bloomquist*, 10 S.W.3d 575 (Mo.App. 2000)[,] and *Kassebaum v. Kassebaum*, 42 S.W.3d 685 (Mo.App. 2001). These cases do not mention unconscionability, but instead discuss the doctrines of impossibility and commercial frustration. They do not apply to the case at bar.

Unconscionability relative to contract law parallels unconscionability relative to separation agreements. Unconscionability is addressed at the time of inception or creation of the contract, not thereafter. *See* Section 400.2-302 RSMo ("If the court as a matter of law finds the contract or any clause of the contract to have been unconscionable *at the time it was made* the court may refuse to enforce the contract") (emphasis added); *State ex rel. Vincent v. Schneider*, 194 S.W.3d 853, 861 (Mo. banc 2006) ("[A] contract, or provision of a contract, is unconscionable if its terms are unconscionable *at the time it was made.*") (emphasis in original).

c.

Joseph argues that Ida has waived her right to maintenance by attempting to have him killed because she knew that killing him would cut off her maintenance obligation. Waiver is the "intentional relinquishment of a known right." *Shahan v. Shahan*, 988 S.W.2d 529, 534 (Mo. banc 1999). "Waiver may be express or it may be implied by conduct that clearly and unequivocally shows a purpose by the [entitled party] to relinquish a contractual right." *Id.* Killing Joseph might have resulted in the termination of Ida's ability to collect maintenance, but her alleged acts do not establish a clear and unequivocal attempt to relinquish her contractual right to maintenance so long as Joseph is living.

d.

Joseph next argues that public policy demands that courts be allowed to modify or terminate non-modifiable maintenance where immoral acts "render the agreement unconscionable." In support of this contention, Joseph relies upon a number of cases following the general rule that "no one shall be permitted to profit by his own fraud, or to take advantage of his own wrong, or to found any claim upon his own iniquity, or to acquire property by his own murder." *Perry v. Strawbridge*, 209 Mo. 621, 108 S.W. 641, 643 (1908) (internal citation omitted).

Missouri courts have followed this policy in a number of cases: *Matter of McCarty*, 762 S.W.2d 458, 461 (Mo.App. 1988) (widow who intentionally killed husband could not benefit from husband's death and receive exempt property, widow's allowance, property held as tenancy by the entirety or tenancy in common, or life insurance proceeds); *In re Estate of Danforth*, 705 S.W.2d 609, 611-12 (Mo.App. 1986) (21-year-old wife who committed fraud in procuring marriage to 75-year-old husband and conspired to murder him to inherit from his estate could not elect to take against his will as a surviving spouse); *Baker v. Martin*, 709 S.W.2d 533, 535 (Mo.App. 1986) (husband who murdered wife could not take as devisee under her will); *Wells v. Harris*, 414 S.W.2d 343, 346 (Mo.App. 1967) (husband who murdered wife could not recover proceeds from wife's life insurance policy); *In re Laspy's Estate*, 409 S.W.2d 725, 730 (Mo.App. 1966) (widow who was convicted of manslaughter for her husband's death could not receive statutory widow's allowance from his estate); *Barnett v. Couey*, 224 Mo.App. 913, 27 S.W.2d 757, 761 (Mo.App. 1930) (when tenant by the entirety murdered co-tenant, estate was converted to a tenancy in common and the felonious tenant could not take the deceased co-tenant's share).

None of these cases [is] analogous to the present case. In each of the above, the death of the victim was a precondition to the killer receiving the benefit. Here, Ida was already entitled to maintenance. Because Joseph's death would result in Ida no longer receiving maintenance, Ida would not profit in this regard if Joseph were murdered. This is a different question than if Ida would be entitled to claim death benefits from an insurance policy or otherwise.

Finally, Joseph asks this Court to extend the holdings in the above cited cases in order to discourage murder. This state's criminal and tort laws already do that.

CONCLUSION

The judgment of the trial court dismissing Count II of Joseph's Motion to Modify is affirmed.

All concur.

CHAPTER 7: PROCREATION

A. Voluntary Limits on Reproduction
3. Abortion

Page 916. Add after *Ayotte v. Planned Parenthood*:

Gonzalez v. Carhart

Supreme Court of the United States, 2007.
550 U.S. ___, 127 S. Ct. 1610.

■ JUSTICE KENNEDY delivered the opinion of the Court.

These cases require us to consider the validity of the Partial-Birth Abortion Ban Act of 2003 (Act), 18 U.S.C. §1531 (2000 ed., Supp. IV), a federal statute regulating abortion procedures. . . . Compared to the state statute at issue in *Stenberg v. Carhart*, [530 U.S. 914 (2000),] the Act is more specific concerning the instances to which it applies and in this respect more precise in its coverage. . . .

. . . .

I

. . . .

B

. . . .

. . . The operative provisions of the Act provide in relevant part:

"(a) Any physician who, in or affecting interstate or foreign commerce, knowingly performs a partial-birth abortion and thereby kills a human fetus shall be fined under this title or imprisoned not more than 2 years, or both. This subsection does not apply to a partial-birth abortion that is necessary to save the life of a mother whose life is endangered by a physical disorder, physical illness, or physical injury, including a life-endangering physical condition caused by or arising from the pregnancy itself. This subsection takes effect 1 day after the enactment.

"(b) As used in this section—

"(1) the term 'partial-birth abortion' means an abortion in which the person performing the abortion—

"(A) deliberately and intentionally vaginally delivers a living fetus until, in the case of a head-first presentation, the entire fetal head is outside the body of the mother, or, in the case of breech presentation, any part of the fetal trunk past the navel is outside the body of the mother, for the purpose of performing an overt act that the person knows will kill the fetus; and

"(B) performs the overt act, other than completion of delivery, that kills the partially delivered living fetus; and

"(2) the term 'physician' means a doctor of medicine or osteopathy legally authorized to practice medicine and surgery by the State in which the doctor performs such activity, or any other individual legally authorized by the State to perform abortions: *Provided, however,* That any individual who is not a physician or not otherwise legally authorized by the State to perform abortions, but who nevertheless directly performs a partial-birth abortion, shall be subject to the provisions of this section.

.   .   .   .   .

"(d)(1) A defendant accused of an offense under this section may seek a hearing before the State Medical Board on whether the physician's conduct was necessary to save the life of the mother whose life was endangered by a physical disorder, physical illness, or physical injury, including a life-endangering physical condition caused by or arising from the pregnancy itself.

"(2) The findings on that issue are admissible on that issue at the trial of the defendant. Upon a motion of the defendant, the court shall delay the beginning of the trial for not more than 30 days to permit such a hearing to take place.

"(e) A woman upon whom a partial-birth abortion is performed may not be prosecuted under this section, for a conspiracy to violate this section, or for an offense under section 2, 3, or 4 of this title based on a violation of this section." 18 U.S.C. §1531 (2000 ed., Supp. IV).

. . . .

II

. . . .

We assume the following principles for the purposes of this opinion. Before viability, a State "may not prohibit any woman from making the ultimate decision to terminate her pregnancy." [*Planned Parenthood of Southeastern Pennsylvania v. Casey*, 505 U.S. 833, 879 (1992) (plurality opinion)]. It also may not impose upon this right an undue burden, which exists if a regulation's "purpose or effect is to place a substantial obstacle in the path of a woman seeking an abortion before the fetus attains viability." *Id.,* at 878. On the other hand, "[r]egulations which do no more than create a structural mechanism by which the State, or the parent or guardian of a minor, may express profound respect for the life of the unborn are permitted, if they are not a substantial obstacle to the woman's exercise of the right to choose." *Id.,* at 877. . . .

III

We begin with a determination of the Act's operation and effect. A straightforward reading of the Act's text demonstrates its purpose and the scope of its provisions: It regulates and proscribes, with exceptions or qualifications to be discussed, performing the intact D&E procedure.

Respondents argue the Act encompasses intact D&E, but they contend its additional reach is both unclear and excessive. Respondents assert that, at the least, the Act is void for vagueness because its scope is indefinite. In the alternative, respondents argue the Act's text proscribes all D&Es. Because D&E is the most common second-trimester abortion method, respondents suggest the Act imposes an undue burden. In this litigation the Attorney General does not dispute that the Act would impose an undue burden if it covered standard D&E.

We conclude that the Act is not void for vagueness, does not impose an undue burden from any overbreadth, and is not invalid on its face.

A

The Act punishes 'knowingly perform[ing]" a "partial-birth abortion." §1531(a) (2000 ed., Supp. IV). It defines the unlawful abortion in explicit terms. §1531(b)(1).

. . . .

B

. . . "As generally stated, the void-for-vagueness doctrine requires that a penal statute define the criminal offense with sufficient definiteness that ordinary people can understand what conduct is prohibited and in a manner that does not encourage arbitrary and discriminatory enforcement." *Kolender v. Lawson*, 461 U.S. 352, 357 (1983)[.] The Act satisfies both requirements.

. . . Doctors performing D&E will know that if they do not deliver a living fetus to an anatomical landmark they will not face criminal liability.

This conclusion is buttressed by the intent that must be proved to impose liability. . . . The Act requires the doctor deliberately to have delivered the fetus to an anatomical landmark. §1531(b)(1)(A) (2000 ed., Supp. IV). Because a doctor performing a D&E will not face criminal liability if he or she delivers a fetus beyond the prohibited point by mistake, the Act cannot be described as "a trap for those who act in good faith." *Colautti* [*v. Franklin*, 439 U.S. 379, 395 (1979)] (internal quotation marks omitted).

Respondents likewise have failed to show that the Act should be invalidated on its face because it encourages arbitrary or discriminatory enforcement. *Kolender, supra*, at 357. Just as the Act's anatomical landmarks provide doctors with objective standards, they also "establish minimal guidelines to govern law enforcement." *Smith v. Goguen*, 415 U.S. 566, 574 (1974). The scienter requirements narrow the scope of the Act's prohibition and limit prosecutorial discretion. . . .

C

We next determine whether the Act imposes an undue burden, as a facial matter, because its restrictions on second-trimester abortions are too broad. A review of the statutory text discloses the limits of its reach. The Act prohibits intact D&E; and, notwithstanding respondents' arguments, it does not prohibit the D&E procedure in which the fetus is removed in parts.

1

The Act prohibits a doctor from intentionally performing an intact D&E. The dual prohibitions of the Act, both of which are necessary for criminal liability, correspond with the steps generally undertaken during this type of procedure. First, a doctor delivers the fetus until its head lodges in the cervix, which is usually past the anatomical landmark for a breech presentation. See 18 U.S.C. §1531(b)(1)(A) (2000 ed., Supp. IV). Second, the doctor proceeds to pierce the fetal skull with scissors or crush it with forceps. This step satisfies the overt-act requirement because it kills the fetus and is distinct from delivery. See §1531(b)(1)(B). The Act's intent requirements, however, limit its reach to those physicians who carry out the intact D&E after intending to undertake both steps at the outset.

The Act excludes most D&Es in which the fetus is removed in pieces, not intact. If the doctor intends to remove the fetus in parts from the outset, the doctor will not have the requisite intent to incur criminal liability. A doctor performing a standard D&E procedure can often "tak[e] about 10-15 'passes' through the uterus to remove the entire fetus." [*Planned Parenthood Fed'n of America v. Ashcroft*, 320 F. Supp. 2d 957, 962 (N.D. Cal. 2004).] Removing the fetus in this manner does not violate the Act because the doctor will not have delivered the living fetus to one of the anatomical landmarks or committed an additional overt act that ills the fetus after partial delivery. §1531(b)(1) (2000 ed., Supp. IV).

. . . .

By adding an overt-act requirement Congress sought further to meet the Court's objections to the state statute considered in *Stenberg*.

Compare 18 U.S.C. §1531(b)(1) (2000 ed., Supp. IV) with Neb. Rev. Stat. Ann. §28-326(9) (Supp. 1999). The Act makes the distinction the Nebraska statute failed to draw (but the Nebraska Attorney General advanced) by differentiating between the overall partial-birth abortion and the distinct overt act that kills the fetus. See *Stenberg*, 530 U.S., at 943-944. The fatal overt act must occur after delivery to an anatomical landmark, and it must be something "other than [the] completion of delivery." §1531(b)(1)(B). This distinction matters because, unlike intact D&E, standard D& E does not involve a delivery followed by a fatal act.

The canon of constitutional avoidance, finally, extinguishes any lingering doubt as to whether the Act covers the prototypical D&E procedure. "'[T]he elementary rule is that every reasonable construction must be resorted to, in order to save a statute from unconstitutionality.'" *Edward J. DeBartolo Corp. v. Florida Gulf Coast Building & Constr. Trades Council*, 485 U.S. 568, 575 (quoting *Hooper v. California*, 155 U.S. 648 (1895)). It is true this longstanding maxim of statutory interpretation has, in the past, fallen by the wayside when the Court confronted a statute regulating abortion. The Court at times employed an antagonistic "'canon of construction under which in cases involving abortion, a permissible reading of a statute [was] to be avoided at all costs.'" *Stenberg, supra*, at 977 (Kennedy, J., dissenting) (quoting *Thornburgh* [*v. Am. Coll. of Obstetricians and Gynecologists*, 476 U.S. 747, 829] (1986) (O'Connor, J., dissenting)). *Casey* put this novel statutory approach to rest. *Stenberg, supra*, at 977 (Kennedy, J., dissenting). *Stenberg* need not be interpreted to have revived it. We read that decision instead to stand for the uncontroversial proposition that the canon of constitutional avoidance does not apply if a statute is not "genuinely susceptible to two constructions." *Almendarez-Torres v. United States*, 523 U.S. 224 (1998)[.] In *Stenberg* the Court found the statute covered D&E. 530 U.S., at 938-945. Here, by contrast, interpreting the Act so that it does not prohibit standard D&E is the most reasonable reading and understanding of its terms.

. . . .

IV

Under the principles accepted as controlling here, the Act, as we have interpreted it, would be unconstitutional "if its purpose or effect is to place a substantial obstacle in the path of a woman seeking an abortion before the fetus attains viability." *Casey*, 505 U.S., at 878 (plurality opinion). The abortions affected by the Act's regulations take place both previability and postviability; so the quoted language and the undue burden analysis it relies upon are applicable. The question is whether the Act, measured by its text in this facial attack, imposes a substantial obstacle to late-term, but previability, abortions. The Act does not on its face impose a substantial obstacle, and we reject this further facial challenge to its validity.

A

The Act's purposes are set forth in recitals preceding its operative provisions. A description of the prohibited abortion procedure demonstrates the rationale for the congressional enactment. . . . The Act expresses respect for the dignity of human life.

Congress was concerned, furthermore, with the effects on the medical community and on its reputation caused by the practice of partial-birth abortion. . . . There can be no doubt that government "has an interest in protecting the integrity and ethics of the medical profession." *Washington v. Glucksberg*, 521 U.S. 702, 731 (1997)[.]

Casey reaffirmed these governmental objectives. . . . Where it has a rational basis to act, and it does not impose an undue burden, the State may use its regulatory power to bar certain procedures and substitute others, all in furtherance of its legitimate interests in regulating the medical profession in order to promote respect for life, including life of the unborn.

The Act's ban on abortions that involve partial delivery of a living fetus furthers the Government's objectives. No one would dispute that, for many, D&E is a procedure itself laden with the power to devalue human life. Congress could nonetheless conclude that the type of abortion proscribed by the Act requires specific regulation because it implicates additional ethical and moral concerns that justify a special prohibition. Congress determined that the abortion methods it proscribed had a "disturbing similarity to the killing of a newborn infant," Congressional Findings (14)(L), in notes following 18 U.S.C. §1531 (2000 ed., Supp. IV), p. 769, and thus it was concerned with "draw[ing]

a bright line that clearly distinguishes abortion and infanticide."
Congressional Findings (14)(G), *ibid.* . . .

Respect for human life finds an ultimate expression in the bond of
love the mother has for her child. The Act recognizes this reality as well.
Whether to have an abortion requires a difficult and painful moral
decision. *Casey, supra,* at 852-853 (opinion of the Court). While we find
no reliable data to measure the phenomenon, it seems unexceptionable to
conclude some women come to regret their choice to abort the infant life
they once created and sustained. Severe depression and loss of esteem
can follow. See *ibid.*

In a decision so fraught with emotional consequence some doctors
may prefer not to disclose precise details of the means that will be used,
confining themselves to the required statement of risks the procedure
entails. From one standpoint this ought not to be surprising. Any number
of patients facing imminent surgical procedures would prefer not to hear
all details, lest the usual anxiety preceding invasive medical procedures
become the more intense. This is likely the case with the abortion
procedures here in issue. See, *e.g.,* [*Nat'l Abortion Fed'n v. Ashcroft,*
330 F. Supp. 2d 436, 466, n.22 (S.D.N.Y. 2004)] ("Most of [the
plaintiffs'] experts acknowledged that they do not describe to their
patients what [the D&E and intact D&E] procedures entail in clear and
precise terms"); see also *id.,* at 479.

It is, however, precisely this lack of information concerning the way
in which the fetus will be killed that is of legitimate concern to the State.
Casey, supra, at 873 (plurality opinion)[.] The State has an interest in
ensuring so grave a choice is well informed. It is self-evident that a
mother who comes to regret her choice to abort must struggle with grief
more anguished and sorrow more profound when she learns, only after
the event, what she once did not know: that she allowed a doctor to
pierce the skull and vacuum the fast-developing brain of her unborn
child, a child assuming the human form.

It is a reasonable inference that a necessary effect of the regulation
and the knowledge it conveys will be to encourage some women to carry
the infant to full term, thus reducing the absolute number of late-term
abortions. The medical profession, furthermore, may find different and
less shocking methods to abort the fetus in the second trimester, thereby

accommodating legislative demand. The State's interest in respect for life is advanced by the dialogue that better informs the political and legal systems, the medical profession, expectant mothers, and society as a whole of the consequences that follow from a decision to elect a late-term abortion.

It is objected that the standard D&E is in some respects as brutal, if not more, than the intact D&E, so that the legislation accomplishes little. What we have already said, however, shows ample justification for the regulation. Partial-birth abortion, as defined by the Act, differs from a standard D&E because the former occurs when the fetus is partially outside the mother to the point of one of the Act's anatomical landmarks. It was reasonable for Congress to think that partial-birth abortion, more than standard D&E, "undermines the public's perception of the appropriate role of a physician during the delivery process, and perverts a process during which life is brought into the world." Congressional Findings (14)(K), in notes following 18 U.S.C. §1531 (2000 ed., Supp. IV), p. 769. There would be a flaw in this Court's logic, and an irony in its jurisprudence, were we first to conclude a ban on both D&E and intact D&E was overbroad and then to say it is irrational to ban only intact D&E because that does not proscribe both procedures. In sum, we reject the contention that the congressional purpose of the Act was "to place a substantial obstacle in the path of a woman seeking an abortion." 505 U.S., at 878 (plurality opinion).

B

The Act's furtherance of legitimate government interests bears upon, but does not resolve, the next question: whether the Act has the effect of imposing an unconstitutional burden on the abortion right because it does not allow use of the barred procedure where "'necessary, in appropriate medical judgment, for [the] preservation of the . . . health of the mother.'" *Ayotte v. [Planned Parenthood of N. New England*, 546 U.S. 320, 327-328 (2006)] (quoting *Casey, supra*, at 879 (plurality opinion)). The prohibition in the Act would be unconstitutional, under precedents we here assume to be controlling, if it "subject[ed] [women] to significant health risks." *Ayotte, supra*, at 328[.] In *Ayotte*[,] the parties agreed a health exception to the challenged parental-involvement statute was necessary "to avert serious and often irreversible damage to [a pregnant minor's] health." 546 U.S., at 328. Here, by contrast, whether the Act creates significant health risks for women has been a contested factual question. The evidence presented in the trial courts and before Congress demonstrates both sides have medical support for their position.

. . . .

There is documented medical disagreement whether the Act's prohibition would ever impose significant health risks on women. See, *e.g.*, [*Planned Parenthood v. Ashcroft*, 320 F. Supp. 2d,] at 1033 ("[T]here continues to be a division of opinion among highly qualified experts regarding the necessity or safety of intact D&E"); see also [*Nat'l Abortion Fed'n*, *supra*, at 482]. . . .

The question becomes whether the Act can stand when this medical uncertainty persists. The Court's precedents instruct that the Act can survive this facial attack. The Court has given state and federal legislatures wide discretion to pass legislation in areas where there is medical and scientific uncertainty. See *Kansas v. Hendricks*, 521 U.S. 346, 360, n. 3 (1997)[;] see also *Stenberg*, *supra*, at 969-972 (Kennedy, J., dissenting); *Marshall v. United States*, 414 U.S. 417, 427 (1974) ("When Congress undertakes to act in areas fraught with medical and scientific uncertainties, legislative options must be especially broad").

This traditional rule is consistent with *Casey*, which confirms the State's interest in promoting respect for human life at all stages in the pregnancy. Physicians are not entitled to ignore regulations that direct them to use reasonable alternative procedures. The law need not give abortion doctors unfettered choice in the course of their medical practice, nor should it elevate their status above other physicians in the medical community. . . .

Medical uncertainty does not foreclose the exercise of legislative power in the abortion context any more than it does in other contexts. See *Hendricks*, *supra*, at 360, n. 3. The medical uncertainty over whether the Act's prohibition creates significant health risks provides a sufficient basis to conclude in this facial attack that the Act does not impose an undue burden.

The conclusion that the Act does not impose an undue burden is supported by other considerations. Alternatives are available to the prohibited procedure. As we have noted, the Act does not proscribe D&E. . . . In addition the Act's prohibition only applies to the delivery of "a living fetus." 18 U.S.C. §1531(b)(1)(A) (2000 ed., Supp. IV). If the intact D&E procedure is truly necessary in some circumstances, it appears likely an injection that kills the fetus is an alternative under the Act that allows the doctor to perform the procedure.

. . . .

. . . Considerations of marginal safety, including the balance of risks, are within the legislative competence when the regulation is rational and in pursuit of legitimate ends. When standard medical options are available, mere convenience does not suffice to displace them; and if some procedures have different risks than others, it does not follow that the State is altogether barred from imposing reasonable regulations. The Act is not invalid on its face where there is uncertainty over whether the barred procedure is ever necessary to preserve a woman's health, given the availability of other abortion procedures that are considered to be safe alternatives.

. . .

■ JUSTICE GINSBURG, with whom JUSTICE STEVENS, JUSTICE SOUTER, and JUSTICE BREYER join, dissenting.

. . . .

Today's decision is alarming. It refuses to take [*Planned Parenthood of Southeastern Pennsylvania v. Casey*, 505 U.S. 833 (1992)] and [*Stenberg v. Carhart*, 530 U.S. 914 (2000)] seriously. It tolerates, indeed applauds, federal intervention to ban nationwide a procedure found necessary and proper in certain cases by the American College of Obstetricians and Gynecologists (ACOG). It blurs the line, firmly drawn in *Casey,* between previability and postviability abortions. And, for the first time since *Roe,* the Court blesses a prohibition with no exception safeguarding a woman's health.

I dissent from the Court's disposition. Retreating from prior rulings that abortion restrictions cannot be imposed absent an exception safeguarding a woman's health, the Court upholds an Act that surely would not survive under the close scrutiny that previously attended state-decreed limitations on a woman's reproductive choices.

I

A

. . . Women, it is now acknowledged, have the talent, capacity, and right "to participate equally in the economic and social life of the Nation." Their ability to realize their full potential, the Court recognized, is intimately connected to "their ability to control their reproductive lives." Thus, legal challenges to undue restrictions on abortion procedures do not seek to vindicate some generalized notion of privacy; rather, they center on a woman's autonomy to determine her life's course, and thus to enjoy equal citizenship stature.

In keeping with this comprehension of the right to reproductive choice, the Court has consistently required that laws regulating abortion, at any stage of pregnancy and in all cases, safeguard a woman's health. See, *e.g., [Ayotte v. Planned Parenthood of N. New England,* 546 U.S. 320, 327-328 (2006)]; *Stenberg,* 530 U.S., at 930[.]

We have thus ruled that a State must avoid subjecting women to health risks not only where the pregnancy itself creates danger, but also where state regulation forces women to resort to less safe methods of abortion. See *Planned Parenthood of Central Mo. v. Danforth,* 428 U.S. 52, 79, 96 S.Ct. 2831, 49 L.Ed.2d 788 (1976) (holding unconstitutional a ban on a method of abortion that "force[d] a woman . . . to terminate her pregnancy by methods more dangerous to her health"). Indeed, we have applied the rule that abortion regulation must safeguard a woman's health to the particular procedure at issue here—intact dilation and evacuation (D&E).[3]

---

[3] . . . . [] Adolescents and indigent women, research suggests, are more likely than other women to have difficulty obtaining an abortion during the first trimester of pregnancy. Minors may be unaware they are pregnant until relatively late in pregnancy, while poor women's financial constraints are an obstacle to timely receipt of services. . . .

In *Stenberg,* we expressly held that a statute banning intact D&E was unconstitutional in part because it lacked a health exception. 530 U.S., at 930, 937. We noted that there existed a "division of medical opinion" about the relative safety of intact D&E, *id.* at 937, but we made clear that as long as "substantial medical authority supports the proposition that banning a particular abortion procedure could endanger women's health," a health exception is required, *id.*, at 938. . . . Thus, we reasoned, division in medical opinion "at most means uncertainty, a factor that signals the presence of risk, not its absence." [*Id.*, at 937.] "[A] statute that altogether forbids [intact D&E] . . . consequently must contain a health exception." *Id.*, at 938.

B

In 2003, a few years after our ruling in *Stenberg,* Congress passed the Partial-Birth Abortion Ban Act—without an exception for women's health. See 18 U.S.C. § 1531(a) (2000 ed., Supp. IV).[4] The congressional findings on which the Partial-Birth Abortion Ban Act rests do not withstand inspection[.] . . .

Many of the Act's recitations are incorrect. For example, Congress determined that no medical schools provide instruction on intact D&E. But in fact, numerous leading medical schools teach the procedure.

More important, Congress claimed there was a medical consensus that the banned procedure is never necessary. But the evidence "very clearly demonstrate[d] the opposite." [*Planned Parenthood Fed'n of Am. v. Ashcroft,* 320 F. Supp. 2d 957, 1025 (N.D. Cal. 2004)]. See also [*Carhart v. Ashcroft,* 331 F. Supp. 2d 805, 1008-09 (D. Neb. 2004)]; [*Nat'l Abortion Fed'n v. Ashcroft,* 330 F. Supp. 2d 436, 488 (S.D.N.Y. 2004)].

Similarly, Congress found that "[t]here is no credible medical evidence that partial-birth abortions are safe or are safer than other abortion procedures." But the congressional record includes letters from numerous individual physicians stating that pregnant women's health would be jeopardized under the Act, as well as statements from nine

---

[4] The Act's sponsors left no doubt that their intention was to nullify our ruling in *Stenberg*[.]

professional associations, including ACOG, the American Public Health Association, and the California Medical Association, attesting that intact D&E carries meaningful safety advantages over other methods. No comparable medical groups supported the ban. In fact, "all of the government's own witnesses disagreed with many of the specific congressional findings." [*Planned Parenthood*, 320 F. Supp. 2d,] at 1024.

C

. . . .

According to the expert testimony [introduced by plaintiffs in the trials courts], the safety advantages of intact D&E are marked for women with certain medical conditions, for example, uterine scarring, bleeding disorders, heart disease, or compromised immune systems. Further, plaintiffs' experts testified that intact D&E is significantly safer for women with certain pregnancy-related conditions, such as placenta previa and accreta, and for women carrying fetuses with certain abnormalities, such as severe hydrocephalus.

Intact D&E, plaintiffs' experts explained, provides safety benefits over D&E by dismemberment for several reasons: *First*, intact D&E minimizes the number of times a physician must insert instruments through the cervix and into the uterus, and thereby reduces the risk of trauma to, and perforation of, the cervix and uterus-the most serious complication associated with nonintact D&E. *Second*, removing the fetus intact, instead of dismembering it *in utero*, decreases the likelihood that fetal tissue will be retained in the uterus, a condition that can cause infection, hemorrhage, and infertility. *Third*, intact D&E diminishes the chances of exposing the patient's tissues to sharp bony fragments sometimes resulting from dismemberment of the fetus. *Fourth*, intact D&E takes less operating time than D&E by dismemberment, and thus may reduce bleeding, the risk of infection, and complications relating to anesthesia.

Based on thoroughgoing review of the trial evidence and the congressional record, each of the District Courts to consider the issue rejected Congress' findings as unreasonable and not supported by the evidence. The trial courts concluded, in contrast to Congress' findings, that "significant medical authority supports the proposition that in some circumstances, [intact D&E] is the safest procedure."

The District Courts' findings merit this Court's respect. Today's opinion supplies no reason to reject those findings. Nevertheless, despite the District Courts' appraisal of the weight of the evidence, and in undisguised conflict with *Stenberg*, the Court asserts that the Partial-Birth Abortion Ban Act can survive "when . . . medical uncertainty persists." This assertion is bewildering. Not only does it defy the Court's longstanding precedent affirming the necessity of a health exception, with no carve-out for circumstances of medical uncertainty; it gives short shrift to the records before us, carefully canvassed by the District Courts. Those records indicate that "the majority of highly-qualified experts on the subject believe intact D&E to be the safest, most appropriate procedure under certain circumstances."

The Court acknowledges some of this evidence, but insists that [because of disagreement about the assessment of risk], the Act can stand. In this insistence, the Court brushes under the rug the District Courts' well-supported findings that the physicians who testified that intact D&E is never necessary to preserve the health of a woman had slim authority for their opinions. They had no training for, or personal experience with, the intact D&E procedure, and many performed abortions only on rare occasions. Even indulging the assumption that the Government witnesses were equally qualified to evaluate the relative risks of abortion procedures, their testimony could not erase the "significant medical authority support[ing] the proposition that in some circumstances, [intact D&E] would be the safest procedure."[6]

---

[6] The majority contends that "[i]f the intact D&E procedure is truly necessary in some circumstances, it appears likely an injection that kills the fetus is an alternative under the Act that allows the doctor to perform the procedure." But a "significant body of medical opinion believes that inducing fetal death by injection is almost always inappropriate to the preservation of the health of women undergoing abortion because it poses tangible risk and provides no benefit to the woman." *Carhart v. Ashcroft*, 331 F. Supp. 2d 805, 1028 (Neb. 2004), aff'd, 413 F. 3d 791 ([8th Cir.] 2005). In some circumstances, injections are "absolutely [medically] contraindicated." 331 F. Supp. 2d, at 1027. The Court also identifies medical induction of labor as an alternative. That procedure, however, requires a hospital stay, rendering it inaccessible to patients who lack financial resources, and it too is considered less safe for many women, and impermissible for others.

II

A

The Court offers flimsy and transparent justifications for upholding a nationwide ban on intact D&E *sans* any exception to safeguard a women's health. Today's ruling, the Court declares, advances "a premise central to [*Casey*'s] conclusion"—*i.e.*, the Government's "legitimate and substantial interest in preserving and promoting fetal life." But the Act scarcely furthers that interest: The law saves not a single fetus from destruction, for it targets only a *method* of performing abortion. And surely the statute was not designed to protect the lives or health of pregnant women. In short, the Court upholds a law that, while doing nothing to "preserv[e] . . . fetal life," bars a woman from choosing intact D&E although her doctor "reasonably believes [that procedure] will best protect [her]." *Stenberg*, 530 U.S., at 946 (Stevens, J., concurring).

As another reason for upholding the ban, the Court emphasizes that the Act does not proscribe the nonintact D&E procedure. But why not, one might ask. . . . "[T]he notion that either of these two equally gruesome procedures . . . is more akin to infanticide than the other, or that the State furthers any legitimate interest by banning one but not the other, is simply irrational." [*Id.*,] at 946-947[.]

Delivery of an intact, albeit nonviable, fetus warrants special condemnation, the Court maintains, because a fetus that is not dismembered resembles an infant. But so, too, does a fetus delivered intact after it is terminated by injection a day or two before the surgical evacuation, or a fetus delivered through medical induction or cesarean[.] Yet, the availability of those procedures—along with D&E by dismemberment—the Court says, saves the ban on intact D&E from a declaration of unconstitutionality. Never mind that the procedures deemed acceptable might put a woman's health at greater risk.

Ultimately, the Court admits that "moral concerns" are at work, concerns that could yield prohibitions on any abortion. See *ante,* at 1633-1634 ("Congress could . . . conclude that the type of abortion proscribed by the Act requires specific regulation because it implicates additional ethical and moral concerns that justify a special prohibition."). Notably, the concerns expressed are untethered to any ground genuinely serving the Government's interest in preserving life. By allowing such concerns to carry the day and case, overriding fundamental rights, the Court dishonors our precedent. See, *e.g., Casey*, 505 U.S., at 850; *Lawrence v. Texas*, 539 U.S. 558, 571 (2003).

Revealing in this regard, the Court invokes an antiabortion shibboleth for which it concededly has no reliable evidence: Women who have abortions come to regret their choices, and consequently suffer from "[s]evere depression and loss of esteem." Because of women's fragile emotional state and because of the "bond of love the mother has for her child," the Court worries, doctors may withhold information about the nature of the intact D&E procedure. The solution the Court approves, then, is *not* to require doctors to inform women, accurately and adequately, of the different procedures and their attendant risks. Instead, the Court deprives women of the right to make an autonomous choice, even at the expense of their safety.

This way of thinking reflects ancient notions about women's place in the family and under the Constitution—ideas that have long since been discredited. Compare, *e.g., Muller v. Oregon*, 208 U.S. 412 (1908), [and] *Bradwell v. State*, 16 Wall. 130, 141 (1873) (Bradley, J., concurring), with *United States v. Virginia*, 518 U.S. 515, 533, 542, n. 12 (1996), [and] *Califano v. Goldfarb*, 430 U.S. 199 (1977).

Though today's majority may regard women's feelings on the matter as "self-evident," this Court has repeatedly confirmed that "[t]he destiny of the woman must be shaped ... on her own conception of her spiritual imperatives and her place in society." *Casey*, 505 U.S., at 852[.]

B

In cases on a "woman's liberty to determine whether to [continue] her pregnancy," this Court has identified viability as a critical consideration. See *Casey*, 505 U.S., at 869-870 (plurality opinion). "[T]here is no line [more workable] than viability," the Court explained in *Casey*, for viability is "the time at which there is a realistic possibility of maintaining and nourishing a life outside the womb, so that the independent existence of the second life can in reason and all fairness be the object of state protection that now overrides the rights of the woman. . . . In some broad sense it might be said that a woman who fails to act before viability has consented to the State's intervention on behalf of the developing child." *Id.*, at 870.

Today, the Court blurs that line, maintaining that "[t]he Act [legitimately] appl[ies] both previability and postviability because . . . a fetus is a living organism while within the womb, whether or not it is viable outside the womb." Instead of drawing the line at viability, the Court refers to Congress' purpose to differentiate "abortion and infanticide" based not on whether a fetus can survive outside the womb, but on where a fetus is anatomically located when a particular medical procedure is performed.

One wonders how long a line that saves no fetus from destruction will hold in face of the Court's "moral concerns." The Court's hostility to the right *Roe* and *Casey* secured is not concealed. Throughout, the opinion refers to obstetrician-gynecologists and surgeons who perform abortions not by the titles of their medical specialties, but by the pejorative label "abortion doctor." A fetus is described as an "unborn child," and as a "baby[;]" second-trimester, previability abortions are referred to as "late-term[;]" and the reasoned medical judgments of highly trained doctors are dismissed as "preferences" motivated by "mere convenience[.]" Instead of the heightened scrutiny we have previously applied, the Court determines that a "rational" ground is enough to uphold the Act[.] And, most troubling, *Casey*'s principles, confirming the continuing vitality of "the essential holding of *Roe*," are merely "assume[d]" for the moment, rather than "retained" or "reaffirmed," *Casey*, 505 U.S., at 846.

III

A

. . . .

Without attempting to distinguish *Stenberg* and earlier decisions, the majority asserts that the Act survives review because respondents have not shown that the ban on intact D&E would be unconstitutional "in a large fraction of relevant cases." But *Casey* makes clear that, in determining whether any restriction poses an undue burden on a "large fraction" of women, the relevant class is *not* "all women," nor "all pregnant women," nor even all women "seeking abortions." [*Id.*] at 895. Rather, a provision restricting access to abortion, "must be judged by reference to those [women] for whom it is an actual rather than an irrelevant restriction," *ibid.* Thus the absence of a health exception burdens *all* women for whom it is relevant-women who, in the judgment of their doctors, require an intact D&E because other procedures would place their health at risk. . . . The very purpose of a health *exception* is to protect women in *exceptional* cases.

. . . .

IV

. . . .

[T]he notion that the Partial-Birth Abortion Ban Act furthers any legitimate governmental interest is, quite simply, irrational. The Court's defense of the statute provides no saving explanation. In candor, the Act, and the Court's defense of it, cannot be understood as anything other than an effort to chip away at a right declared again and again by this Court—and with increasing comprehension of its centrality to women's lives. When "a statute burdens constitutional rights and all that can be said on its behalf is that it is the vehicle that legislators have chosen for expressing their hostility to those rights, the burden is undue." *Stenberg*, 530 U.S., at 952 (Ginsburg, J., concurring) (quoting *Hope Clinic v. Ryan*, 195 F. 3d 857, 881 (7th Cir. 1999) (Posner, C. J., dissenting)).

. . . .

NOTE:

In light of its ruling in *Gonzalez v. Carhart*, 550 U.S. __, 127 S. Ct. 1610, 1619, 1629-31 (2007) (*Carhart II*), the Supreme Court vacated and remanded a Fourth Circuit decision involving a Virginia ban on what was statutorily described as "partial birth infanticide." *Herring v. Richmond Med. Ctr. for Women*, 550 U.S. ___, 127 S. Ct. 2094 (2007). In a split decision, the Fourth Circuit declared the Virginia law unconstitutional for a second time. (For the earlier decision, see *Richmond Med. Ctr. for Women v. Hicks*, 409 F.3d 619 (4th Cir. 2005).) The majority opinion in the case explained that the Virginia statute outlawed "intact dilation and evacuation" without the same (kind of) *scienter* element that the *Carhart II* Court had held saved the federal "Partial-Birth Abortion Act" from constitutional demise. *Richmond Med. Ctr. for Women v. Herring*, 527 F.3d 128 (4th Cir. 2008). "[T]he Virginia Act has no provision requiring intent at the outset of the procedure[, and] . . . thus imposes criminal liability on a doctor who sets out to perform a standard D&E that by accident becomes an intact D&E." *Id.* at 131. The statute, the court continued, "thereby expos[es] all doctors who perform standard D&Es to prosecution, conviction, and imprisonment," *id.*, and, as a result, imposes "'an undue burden upon a woman's right to make an abortion decision,' in violation of the Constitution." *Id.* at 135 (quoting *Stenberg v. Carhart*, 530 U.S. 914, 945-46 (2000), and citing *Gonzalez v. Carhart*, 550 U.S. __, 127 S. Ct. 1610, 1619, 1629-31 (2007)).

C. Involuntary Limits on Reproduction
2. Indirect Restrictions

Page 954. Add after *International Union, UAW v. Johnson Controls*:

North Coast Women's Care Medical Group v. Superior Court

California Court of Appeals, 2006.
40 Cal. Rptr. 3d 636.

■ O'ROURKE, J.

. . . .

Factual and Procedural Background

. . . After [Guadalupe] Benitez tried unsuccessfully for about two years to become pregnant through intravaginal insemination (IVI) performed at home, her primary care physician referred her to North Coast [Women's Care Medical Group (North Coast)] for fertility treatment.

In August 1999, Benitez began fertility treatment with Dr. [Christine] Brody. Benitez informed Dr. Brody of her sexual orientation at their first meeting. Dr. Brody told Benitez that if her treatment reached the point where [intrauterine insemination (IUI)] was the next recommended step, Dr. Brody would not perform the procedure because it would be against her religious beliefs. Dr. Brody's explanation of why her religious beliefs precluded her from performing IUI for Benitez is a matter of dispute. Benitez claims Dr. Brody told her it was against her religious beliefs to perform IUI for a lesbian. Dr. Brody claims she told Benitez it was against her religious beliefs to perform IUI for any unmarried woman, regardless of sexual orientation, and she was certain [that her colleague] Dr. [Douglas] Fenton would share her religious convictions regarding the IUI issue because they attended the same church.[2] In any event, Dr. Brody told Benitez that other doctors at North Coast would be available to perform IUI on Benitez if it became necessary, and with that understanding, Benitez began treatment with her.

    . . . .

    . . . During [a] visit [in March 2000], Benitez told Dr. Brody she wanted to use fresh sperm donated by a friend instead of frozen sperm for her IUI, as she understood using fresh sperm was more likely to result in pregnancy. At Dr. Brody's direction, Benitez's friend underwent blood tests for certain conditions, including hepatitis and HIV. Benitez underwent laparoscopic surgery [recommended by Dr. Brody] in April 2000. The surgery revealed no problem that would interfere with her fertility.

The parties relate different versions of the events leading to North Coast's referral of Benitez to an outside physician. Dr. Brody and Dr. Fenton aver that "live non-spousal donor sperm" had never been used at North Coast and that no North Coast patient before Benitez had ever requested to use such sperm for IUI. Consequently, an inquiry into the requirements for using such sperm was necessary to ensure that North Coast did not violate any laws. According to Dr. Brody, because Benitez was aware that the details and protocol of preparing the live non-spousal donor sperm had not been clarified as of July 5, 2005, the date of

---

[2] Dr. Brody claims she told Benitez that with the exception of participating in IUI, she would provide care to Benitez from ovulation induction through term delivery.

Benitez's last office visit with Dr. Brody before Dr. Brody left on a vacation, Benitez decided to proceed with IUI using frozen, pre-washed, IUI-ready sperm from a sperm bank. Dr. Brody noted this in her dictated chart notes of July 5, 2005, but the dictated notes were not placed in Benitez's chart until after Dr. Brody returned from her vacation on July 17, 2005.

According to defendants, the absence of Dr. Brody's July 5 notes from Benitez's chart during her vacation caused a misunderstanding between Benitez and Dr. Fenton that resulted in Dr. Fenton's referral of Benitez to an outside physician. While Dr. Brody was on vacation, Benitez called her office to obtain a refill of her Clomid prescription in anticipation of undergoing IUI about 14 days later. Because Dr. Brody was away, Benitez was referred to Dr. Fenton, who thought Benitez still intended to undergo IUI with live non-spousal donor sperm. Dr. Fenton claims Benitez did not tell him she had agreed during her last office visit with Dr. Brody to undergo IUI with frozen, IUI-ready sperm. If live donor sperm rather than frozen, IUI-ready sperm is used for IUI, the live sperm must go through a preparation process that only two people at North Coast—Dr. Fenton and nurse Dana Landsparger—were qualified and licensed to perform. Because it was against Dr. Fenton's moral and religious beliefs to perform IUI or prepare live donor sperm for Benitez, he asked Landsparger if she would be willing to prepare the live donor sperm for Benitez's IUI. Landsparger informed Dr. Fenton that it was also against her moral and religious beliefs to prepare live donor sperm for Benitez. Unaware that Benitez was willing to undergo IUI with frozen IUI-ready sperm, Dr. Fenton referred her to outside physician Dr. Michael Kettel for IUI. Dr. Fenton asserts that had he known Benitez was willing to proceed with frozen sperm, the referral would have been unnecessary because there were two other doctors at North Coast who could have performed IUI for Benitez with frozen sperm. He claims he told Benitez that North Coast would absorb any additional costs she incurred as a result of the referral.

According to Benitez, in May 2000, Dr. Brody told her North Coast did not have a "tissue license" required by state law for insemination with known-donor sperm. When Benitez visited Dr. Brody on July 5 and tested negative for pregnancy, Dr. Brody promised she would undergo IUI at North Coast, but with frozen sperm because North Coast still did not have a tissue license. Dr. Brody told Benitez to call the office when her menstrual cycle resumed so Dr. Brody could prescribe Clomid, to be followed by IUI when Benitez ovulated.

On July 7, 2000, Benitez began her menstrual cycle and telephoned Dr. Brody's office for a refill of her Clomid prescription. A receptionist relayed Benitez's request to Dr. Fenton because Dr. Brody was on vacation. Later that day, "Shirley" at North Coast telephoned Benitez and told her Dr. Fenton would not refill her prescription. The following day, Dr. Fenton telephoned Benitez and told her that due to the beliefs of Dr. Brody and other North Coast staff members, he could not help her. He explained that Dr. Brody and her staff did not feel comfortable with Benitez's sexual orientation and that although he personally had no bias against performing IUI for her, she would not be treated fairly at North Coast and would not get timely care from staff members who had objections to her sexual orientation. Dr. Fenton offered to refer Benitez to an outside physician, telling her she was entitled to care that was not discriminatory.

Benitez claims she had to beg Sharp for an "off plan" referral to another obstetrician and gynecologist, and that although Sharp ultimately authorized reproductive therapy with Dr. Kettel, the cost of receiving treatment from him was substantially greater than the cost of continuing treatment with North Coast would have been. In her answer to the petition for writ of mandate, Benitez denies that Dr. Fenton offered to pay the additional costs she incurred as a result of his referral to Dr. Kettel and alleges defendants have not paid any of those costs. In her first amended complaint, Benitez alleges she ultimately became pregnant under Dr. Kettel's care by the process of in vitro fertilization. Benitez eventually gave birth to a healthy boy.

Benitez filed the instant action in August 2001. In the first cause of action of her first amended complaint she alleges defendants violated the Unruh Act[,] Civ.Code, § 51[,][3] by discriminating against her on the

---

[3] . . . Civil Code section 51, subdivision (b) provides: "All persons within the jurisdiction of this state are free and equal, and no matter what their sex, race, color, religion, ancestry, national origin, disability, or medical condition are entitled to the full and equal accommodations, advantages, facilities, privileges, or services in all business establishments of every kind whatsoever." Civil Code section 52, subdivision (a), provides: "Whoever denies, aids or incites a denial, or makes any discrimination or distinction contrary to Section 51 . . . is liable for each and every offense for the actual

basis of her sexual orientation.[4] Defendants answered the first amended complaint and asserted . . . that Benitez is barred from recovery because their alleged misconduct was "justified and protected by [their] rights of free speech and freedom of religion" under the federal and state Constitutions. Benitez moved for summary adjudication of [that] . . . defense and the court granted the motion, precluding defendants from raising the defense at trial.

[The court of appeals ordered the superior court to vacate its order granting Benitez's motion and to deny it as to Drs. Brody and Fenton.]

NOTE:

The Court of Appeals' decision has been appealed to the California Supreme Court, where it is now pending.

The following arguments appear in the Opening Brief filed on behalf of Guadalupe T. Benitez with the California Supreme Court, Opening Brief on the Merits of Plaintiff and Real Party in Interest Guadalupe T. Benitez at 8-12, 26-27, N. Coast Women's Care Med. Group v. Super. Ct., No. S142892 (Cal. Sep. 21, 2006):

> The Unruh Act prohibits a physician from discriminating against his or her patients based on personal characteristics such as their race, national origin, religion, sex or sexual orientation. . . .

> Nevertheless, sexual orientation discrimination has persisted in California, requiring occasional reminders by the courts—in various contexts demonstrating the range of discrimination lesbians and gay men frequently encounter in daily life—that the Unruh Act prohibits businesses from acting on anti-gay bias. . . .

---

damages, and any amount that may be determined by a jury, or a court sitting without a jury, up to a maximum of three times the amount of actual damage but in no case less than four thousand dollars ($4,000), and any attorney's fees that may be determined by the court in addition thereto, suffered by any person denied the rights provided in Section 51[] . . . ."

[4] Plaintiff's first amended complaint also includes causes of action against defendants for breach of contract, deceit, negligence and intentional infliction of emotional distress.

The decision in *Washington v. Blampin*, 226 Cal.App.2d 604 (1964)[,] is illustrative. In that case, a doctor refused to provide medical services to an African-American girl because of her race. *Id.* at p. 605. In defending against an Unruh Act claim, the doctor argued that, as a professional, he could not be required to treat an "unwelcome" patient. *Id.* at p. 608. The Court of Appeal rejected that argument, holding that "the personal nature of the physician-patient relationship creates no obstacle to a recovery of damages when service is refused by reason of the plaintiff's race or color." *Ibid.*

There can be no principled distinction between *Washington v. Blampin* and the present case. So long as a physician or medical group offers services to the general public, the Unruh Act tolerates no invidious distinctions among patients, who "are entitled to the full and equal . . . services" offered to the public. "Our modern society has become so interdependent and interrelated that those who perform a significant public function may not erect barriers of arbitrary discrimination in the marketplace." *In re Cox*, 3 Cal.3d 205, 218 (1970)[.]

North Coast, Brody and Fenton offer gynecological and obstetrical services to the public for a fee. They have chosen to specialize in treating infertility, and thus offer IUI and related services. Having chosen that practice area, these defendants cannot reasonably claim an excuse from complying with the laws applicable to such practice, including the Unruh Act. As the superior court correctly observed, the civil rights law "permits [d]efendants free rein to operate their business as long as they do not discriminate." See order granting summary adjudication of defendants' religious defense. Having chosen to offer IUI to their heterosexual patients, they must do so equally for their lesbian patients. "When followers of a particular sect enter into commercial activity as a matter of choice, the limits they accept on their own conduct as a matter of conscience and faith are not to be superimposed on the statutory schemes which are binding on others in that activity." *Ibid.* (quoting *Catholic Charities of Sacramento, Inc. v. Superior Court*, 32 Cal.4th 527, 565 (2004)).

. . . .

Defendants claimed below that the free exercise of the First Amendment to the United States Constitution exempts them from the Unruh Act. Under the federal Constitution, neutral laws of general application that do not target religious beliefs or practices are to be enforced as long as they serve a legitimate state purpose in a rational manner. See *Employment Division v. Smith*, 494 U.S. 872 (1990). The Unruh Act easily satisfies this test.

Petitioners' claim of religious exemption from the Unruh Act is directly contrary to *Employment Division v. Smith*, which held that the free exercise clause did not prohibit the application of Oregon's drug laws to ceremonial ingestion of peyote. In *Employment Division v. Smith*, the respondents contended "that their religious motivation for using peyote places them beyond the reach of a criminal law that is not specifically directed at their religious practice." 494 U.S. at p. 878. Similarly here, defendants contend that their religious motivation for discriminating against lesbians places them beyond the reach of the Unruh Act, which likewise is not specifically directed at their religious practice.

Employment Division v. Smith rejected the respondents' contention in language equally applicable here: "We have never held that an individual's religious beliefs excuse him from compliance with an otherwise valid law prohibiting conduct that the State is free to regulate. On the contrary, the record of more than a century of our free exercise jurisprudence contradicts that proposition." *Id.* at pp. 878-79. "'Conscientious scruples have not, in the course of the long struggle for religious toleration, relieved the individual from obedience to a general law not aimed at the promotion or restriction of religious belief. The mere possession of religious convictions which contradict the relevant concerns of a political society does not relieve the citizen from the discharge of political responsibilities (footnote omitted).'" *Id.* at p. 879 (quoting *Minersville School Dist. Bd. of Ed. v. Gobitis*, 310 U.S. 586, 594-595 (1940)).

Thus, *Employment Division v. Smith* noted, the United States Supreme Court has "consistently held that the right of free exercise does not relieve an individual of the obligation to comply with a 'valid and neutral law of general applicability on the ground that the law proscribes (or prescribes) conduct that his religion prescribes (or proscribes).'" 494 U.S. at p. 879 (quoting *United States v. Lee*, 455 U.S. 252, 263, fn. 3 (1982)). For example, as further noted in *Employment Division v. Smith, supra,* 484 U.S. at page 879, the U.S. Supreme Court has:

- "held that a mother could be prosecuted under the child labor laws for using her children to dispense literature in the streets, her religious motivation notwithstanding[,]" citing *Prince v. Massachusetts*, 321 U.S. 158 (1944);

- "upheld Sunday closing laws against the claim that they burdened the religious practices of persons whose religions compelled them to refrain from work on other days[,]" citing *Braunfeld v. Brown*, 366 U.S. 599 (1961);

- "sustained the military Selective Service System against the claim that it violated free exercise by conscripting persons who opposed a particular war on religious grounds[,]" citing *Gillette v. United States*, 401 U.S. 437, 461 (1971); and

- "rejected the claim" by an Amish employer seeking "exemption from collection and payment of Social Security taxes on the ground that the Amish faith prohibited participation in governmental support programs[,]" citing *United States v. Lee, supra*, 455 U.S. at pp. 258-61.

Employment Division v. Smith explained that "[t]he rule respondents favor would open the prospect of constitutionally required religious exemptions from civic obligations of almost every conceivable kind—ranging from compulsory military service, to the payment of taxes, to health and safety regulation such as manslaughter and child neglect laws, compulsory vaccination laws, drug laws, and traffic laws, to social welfare legislation such as minimum wage laws, child labor laws, animal cruelty laws, environmental protection laws, and laws providing for equality of opportunity for the races." *Id.* at pp. 888-889 (citations omitted). To this list can be added anti-discrimination laws like the Unruh Act.

Employment Division v. Smith concluded that "[r]espondents urge us to hold, quite simply, that when otherwise prohibitable conduct is accompanied by religious convictions, not only the convictions but the conduct itself must be free from government regulation. We have never held that, and decline to do so now." *Id.* at p. 882. This court likewise should decline to do so here. Religious convictions are no excuse for violating anti-discrimination laws, just as they created no exemption from the civic obligations described in *Employment Division v. Smith.* To hold otherwise and permit individual religious beliefs to excuse acts contrary to a general law "would be to make the professed doctrines of religious belief superior to the law of the land, and in effect to permit every citizen to become a law unto himself." *Catholic Charities, supra,*

32 Cal.4th at p. 548 (quoting *Employment Division v. Smith, supra,* 494 U.S. at p. 879).

. . . .

In briefing and oral argument before the Court of Appeal, defendants relied on a California appellate decision and three statutes granting physicians a right of conscience to refuse a requested service in certain circumstances. The appellate decision, *Conservatorship of Morrison,* 206 Cal.App.3d 304, 310-311 (1988), held that a physician lawfully could refuse, on grounds of conscience, to remove a feeding tube from a persistently vegetative patient at her conservator's direction if the patient could be transferred to the care of another physician who would follow the conservator's direction. The three statutes prescribe rights to refuse, as a matter of conscience, to perform an abortion[,] Health & Saf. Code, § 123420, subd. (a), to comply with a health care directive or decision[,] Prob. Code, § 4734, and to fill certain pharmaceutical prescriptions[,] Bus. & Prof. Code, § 733, subd. (b)(3). But these authorities do not allow doctors to *violate the law* according to conscientious objections. Rather, they expressly make certain refusals lawful, avoiding any conflict with the Unruh Act by respecting objections to particular *treatments* without sanctioning discriminatory refusals to treat particular groups of *people.*

Thus, a doctor may refuse all requests to withdraw artificial life support, but may not refuse such a request just for people of color or just for lesbian and gay patients while complying with the wishes of white or heterosexual patients. Similarly, a doctor may refuse to perform all abortions, but may not refuse to do so just because of a patient's national origin or sexual orientation. That is the law in California, and it is in complete harmony with [American Medical Association's] ethical rules.

. . . .

The following arguments appear in the Answer Brief on the Merits filed on behalf of Petitioners Dr. Christine Z. Brody and Dr. Douglas K. Fenton, Answer Brief on the Merits at 40-42, 45-48, 50-53, N. Coast Women's Care Med. Group v. Super. Ct, No. S142892 (Cal. Dec. 21, 2006):

. . . .

There is nothing radical about defendants' conduct or a rule that would protect it. Defendants reasonably accommodated plaintiff. They were candid from the onset of plaintiff's relationship with North Coast; they provided her the treatment they said they would provide; they referred her to another physician for treatment they were unable to provide; they agreed to pay any additional cost for such referral.

Rather, it is plaintiff that demanded that the physicians perform an IUI upon her. It is plaintiff who is trying to prohibit the doctors from assisting other women in the future. Finally, it is plaintiff who is unwilling to offer any accommodations.

Nobody contends that health care providers do not have the right to refuse to provide care in certain circumstances based upon their conscience. Plaintiff claims, however, that doctors should be bound by the lines she draws rather than the boundaries of their faith. She is implicitly arguing that her perceived rights are more important than the doctors' rights.

However, to the extent that this case is viewed as a matter of conflicting rights, reasonable accommodation, including patient referral, is an attractive means to resolve the matter when a physician has an objection based upon her conscience. Accommodation is found in a variety of analogous contexts. For example, the Health and Safety Code allows physicians to refuse to perform abortions based on a "moral, ethical, or religious basis."

For another example, subdivision (a) of Probate Code section 4734 provides that "A health care provider may decline to comply with an individual health care instruction or health care decision for reasons of conscience." If so, the provider must promptly inform the patient and "[i]mmediately make all reasonable efforts to assist in the transfer of the patient to another health care provider or institution that is willing to comply with the instruction or decision."

Even in the context of end-of-life treatment, a physician cannot be forced to provide care that conflicts with his moral beliefs. In *Conservatorship of Morrison*, 206 Cal.App.3d 304 (1988), the court held that "a conservator can authorize the removal of a nasogastric feeding tube from a conservatee who is in a persistent vegetative state, but cannot require physicians to remove the tube against their personal moral objections if the patient can be transferred to the care of another physician who will follow the conservator's direction." *Id.* at 306-307.

The court emphasized that "no physician should be forced to act against his or her personal moral beliefs if the patient can be transferred to the care of another physician." *Id.* at 311.

The state also provides for pharmacists who object to filling certain prescriptions on religious grounds, so as long as reasonable accommodation is made.

Accommodation and mutual respect is the epitome of our multi-cultural community. "[T]his desire to accommodate faiths at odds with the government is the most important distinguishing feature of American church-state separation." [Michael] McConnell, *Freedom From Persecution [or Protection of the Rights of Conscience?: A Critique of Justice Scalia's Historical Arguments in* City of Boerne v. Flores], 39 WM. & MARY L. REV. [819,] 832 [(1998)].

. . . .

Dr. Fenton and Dr. Brody clearly stated that their religious beliefs prohibit them from artificially inseminating an unmarried woman because to do so would make them the active agent for conceiving a pregnancy out of wedlock.

A law "substantially burdens a religious belief if it 'conditions receipt of an important benefit upon conduct proscribed by a religious faith, or where it denies such a benefit because of conduct mandated by religious belief, thereby putting substantial pressure on an adherent to modify his behavior and to violate his beliefs . . . .'" *Catholic Charities [of Sacramento, Inc. v. Superior Court,* 32 Cal.4th [527,] 562 [(2004).]

Liability in civil litigation burdens a religious belief. *Molko v. Holy Spirit Assn.,* 46 Cal.3d 1092, 1117 (1989). Forcing someone to choose between performing an IUI (against her religious belief) or facing civil liability places a substantial burden upon the defendants' religious beliefs. . . .

An affirmative obligation or prohibition, combined with sanctions, is an even greater burden on Constitutional rights than a denial of benefits.

Here, Dr. Brody and Dr. Fenton faced the choice of agreeing to perform an IUI upon plaintiff in violation of their sincerely-held religious belief, or face a monetary sanction in the form of money damages and potentially attorneys' fees for allegedly violating the Unruh Act. The fees alone are alleged by plaintiff to be in the hundreds of thousands of dollars now. This undoubtedly is a substantial burden upon their religious beliefs because it places them in a situation of having to choose between paying a civil judgment or adhering to their religious beliefs.

. . . .

Plaintiff claims that Dr. Brody and Dr. Fenton can merely stop performing IUIs altogether to avoid any conflict with their religious beliefs. This is tantamount to claiming that, in the context of any profession, individuals lose their constitutionally guaranteed liberty of conscience.

The California Constitution puts no such limitation on the free exercise and enjoyment of religion. Most certainly, it does not limit it to private observance, nor does it qualify this guarantee as being inapplicable in the context of a professional activity. . . . [T]he obligations of a religious adherent do not end at the doors of a place of worship. Rather, those beliefs are fulfilled through daily conduct in society and at work, in both private and professional contexts. Religion, by its very nature, is existent in society.

By the same token the Unruh Act cannot limit an individual's employment opportunities. "An individual's freedom of opportunity to work and earn a living has long been recognized as one of the fundamental and most cherished liberties enjoyed by members of our society . . . ." *Gay Law Students' Association v. Pacific Telephone & Telegraph Company*, 24 Cal.3d 458, 470 (1979) (citations omitted). "It is axiomatic that the right of an individual to engage in any of the common occupations of life is among the several fundamental liberties protected by the due process and equal protection clauses of the Fourteenth Amendment." *Hughes v. Board of Architectural Examiners*, 17 Cal.4th 763, 788 (1998).

Dr. Brody and Dr. Fenton's rights to choose their profession would be substantially impeded if they were forced to limit the nature of their services to their patients. While fertility treatments make up a small percentage of both doctors' practices, nevertheless, it is important for the doctors to have the option to provide these services.

It is equally important for patients in San Diego County to have an alternative to an expensive fertility treatment center where treatments cost as much as $25,000. This is important for all women who seek fertility treatment.

Plaintiff proposes an all or nothing rule, whereby the doctors are required to perform IUI upon everyone if they provide it to anyone. Stated alternatively, because the doctors provided IUIs in the past, they must perform an IUI upon plaintiff. It would impose a substantial burden on the defendant physicians to compel them to conduct an intimate medical procedure contrary to their conscience. . . .

. . . .

The Unruh Act and the physician defendants' religious belief can be easily accommodated by interpreting a religious exemption to the Unruh Act. If physicians choose, based upon their liberty of conscience, not to perform a particular medical procedure and arrange for a referral of the patient to a qualified medical provider to provide that treatment, then the interests of both parties are protected. This is a very narrow exception that will apply only to physicians. Without such a ruling, the Unruh Act as applied to Dr. Fenton and Dr. Brody would fail strict scrutiny and be unconstitutional.

While California has an interest in limiting discrimination based upon sexual orientation, as evidenced by the Unruh Act, that interest cannot be considered greater than the interest in protecting freedom of religion. In fact, by its own terms, the Unruh Act prohibits discrimination based upon religious beliefs and sexual orientation, among a series of other categories of prohibited conduct. "'Religion' includes all aspects of religious belief, observance, and practice." Thus, according to the terms of the Unruh Act, at a minimum, religion and sexual orientation deserve equal protection.

However, unlike the Unruh Act, the California Constitution specifically guarantees the free exercise and enjoyment of religion. A prohibition upon sexual orientation discrimination is not enshrined within a parallel Constitutional guarantee.[*] As between the two rights at issue, if anything, the guaranteed free exercise and liberty of

---

[*] [Ed.: This brief was filed before the California Supreme Court's decision in *In re Marriage Cases*, 183 P.3d 384 (Cal. 2008), excerpted in this Supplement, *supra*, Chapter 2, Section A, at pages 10-29.]

conscience carries greater weight than the State's interest in ending sexual orientation discrimination.

. . . .

The rule announced from this case will impact physicians and patients alike. If this Court announces a rule that allows physicians and patients to accommodate one another's interests through referrals to qualified doctors, there will be greater access to care. Doctors will be able to provide care up to their religious objection. For example, a physician might be able to assist the patient to get pregnant through IVI or some other procedure. In this way, patients like Benitez will have access to a greater number of physicians.

This will not only benefit lesbian patients, but it will equally benefit single heterosexual women through greater access to care.

D. Problems Posed by New Reproductive Techniques

Page 1016. Add after Note 3:

4. See also North Coast Women's Care Medical Group v. Superior Court, 40 Cal. Rptr. 3d 636 (Ct. App. 2006), now pending in the California Supreme Court, discussed in this Supplement, *supra*, Chapter 7, Section C, at pages 142-55.

CHAPTER 8: PARENTS AND CHILDREN

B. Encroachments on the Doctrine of Family Privacy
3. Criminal Law

Page 1047. Add after *Connecticut v. Miranda*:

State v. Gewily

Connecticut Supreme Court, 2006.
911 A.2d 293.

■ PALMER, J.

A jury found the defendant, Mostafa Gewily, guilty of one count of risk of injury to a child in violation of General Statutes (Rev. to 2001) § 53-21(a)(1)[1] and one count of custodial interference in the first degree in violation of General Statutes § 53a-97. The trial court rendered judgment in accordance with the jury verdict,[2] and the defendant appealed,[3] claiming that the evidence was insufficient to support his conviction of

---

[1] General Statutes (Rev. to 2001) § 53-21 (a) provides in relevant part: "Any person who (1) wilfully or unlawfully causes or permits any child under the age of sixteen years to be placed in such a situation that the life or limb of such child is endangered, the health of such child is likely to be injured or the morals of such child are likely to be impaired, or does any act likely to impair the health or morals of any such child . . . shall be guilty of a class C felony."

All references to § 53-21 in this opinion are to the revision of 2001.

[2] The trial court imposed consecutive sentences of ten years imprisonment on the count of risk of injury to a child and five years imprisonment on the count of custodial interference in the first degree, for a total effective sentence of fifteen years imprisonment.

[3] The defendant appealed from the judgment of the trial court to the Appellate Court, and we transferred the appeal to this court pursuant to General Statutes § 51-199 (c) and Practice Book § 65-1.

risk of injury to a child.[4] We disagree and, therefore, affirm the judgment of the trial court.

The jury reasonably could have found the following facts. The defendant, an Egyptian national, married his wife, Maria Gewily (Maria), in 1994. Shortly after their marriage, the couple began living in Meriden in the home of Maria's mother. In March, 1998, Maria gave birth to S, the couple's only child.

Not long after S's birth, the couple's marriage began to deteriorate, and the defendant became verbally and physically abusive to Maria. On one occasion, Maria called the police after the defendant slapped her and knocked her down. When the defendant learned that Maria had called the police, he threatened to kill her. Although the defendant never was verbally or physically abusive to S directly, S often was present when the defendant was abusive to Maria.

In December, 2000, the defendant and Maria began living apart. Maria continued to reside with S at her mother's home in Meriden, and the defendant moved to West Haven. Maria, however, regularly took S to visit the defendant at his West Haven residence, where Maria and S frequently stayed overnight. According to Maria, her reason for bringing S to stay with the defendant was to ensure that S would continue to have a relationship with his father.

After the defendant and Maria separated, S became more and more reluctant to spend time with the defendant. On one occasion, while S was waiting at home for the defendant to pick him up for a scheduled visit, S told his grandmother, Maria's mother, that he did not want to go with the defendant. S also informed her that she should not go outside when the defendant arrived because the defendant had told S that he was "going to cut [his grandmother's] head off and [her] stomach with a big knife." The defendant's threat against S's grandmother was only one of a number of such threats that the defendant had made against Maria and her mother. In fact, the defendant was so upset about his separation and possible divorce from Maria that he told one of Maria's relatives that "he

---

[4] The defendant has not challenged his conviction of custodial interference in the first degree.

would kill [S] . . . while [Maria] watched, and then he would kill her, and then he would kill himself before the divorce happened."

In October, 2001, approximately one year after the couple's separation, Maria filed for divorce. Shortly thereafter, on November 9, 2001, Maria obtained a restraining order prohibiting the defendant from entering her home and from threatening, assaulting or otherwise harassing her. Pursuant to the order, Maria was awarded temporary custody of S. The order, however, permitted the defendant unsupervised visitation with S on Sundays from noon until 4 p.m., and on Mondays from noon until 5 p.m.

On Sunday, December 9, 2001, the defendant picked up S in accordance with the visitation order and informed Maria that he probably would take S to a shopping mall. The defendant, however, did not return with S by 4 p.m. as the order required. Maria finally called the Meriden police department at approximately 7 p.m. and reported that the defendant had not returned with S as the order required. The officer with whom Maria spoke advised her to wait a few more hours to be sure that the defendant was not unavoidably late due to circumstances beyond his control.

At approximately 10 p.m. that evening, Maria called the Meriden police department again and informed a duty officer that the defendant still had not returned with S. The Meriden police then contacted the West Haven police department, which dispatched an officer to the defendant's apartment. Upon arriving there, the West Haven officer was informed by one of the defendant's neighbors that he had moved out at least one week earlier.

In the early morning hours of December 10, 2001, Maria received a telephone call from the defendant. When Maria asked the defendant where he was, the defendant implied that he was at a casino. Maria, however, could hear background noises that led her to believe that he was at an airport. Moreover, when the defendant permitted Maria to speak with S, S asked her if she was going to "come on the airplanes . . . ." In fact, airline records revealed that the defendant and S had flown from New York to Cairo, Egypt, arriving on December 10, 2001.

The defendant next contacted Maria on December 15, 2001. He told her that he and S were in California but did not permit her to speak to S. Maria did not hear from the defendant again until December 24, 2001, at which time the defendant informed her that he had taken S to Cairo. The defendant allowed Maria to speak with S, who again inquired of Maria whether she would be "coming over . . . ." In an effort to avoid upsetting S, Maria explained that she would see him soon.

The next day, the defendant telephoned Maria but did not allow her to speak with S. In that conversation, the defendant blamed Maria for the family's separation and threatened to reenter the United States under an alias and kill her.

From December, 2001, until the summer of 2002, the defendant telephoned Maria at least twenty times. Only occasionally, however, did the defendant permit Maria to talk with S. When Maria was permitted to speak with S, their conversation focused on whether she would be "coming over." Maria repeatedly tried to comfort S by reassuring him that she would be visiting him soon. Although the defendant provided Maria with a telephone number that she could use to contact him in Egypt, Maria was not always able to get through to S when she used that number.

Maria stopped receiving telephone calls from the defendant in the summer of 2002. Maria also abandoned her efforts to communicate with S because the defendant had made it so difficult for her to do so, emotionally and otherwise. Meanwhile, in March, 2002, Maria's divorce from the defendant became final. The divorce decree awarded full custody of S to Maria.

Approximately one year after taking S from his home in Meriden and relocating to Egypt, the defendant returned to the United States. On December 24, 2002, the defendant was arrested at John F. Kennedy International Airport in New York. He did not, however, have S with him.

On one occasion following his arrest, the defendant, who was incarcerated in lieu of bail pending trial, placed a telephone call from prison to Esam Awad, a friend and former coworker. During that conversation, the defendant explained to Awad that he was concerned about S's well-being. In light of that concern, the defendant provided Awad with a Cairo telephone number and asked Awad to call it to find out if S was alright. The defendant also instructed Awad to inform the woman who answered the telephone that she was not to release S to anyone without the defendant's prior approval. Awad followed the defendant's instructions and was informed by the woman with whom he spoke that S was "good" and "feeling well . . . ."

Since his arrest, the defendant steadfastly has refused to disclose S's location. Despite efforts by the Federal Bureau of Investigation and the United States Department of State to locate S, his whereabouts remain unknown.[6] With these facts in mind, we turn to the defendant's claim that the evidence was inadequate to support his conviction of risk of injury to a child.

The defendant's claim of evidentiary insufficiency is twofold: first, that the state presented no evidence concerning the actual status of S's health; and second, that the state failed to establish that the defendant had created a situation likely to be harmful to S's health. We reject the defendant's first argument because the state was not required to present evidence of S's health. We also reject the defendant's second argument because the evidence amply supports the jury's finding that the defendant caused S to be placed in a situation likely to be detrimental to his health.

     . . . .

A person is guilty of violating General Statutes (Rev. to 2001) § 53-21(a)(1) if that person "wilfully or unlawfully causes or permits any child under the age of sixteen years to be placed in such a situation that the life or limb of such child is endangered, the health of such child is likely to be injured or the morals of such child are likely to be impaired, or does any act likely to impair the health or morals of any such child . . . ." As we

---

[6] Evidence adduced at trial indicated that Egypt is not a signatory to the Hague Convention, an international treaty that establishes, *inter alia*, the legal rights and procedures pursuant to which a child unlawfully removed from his or her home country may be returned to that country. Because Egypt is not a party to the Hague Convention, it has not been possible to invoke the provisions of that treaty for the purpose of seeking S's return to the United States.

recently have observed, "[a]lthough it is clear that [t]he general purpose of § 53-21 is to protect the physical and psychological well-being of children from the potentially harmful conduct of [others] . . . we long have recognized that subdivision (1) of § 53-21[(a)] prohibits two different types of behavior: (1) deliberate indifference to, acquiescence in, or the creation of situations inimical to the [child's] moral or physical welfare . . . and (2) acts directly perpetrated on the person of the [child] and injurious to his [or her] moral or physical well-being." Thus, "the first part of § 53-21(1)[(a)] prohibits the creation of *situations* detrimental to a child's welfare, while the second part proscribes injurious *acts* directly perpetrated on the child." In the present case, we are concerned with the portion of § 53-21(a)(1) relating to the creation of a situation likely to be detrimental to the health of a child.[7] Finally, in addressing a challenge to a finding that the conduct of the accused had caused psychological harm to a child in violation of § 53-21, we recently observed that the fact finder is not required to "make a determination as to the precise nature or severity of the injury"; rather, the fact finder need only decide whether the accused placed the child in a situation that was likely to be psychologically injurious to that child.

The defendant's argument that the state was required to prove that S's health actually was impaired by the defendant's conduct is contrary both to the applicable statutory language and to the cases interpreting that language. Pursuant to the portion of § 53-21(a)(1) under which the defendant was charged, the state was required to establish only that the defendant wilfully had caused or permitted S to be placed in a situation that likely would be injurious to S's health; the state was not required to prove that S, in fact, had been harmed or injured as a result of the defendant's conduct. In other words, actual injury is not an element of the "situation" prong of § 53-21(a)(1). Because that provision focuses on the conduct of the accused rather than the harm that the child actually may have suffered, we reject the defendant's claim that he is entitled to a judgment of acquittal with respect to the risk of injury count on the ground that the state failed to adduce evidence of the status of S's health.

---

[7] The state alleged in its information that the defendant had "[wilfully] caused or permitted a child under the age of sixteen years to be placed in such a situation that the health of such child is likely to be injured, in violation of [§] 53-21(a)(1) . . . ."

The defendant also contends that the evidence was insufficient to establish that he wilfully created a situation that was likely to be harmful to S's health. In particular, the defendant asserts that, because there is virtually nothing in the record detailing the specific circumstances under which S has lived since he was removed from Maria's custody, the jury necessarily was required to rely on conjecture and speculation in determining whether the defendant had caused S to be placed in a situation likely to be detrimental to his health. As the state aptly notes, the crux of the defendant's argument is that, because the defendant's abduction and prolonged concealment of S since that abduction have prevented the state from establishing the status of S's health, there was insufficient evidence to support the jury's finding that S's emotional or psychological condition was likely to have been impaired as a result of the situation in which he had been placed by the defendant. This contention also is without merit.

The state established that, as a result of the defendant's conduct, S was suddenly and indefinitely deprived of the love and affection of Maria, his mother and custodial parent, when he was only three years old. The jury reasonably could conclude that that separation, coupled with the fact that S found himself in entirely new surroundings in a foreign country, was likely to be highly traumatic to S and, therefore, harmful to his mental and emotional health. Although it is true that, on occasion, the defendant permitted Maria to speak with S on the telephone, those sporadic conversations were no substitute for the care and affection that S would have received from Maria if the defendant had not taken S from her in blatant violation of the court-ordered custodial arrangements. Indeed, in Maria's conversations with S, he regularly inquired about when she was coming to see him, revealing his distress about their separation. Moreover, the defendant so closely monitored and regulated Maria's conversations with S that Maria, out of frustration and despair, eventually abandoned her efforts to communicate with S by using the telephone number that the defendant had given to her.

We previously have noted, albeit in a somewhat different context, that significant harm is likely to result from the forced separation of a child from his or her parents. In *In re Juvenile Appeal* (83-CD), 455 A.2d 1313 (1983), we observed that "[u]ninterrupted home life comports . . . with each child's biological and psychological need for unthreatened and unbroken continuity of care by his parents." We also have observed that children who are separated from their parents may "suffer anxiety and depression . . . [and] are forced to deal with new caretakers, playmates, school teachers, etc. As a result they often suffer emotional damage and their development is delayed." (Internal quotation marks omitted.) . . . S's repeated questions to Maria about when she would be coming to see him reveal that S had developed a strong bond with Maria, such that losing contact with her undoubtedly was especially worrisome and painful for S. In light of the defendant's current circumstances, moreover, the jury was entitled to conclude that the end result of the defendant's unlawful conduct was to deprive S of the love, support and companionship of *both* of his parents.

Finally, in view of the court order awarding custody of S to Maria, the jury reasonably could have found that it was not in S's best interests to be forced to reside with the defendant. Indeed, the state demonstrated that the defendant had a violent and threatening disposition, and that he displayed that temperament in S's presence. As a result, S increasingly—and justifiably—feared spending time with the defendant. Under such circumstances, the jury reasonably could have concluded that it was unhealthy for S to reside with the defendant, in a foreign country, without any opportunity to be with his mother. Contrary to the defendant's claim, therefore, the evidence adduced by the state was more than adequate to permit a finding beyond a reasonable doubt that the defendant, in abruptly and unlawfully abducting S from his home in Meriden and relocating him to Egypt, thereby depriving him of contact with his custodial parent, wilfully caused S to be placed in a situation likely to be harmful to his mental health and well-being in violation of § 53-21(a)(1).

The judgment is affirmed.

CHAPTER 9: GROWING UP IN THE LAW

E. Age and Criminal Law

Page 1179. Add after Note:

State ex rel. Z.C.

Supreme Court of Utah, 2007.
165 P.3d 1206.

■ PARRISH, JUSTICE:

BACKGROUND

When she was thirteen years old, Z.C. engaged in consensual[1] sex with a twelve-year-old boy and became pregnant. The state prosecutor chose to file delinquency petitions against both Z.C. and the boy for sexual abuse of a child under Utah Code section 76-5-404.1, a crime that would constitute a second degree felony if committed by an adult. The twelve-year-old boy was adjudicated delinquent and given probation. Z.C. moved to dismiss the delinquency petition filed against her on the grounds that it violated her constitutional rights and that the legislature could not have intended such a result. The juvenile court denied Z.C.'s motion.

Z.C. then entered an admission to the delinquency petition on condition that she be able to appeal the denial of her motion to dismiss. As a result of her admission, the juvenile court adjudicated Z.C. delinquent for sexual abuse of a child but imposed a relatively light punishment. The court ordered her to obey the reasonable requests of her parents, to write an essay regarding her child and the effect of her actions on the child, to have no unsupervised contact with the father of her child, to provide a DNA sample, and to pay a $75 DNA processing fee.

---

[1] Throughout this opinion, we employ the term "consensual" in its conventional, rather than its legal, sense. Children under the age of fourteen cannot legally consent to intercourse or sexual touching in the state of Utah. Utah Code Ann. § 76-5-406(9) (2003).

Z.C. appealed to the Utah Court of Appeals, which, "with some reluctance," affirmed the juvenile court. *State ex rel. Z.C.,* 2005 UT App 562, ¶ 1, 128 P.3d 561. We granted certiorari to review the court of appeals' decision.

ANALYSIS

Z.C. presents two arguments to this court. First, Z.C. asserts that it was not the legislature's intent that a child be charged with sexual abuse of a child for engaging in consensual sexual activity with another child. Second, Z.C. asserts that if this were the legislature's intent, Utah Code section 76-5-404.1 violates her state constitutional right to the uniform operation of the law. *See* Utah Const. art. I, § 24.

We address the statutory claim first[.] . . . In so doing, we find that the plain language of Utah Code section 76-5-404.1 allows Z.C. to be adjudicated delinquent for child sex abuse. However, we also find that applying the statute to treat Z.C. as both a victim and a perpetrator of child sex abuse for the same act leads to an absurd result that was not intended by the legislature. As such, we reverse the court of appeals and vacate Z.C.'s delinquency adjudication. We therefore need not reach her constitutional claim.

I. THE PLAIN LANGUAGE OF UTAH CODE
SECTION 76-5-404.1

. . . .

Utah's child sex abuse statute, which deals with sexual touching that does not amount to rape of a child,[2] reads as follows:

> (1) As used in this section, "child" means a *person* under the age of 14.

---

[2] "A person commits rape of a child when the person has sexual intercourse with a child who is under the age of 14." Utah Code Ann. § 76-5-402.1(1) (2003). Z.C. admitted having intercourse with a twelve-year-old boy and did, in fact, become pregnant. Under the literal language of the statute, therefore, both Z.C. and the twelve-year-old boy could have been adjudicated delinquent for rape of a child, a first degree felony if committed by an adult, which carries a minimum six-year sentence without parole and may be punished by life imprisonment without possibility of parole. *Id.* §§ 76-5-402.1(2), 76-3-406.

(2) A *person* commits sexual abuse of a child if, under circumstances not amounting to rape of a child, object rape of a child, sodomy upon a child, or an attempt to commit any of these offenses, the actor touches the anus, buttocks, or genitalia of any child, the breast of a female child, or otherwise takes indecent liberties with a child, or causes a child to take indecent liberties with the actor or another with intent to cause substantial emotional or bodily pain to *any person* or with the intent to arouse or gratify the sexual desire of *any person* regardless of the sex of any participant.

Utah Code Ann. § 76-5-404.1(1)-(2) (2003) (emphasis added).

. . . .

. . . [U]nder the plain language of the statute, a child is a person and may be adjudicated delinquent for sexually touching another child with the requisite intent.

II. ABSURD RESULT

Normally, where the language of a statute is clear and unambiguous, our analysis ends; our duty is to give effect to that plain meaning. However, "[a]n equally well-settled caveat to the plain meaning rule states that a court should not follow the literal language of a statute if its plain meaning works an absurd result." *Savage v. Utah Youth Vill.,* 2004 UT 102, ¶ 18, 104 P.3d 1242. The absurd results canon of statutory construction recognizes that although "the plain language interpretation of a statute enjoys a robust presumption in its favor, it is also true that [a legislative body] cannot, in every instance, be counted on to have said what it meant or to have meant what it said." *FBI v. Abramson,* 456 U.S. 615, 638, 102 S.Ct. 2054, 72 L.Ed.2d 376 (1982) (O'Connor, J., dissenting).

In defining the parameters of what constitutes an absurd result, we note the inherent tension in this canon of construction between refraining from blind obedience to the letter of the law that leads to patently absurd ends and avoiding an improper usurpation of legislative power through judicial second guessing of the wisdom of a legislative act. *See West Jordan v. Morrison,* 656 P.2d 445, 446 (Utah 1982) ("[I]t is not the duty of this Court to assess the wisdom of the statutory scheme.") . . . Thus, as is common to all rules of statutory construction, the guiding star of the absurd results doctrine is the intent of the pertinent legislative body, which limits the application of this canon of construction. Rather than controverting legislative power, the absurd results doctrine functions to preserve legislative intent when it is narrowly applied. *Pub. Citizen v. United States Dep't of Justice,* 491 U.S. 440, 470, 109 S.Ct. 2558, 105 L.Ed.2d 377 (1989) (Kennedy, J., concurring)[.] Therefore, in deference to Congress, the Supreme Court has noted that this canon of statutory interpretation applies only where the result is so absurd that "'Congress could not *possibly* have intended'" it. *Pub. Citizen,* 491 U.S. at 470, 109 S.Ct. 2558 (Kennedy, J., concurring) (quoting *FBI,* 456 U.S. at 640, 102 S.Ct. 2054 (O'Connor, J., dissenting)).

Other than the directive that a result must be so absurd that the legislative body which authored the legislation could not have intended it, there is no precise legal standard to determine what legislatures would consider to be an absurd result. *See* Veronica M. Dougherty, *Absurdity and the Limits of Literalism: Defining the Absurd Result Principle in Statutory Interpretation,* 44 Am. U. L. Rev. 127, 128 (1994). This comes as no surprise because the absurd, by definition, evades neat categorization. . . .

. . . .

. . . [W]e examine whether Utah Code section 76-5-404.1 has been applied so as to produce an absurd result in this case. Because we conclude that the legislature could not possibly have intended to punish both children under the child sex abuse statute for the same act of consensual heavy petting,[6] we hold that applying the plain language of the statute in this case produces an absurd result.

Sexual abuse of a child is one of the most heinous crimes recognized by our penal code. The gravity of this crime is reflected by the fact that it is punished as a second degree felony if committed by an adult. Child

---

[6] It is undisputed that Z.C. and the boy engaged in more than just sexual touching, but we must analyze the absurd result question in the context of the law actually applied and the act with which the State chose to charge Z.C., not the law that might have been applied or the act with which the State could have charged Z.C.

sex abuse merits serious penalties because of the extreme psychological harm that the perpetrator causes the victim. Therefore, like all forms of sexual assault, child sex abuse presupposes that a single act of abuse involves a victim, whom the statute endeavors to protect, and a perpetrator, whom the statute punishes for harming the victim.

The State, however, applies Utah Code section 76-5-404.1 in an unprecedented manner. By filing delinquency petitions for child sex abuse against both participants for sexually touching one another, the State treats both children as perpetrators of the same act. In this situation, there is no discernible victim that the law seeks to protect, only culpable participants that the State seeks to punish.[8] We know of no other instance in which the State has attempted to apply any sexual assault crime to produce such an effect.[9]

We acknowledge that the legislature has demonstrated its intent to punish both participants in victimless, extramarital sexual activity under Utah's adultery and fornication statutes. *Id.* §§ 76-7-103, -104. However, these statutes differ from sexual assault crimes, such as child sex abuse, in both the theory and degree of punishment. Rather than punishing an actor who has perpetrated a crime against a victim, these laws demonstrate the legislature's disapproval of the acts of both participants for violating a moral standard. Because these crimes do not involve a victim, they involve a lesser degree of punishment. Both adultery and fornication are punishable as class B misdemeanors. Utah Code Ann. §§ 76-7-103(2), -104(2) (2003). Thus, while the legislature clearly could have intended some degree of simultaneous culpability for both Z.C. and the twelve-year-old boy under the fornication statute in order to discourage their admittedly reckless and age-inappropriate behavior, it is absurd to conclude that the legislature intended to simultaneously punish both children for child sex abuse, a crime that clearly envisions a perpetrator and a victim.

A review of the floor debates regarding the 1983 enactment of the Child Kidnaping and Sexual Abuse Act, L.1983, ch. 88, § 24, which

---

[8] . . . [W]e conclude that the State's double prosecution of these children is best characterized as charging both as perpetrators for the same act.

[9] The primary fail-safe against the absurd application of criminal law is the wise employment of prosecutorial discretion, a quality that is starkly absent in this case. . . .

created Utah Code section 76-5-404.1, reveals no evidence that the legislature contemplated application of the statute to situations where the same child was both victim and perpetrator. Although we generally do not consult legislative history where the meaning of the statute is clear, after finding that the plain meaning has been applied in an absurd manner, we seek to confirm that the absurd application was indeed unintended by the legislature.

Recent legislative developments bolster our conclusion that the children's simultaneous delinquency adjudications could not have been intended by the legislature. In reaction to the court of appeals' disposition in this case, the legislature passed a bill that amended the diversion statute to avoid the application of the child sex abuse statute in similar cases. *See* Juvenile Offenses Diversion Amendment, L.2006, ch. 166, § 1 (codified as amended at Utah Code Ann. § 77-2-9(2) (Supp.2006)). Although the previous version of the statute forbade diversions for crimes "involving a sexual offense against a victim who is under the age of 14," Utah Code Ann. § 77-2-9 (2003), the amended version allows diversions for sexual offenses committed by individuals under the age of sixteen as long as "the person did not use coercion or force; there is no more than two years' difference between the ages of the participants; and it would be in the best interest of the person to grant diversion," *id.* § 77-2-9(2) (Supp.2006). . . . The underlying purpose of the amendment was undoubtedly to prevent future delinquency adjudications similar to Z.C.'s. In fact, the sponsor of the bill in the House stated, "I think most of us would agree that when twelve and thirteen years olds get involved in this kind of behavior it's certainly not something we want to allow or encourage. We also probably do not want to convict them both of 'rape of a child'. . . ." Comments of Rep. Fowlke, House floor debate on S.B. 167, March 1, 2006.

We conclude that the legislature could not have intended the child sex abuse statute to be applied to punish Z.C. for the conduct at issue. And the fact that this is a juvenile court disposition, in which the judge enjoys considerable latitude in crafting punishments and assigning state services designed to help the child, does not change our conclusion. No amount of judicial lenity to compensate for the absurd application of the law changes the fact that the application of the law was absurd to begin with. Moreover, labeling Z.C. with the moniker of "child abuser," even within the juvenile court system, can have serious consequences that were not intended by the legislature. A delinquency adjudication for sexual abuse of a child can lead to sentencing enhancements for any offenses Z.C. might commit while she is a juvenile or even as an adult if her juvenile record is not expunged. Such an adjudication also has the potential to affect any civil proceedings related to the custody of her child or any future attempts to seek child support from the father.

We therefore vacate Z.C.'s adjudication. We stress, however, that our holding is narrowly confined to the application of Utah Code section 76-5-404.1 in situations where no true victim or perpetrator can be identified. Even among children under the age of fourteen, there are unfortunately situations where an older or more physically mature child abuses a younger or smaller child. In cases where there is an identifiable distinction between the perpetrator and the victim, it is manifestly logical to conclude that the legislature intended to include such acts within the scope of Utah Code section 76-5-404.1. In Z.C.'s case, however, where both children were under the age of fourteen and were of similar age, where both children met the intent requirement of the statute, and where there was no evidence of any coercion or force, we conclude that application of the child sex abuse statute produces an absurd result.[10]

CONCLUSION

Even though the plain language of section 76-5-404.1 allows Z.C. to be adjudicated delinquent for sexual abuse of a child, we conclude that the filing of delinquency petitions against both participants produces an absurd result not intended by the legislature because, like all sexual assault crimes, the statute presupposes a perpetrator and a victim. We therefore hold that the juvenile court erred in denying Z.C.'s motion to dismiss the delinquency petition. We remand this matter to the court of appeals with instructions to remand it to the juvenile court to vacate Z.C.'s delinquency adjudication.

---

[10] Our analysis would likewise apply to all cases similar to Z.C.'s even if the State elected to charge only one of the minors involved. We hold that the application of Utah Code section 76-5-404.1 is absurd where no true perpetrator or victim exists. And the State may not create a perpetrator and a victim through selective prosecution. Rather, charges against the perpetrator must be based upon a material gap in the maturity of the two participants, evidence of coercion or force, or a wider age differential than exists in this case.

CHAPTER 10: CHILD ABUSE AND NEGLECT

A. What Should the Standards Be for Intervening Between Parent and Child?
2. Defining Child Neglect
a. Standard

Page 1222. Add after *In re Pope*:

In re Brittany T.

Family Court of New York, Chemung County, 2007.
835 N.Y.S.2d 829.

■ BROCKWAY, J.

This court is called upon to once again ultimately determine whether it is in the best interest of a morbidly obese child, who also suffers from numerous comorbidities, to be removed from parents who have consistently failed to address her severe medical concerns and who have also failed to ensure her proper school attendance. No reported case law exists in New York on this issue. For the reasons set forth below, the court decides that removal is appropriate and necessary.

An (amended) petition was filed March 23, 2006 by the Chemung County Department of Social Services. The department seeks to have the court find the respondents, Shawna T. and Robert T. (hereinafter the respondents) in willful violation of this court's order of disposition dated August 4, 2003, which was subsequently extended on June 24, 2004, February 14, 2005 and February 7, 2006 (the latter for a period of one year, which is currently pending extension). The petition also seeks placement of the child with the Department.

By way of history, the court's records reflect that the initial 90-day progress report included several serious concerns about the respondents' lack of progress. The court therefore returned the matter for review on November 24, 2003. At that appearance, the respondents consented to the immediate placement of the child, Brittany T. (date of birth 1994) with the Department through a kinship foster care placement with a maternal aunt. The court granted the placement due to serious and continuing health concerns related to the child's morbid obesity and the parents' lack of consistency and commitment in addressing both her medical and physical needs as well as school attendance issues. On April 19, 2004, the child was returned to the parents but reentered foster care by order of this court dated October 19, 2004. On October 21, 2004[,] the department filed a violation petition against the respondents. The violation petition resulted in a six-month adjournment in contemplation of dismissal (ACD) being granted on February 14, 2005. Conditions of the ACD included the parties consenting to the child remaining in (kinship) foster care and a requirement that they continue to follow the original terms and conditions. The child was returned to the parents' care and custody on or about September 5, 2005. From the credible court records and evidence, it can be concluded that during these periods, the child's weight underwent significant changes, which can be summarized as follows:

Appx Date(s)	Residence	Appx Age	Appx Weight
Oct 2002	Parents	8.8	237
Nov 2003	Consent Removal	9.9	261
April 2004	Returned to Parents	10.2	252
Oct 2004	Removal	10.8	255
Nov 2004	Started @ Geisinger	10.9	256
Sept 2005	Returned to Parents	11.7	238
Mar 2006	Instant Violation	12.1	263
May 2006	With Parents	12.3	266

Department's Case

The instant petition alleges that the respondents have again willfully and without just cause violated terms and provisions of the court's dispositional order by, inter alia, failing to ensure that the child attend school on a regular basis and on time, failing to take the child at least two to three times per week to the gym, failing to actively and honestly attend and participate in a nutrition and education program, failing to cooperate with the referred programs, and failing to sign necessary releases of information. Specifically, it is alleged that the respondents violated terms 18, 21, 22 (incorrectly referred to as number 24 in the petition), 23, 26 and 27. Several days of fact-finding occurred over a period of many months.

. . . .

Term[s] 22 [and 27]

Term 22 provides that the respondents "shall use all resources available to ensure the mental, physical and emotional well-being of the child"; term 27 requires that the parents "buy a membership in a local gym and take the child to this gym at least two to three times a week."

Mark Monichetti, director of Elmira Fitness Center, testified regarding Brittany's enrollment at the center and her attendance thereat. Records of attendance are made through an identity card with a bar code on it. Based upon logs for the period August 12, 2005[,] through February 27, 2006[,] and created through the use of the child's card, the credible evidence establishes that Brittany did not attend the gym two to three times per week. Nor were any valid explanations for said failure adduced at hearing.

Term 23

Term 23 requires the respondents to

"take all actions necessary to ensure that the children [*sic*], if of appropriate age, attend school regularly and complete all homework assignments. The respondents shall communicate and cooperate with the children's [*sic*] school to ensure the children [*sic*] are in an appropriate classroom setting. The Respondent shall account for all absences or tardies with a note personally provided by the Respondents to the appropriate school official. Absences of three or more days in succession shall be accounted for by a note from a health care provider personally provided by the Respondent to the appropriate school official."

With respect to this requirement, the department presented the testimony of Rose Kramarik, principal of Broadway Middle School. Ms. Kramarik testified that from the commencement of the 2005-2006 school year through March 23, 2006, the child was absent 18 days and was tardy on 25 days out of a possible 68 days. Ms. Kramarik testified that in order for an absence to be considered "excused" the parent simply needs to supply the school with a note explaining the reason for the child's absence. Seventeen absent days were "excused" and one day of absence was "unexcused." The child was illegally tardy (late coming to school) 25 times from the beginning of the school year until March 23, 2006, when the instant petition was filed. In summary, she said the child was either absent or tardy 48 out of 68 school days. The department also introduced the child's attendance logs documenting the aforesaid absences and tardies.

Term 26

This term requires the respondents to "actively and honestly attend and participate in a nutrition program education program [*sic*] approved by the Department. They shall actively and honestly follow any and all recommendations, attend all meetings until successfully discharged and fully comply with any recommended after care and/or discharge plans. The respondents shall utilize the skills and techniques taught in said program during contact with the child."

Bruce Brennan, a registered dietician employed by the Nutrition Clinic in Elmira, New York, testified that Shawna and Brittany T. first became involved with the Clinic in August 2005 and with him personally in January 2006. His first appointment with them was scheduled for January 12, 2006. Respondent Shawna T. did attend the first session and thereafter cancelled the following three appointments. Brennan testified that one appointment was cancelled due to weather and one appointment was cancelled due to Mrs. T. ostensibly being treated at the emergency room. No explanation was offered for the third cancelled appointment. Ms. Carlyle during her testimony on this point had also expressed concern over Brittany's weight increasing from 238 pounds to 263 pounds during the relatively short period of time from October 2005 until April 2006, despite involvement with the Nutrition Clinic.

Also generally testifying on behalf of the Department, and probably most compelling, was Dr. William J. Cochran. Cochran is a Board certified pediatric gastroenterologist and nutritionist. He is currently the director of the pediatric weight management program and vice-chairman of the department of pediatrics at Geisinger Health Systems (Danville, Pa). Cochran was formerly on the faculty of the Baylor College of Medicine (Houston, Tex) and has lectured and written extensively (including a book) on pediatric obesity.

Cochran had first started working with the child and respondents by doing an evaluation in November 2004. Extensive testing, interviewing and teaching has been done with Brittany, and he has been monitoring her weight management program. Genetic and psychiatric disease syndromes were ruled out by Cochran; rather, he deemed the obesity as simply due to excessive caloric intake and a sedentary lifestyle.

Cochran credibly testified that the child currently suffers from morbid obesity and associated co-morbidities. One is considered morbidly obese in medical literature and by practitioners when one's body mass index (BMI) exceeds 40. An ideal BMI is 18-25; Brittany's BMI is 50. Co-morbidities are other disorders or diseases accompanying a primary diagnosis. In Brittany, these include those typically found with morbid obesity: gallstones, excessive fat in her liver with resultant fatty liver disease (which, he said, could eventually develop into nonalcoholic cirrhosis of the liver), sleep apnea, intermittent high blood pressure, pain in her knee joints, insulin resistence (indicating an increased risk of developing diabetes) and Acanthosis Nigricans (darkening and thickening of the skin around her neck associated with insulin resistance). Additionally, he testified as to the significant social and psychological impact such morbidity has. This is accentuated for females. According to the doctor, Brittany had, indeed, recently been exhibiting signs of depression.[4]

The program in which Brittany has participated through Cochran is a multidisciplinary one. It consists of 15 sessions, and involves behavior modification, lifestyle changes, dietary assistance, and exercise therapy. Cochran expressed his concern that after two and a half years, the

---

[4] As discussed below, it also likely explains much of her school attendance deficiencies.

attempts to deal with Brittany and the parents regarding her obesity have, overall, been "unsuccessful." Very much concerning to Cochran was that in the Fall of 2005 (when the child left his program and was returned to the respondents), she weighed 238; by February of 2006 (when she was ordered to reenter it), she weighed in at 261, a gain of approximately five pounds per month. This all occurred while a weight loss of one to two pounds per month had been achieved and was a realistic expectation for the future. She returned to the program having gained "twenty (20) some odd pounds more than when she left," the "exact opposite of where she should be." Cochran opined that in his expert opinion, if the child does not receive the necessary and proper attention for her morbid obesity she would be expected to have continued weight increase and her health would deteriorate further and that these medical concerns were "life-limiting." Moreover, her risks are exacerbated by the family history of hypertension, heart disease, stroke and diabetes.

Cochran, who testified April 7, 2006, had a personal discussion with Brittany and the mother regarding caloric intake, proper foods, and the need for vigorous exercise and lifestyle changes. He testified that it is important that the parents be role models regarding lifestyle and weight reduction habits. Typical of his concerns was an incident he described in November of 2004. He testified that he had just spent a long session with Brittany and Mrs. T. regarding Brittany's health, including appropriate eating and foods, regarding which the mother said she understood. Right after the appointment, he went to an eating establishment across from the hospital. There, he saw Brittany eating french fries and a "hamburger or something of that nature." This, he said, "would not have been the type of foods I would have hoped her to be consuming after sitting down and just talking about the problem." More recently, he noted, food logs continue to reflect regular ingestion by the child of foods he would certainly not recommend, including "lots of chicken nuggets, lots of pop tarts, hot dogs and pizza."

The Respondents' Case

. . . .

Testifying on behalf of respondent Robert T. was Carolyn Hodges, director of the Sol Stone Center for Eating Disorders in Elmira and also a director of the Nutrition Clinic. Hodges is a clinical dietician with a Master's in Nutrition from Marywood College. She testified that she is familiar with Brittany's participation in the program and had seen some improvement in Brittany over time. Hodges testified that it is essential for the parents to actively participate with the child in the nutrition program in order for the program to be effective. Hodges explained that Brittany suffers from a significant amount of emotional distress related to her excessive weight and concurred with the other experts' testimony that Brittany's excessive weight has a detrimental effect on her physical and emotional well-being. During the period she has worked with the family, she felt that Brittany was making progress. She opined that she knew of no children removed from their homes due to weight and that she felt that being with any parent was better than being with no parent at all.

The respondents testified on their own behalf. Court records indicate the father (date of birth 1966) is now approaching 41 years of age. He is confined to a wheelchair and, he testified, suffers from cardiomyopathy, muscular dystrophy, arthritis and scoliosis. He asserted that "all" the family follow a dietary regime. He further testified that Brittany bowls weekly, has attended school dances and has walked to school once. Much of Brittany's tardiness, he said, was because he thought school started at 8:15, not 8:00. He also proffered that Dr. Sobel had told the parents that Brittany's average physical "health has been fine."

The mother, according to court records, is soon to be 32 years of age (date of birth 1972). The court has observed throughout the past four years that Mrs. T. herself is very obese (the April 6, 2006 DSS 30-day report to the court indicated that her weight at the nutrition clinic on April 5, 2006 was 436 pounds). Moreover, at least fairly recently, the court has observed that the mother suffers from some very audible breathing difficulties. The mother expressed during testimony (as she had to Dr. Cochran several years earlier) a seeming understanding of caloric intake, the keeping of accurate food logs, the importance of exercise and the like. She offered that there were numerous difficulties during the period of supervision including such things as weather and transportation troubles and a hospital stay for herself for gallstones. She was aware that Brittany often had snacks after school and after dinner in the evening and that the child was known to "sneak food" at home. She also attributed some of the compliance difficulties to Brittany getting "frustrated" at "all she needs to do" and that the child "hates all of what the court has ordered the parents to do." On a positive note, the mother indicated that Brittany was now enjoying and doing better in school, to which she or her husband regularly drive her the half mile.

Distilled to its essence, the parents disagreed with particular dates and times, but did not refute that there have been missed appointments, missed school days and numerous tardies. While not disputing that they have not thoroughly complied with the court's dispositional order, they indicated they had tried their best. Essentially, however, they each offered numerous excuses for their noncompliance and argued that the child has not been negatively impacted by their noncompliance. The court frankly finds the respondents' explanations regarding their inability to comply with the terms to be spurious, unpersuasive and largely lacking credibility.

Law on Violation

A petition alleging a violation of an order of supervision can be sustained if the court is satisfied by competent proof that the violation was done "willfully and without just cause." Family Ct Act § 1072. Not statutorily specified, however, is the level of proof needed. Family Court Judge Marilyn O'Connor in *Matter of L.M.*, 824 NYS2d 768 (Fam Ct, Monroe County 2006) discusses this statutory void. As she notes, "[t]he degree of proof required in a particular type of proceeding 'is the kind of question which has traditionally been left to the judiciary to resolve.'["] . . . Judge O'Connor concludes (properly, in this court's opinion) that "[s]ince a respondent faces the potential of a jail term and loss of freedom for a violation of an order of supervision . . ." a "clear and convincing evidence" standard must be met in order to establish a willful violation of an order of supervision under Family Ct Act § 1072 (id.).

Additionally, it is well established that terms to be enforced must sufficiently apprise a respondent what is required of him, her or them. Here, the terms are very clear. Moreover, it is equally clear that a willful violation is supported by one's failure to regularly attend and meaningfully participate in programs, as it indicates an unwillingness or inability to take the steps necessary to assume responsibility for one's children.

Discussion and Conclusions as to Violation

With respect to the alleged violation of term 26, the court finds that several of the missed appointments at the nutrition clinic may have been with just cause and thus so much of the violation of term 26 as is based thereon, is not sustained. With respect to the rest of term 26 and all of the other terms, however, their willful violation is sustained by competent, credible evidence which is ample, clear and convincing. The respondents' failures regarding those established to have been violated are further found, by equally clear and convincing evidence, to have been without just cause. All of this has convincingly and patently had a very negative physical, emotional and mental impact on Brittany.

In arriving at these conclusions, it is startling to read the original neglect petition of February 21, 2003 (when Brittany was about to turn nine). That petition alleged, *inter alia*, that:

> "Brittany T. has a severe weight problem and weighs in excess of 240 pounds. Brittany has been seen by a variety of doctors and all of the physicians involved are very concerned about her health due to the fact that she is morbidly obese. Despite these doctors' concerns, Mr. and Mrs[.] T. have been uncooperative with service providers and have shown a lack of follow through with these services. [Physicians] have made numerous recommendations to Mr. and Mrs. T. in the past and none of these recommendations were ever followed through with. . . [.] It has been determined by [the physicians] involved that Brittany's weight problems are not organic in nature and are the result of poor parental modeling and control of food intake. Physicians have seen a pattern of alarming behavior on the part of Mr. and Mrs. T. regarding their attitude toward Brittany's morbid obesity and her extremely poor attendance in school. Brittany has had attendance problems at school ever since she began kindergarten. Many of these absences have been unexcused absences and the family refuses to ensure that Brittany attend school, even [on] a semi regular basis. . . [.] When Robert and Shawna have enrolled Brittany in programs in the past, they have not continued with these programs and have multiple excuses as to why they do not continue. . . [.]"

Shockingly, it is truly as if nothing (except weight gain) has changed in the past three-plus years. This court on many, many occasions has expressed its concern with respect to the lack of commitment and motivation demonstrated by the respondents in effectively and wholeheartedly addressing their daughter's school issues (at least until the eve of trial) and her morbid obesity. The latter concern continues unabated, along with its concomitant health complications. It is inconceivable to this court that the respondents continue to disregard the medical and other advice of their experts. This is despite the myriad services which the department has actively and repeatedly urged. Furthermore, CASA, too, has been intimately involved with and assisted the family since its assignment in October 2004. Even more incredible is that this has continued in spite of respondents' knowing that their jailing and/or their daughter's removal from home were more immediate likelihoods than Brittany's probable premature death.

The long history of this unfortunate case demonstrates that the respondents have unequivocally evinced an unwillingness to follow doctors' and others' advice, so as to justify a finding that they willfully violated the terms of the order of disposition. The respondents' continued noncompliance in ensuring Brittany's regular school attendance and in assuring their active and diligent cooperation with, and participation in, programs designed to aggressively address the child's morbid obesity, only amplifies the willfulness of their violation. The court recognizes the physical limitations of the respondents but finds that this neither excuses nor prohibits them from executing their parental and court-ordered responsibilities.

Law on Disposition of Violation

. . . .

In regard to removal of a child due to morbid obesity and its related health concerns, the court has found no similar reported cases in this state. In a very similar matter (involving a 461-pound 16 year old), the Court of Common Pleas of Northumberland County, Pennsylvania (Charles Saylor, J.) found that because of the parent's limitations and the lack of attention in addressing the child's medical appointments and schooling, it was clear that best interests required the continued placement of the child in foster care until such time as the parent could "demonstrate the ability to offer the required assistance and support to her son," and until "new eating habits, education and exercise programs become more ingrained and of a habitual nature." Courts in several other states (California, Iowa, Indiana, New Mexico and Texas) have also recognized morbid obesity as an actionable issue. *See*, Patel, *Super-Sized Kids: Using the Law to Combat Morbid Obesity in Children*, 43 Fam[.] Ct[.] Rev[.] 164 (2005). The Iowa case appears to involve a child strikingly similar in age, height and weight to Brittany. Removal was ordered in that case as well. *In re L.T.*, 494 N.W.2d 450 (Iowa Ct App 1992).

Discussion and Conclusions as to Disposition

It is clear in New York that a child is neglected when his or her "physical, mental or emotional condition has been impaired as a result of the failure of his or her parent to exercise a minimum degree of care in supplying the child with adequate education or medical care, though financially able to do so." Family Ct Act § 1012(f)[i][A]. The respondents, due to their continued failures with respect to Brittany's educational and medical needs, have not provided that minimum degree of care, which is measured against the behavior of reasonable and prudent parents faced with the same circumstances.

This court is cognizant of potential concerns regarding the power of the State to drastically intervene in the regulation of family affairs with respect to morbid obesity. It is also very aware of the emotional impact that disruptions in the parent-child relationship may have. This court also agrees and holds that state intervention would generally "not be justified . . . simply because a child was overweight, or did not simply engage in a healthy and fit lifestyle." However, where, as here, there are clear medical standards and convincing evidence that there exist severe, life-limiting dangers due to parental lifestyle and persistent neglect, removal is justified. This is no less a cause for determining neglect and ordering removal than is a matter where a child is at risk of life-limiting consequences due to malnourishment, inadequate supervision or other heretofore well-established bases for removal. Indeed, "the obesity must be of a severe nature reaching the life threatening or morbid state, which has also manifested itself in physical problems, such as those present here, or mental problems."

In so deciding, of course, the court notes that less-drastic remedies should generally be attempted first. In the instant matter, as noted above, absolutely every thing and every effort has been attempted—not for months, but for years. The court finds that Brittany's continued residency in the home is contrary to her health, welfare and safety and that the best interest of the child warrants her removal from the care and custody of the parents and placement once again with the department. The court finds that the department has employed not only reasonable but, indeed, extraordinary efforts to prevent or eliminate this need.

Therefore, it is hereby ordered that the respondents are found in willful violation of this court's dispositional order dated April 24, 2003 (as subsequently extended by this court); and it is further ordered that the child Brittany T. shall, pursuant to § 1055 of the Family Court Act, be placed in the custody of the Commissioner of the Chemung County Department of Social Services within seven court days of the entry of this order; and it is further ordered that the parents shall be authorized to jointly visit the child at the Human Resources Building, or where the child might be placed, or other fitting place chosen by the Department, twice per week, totaling no less than four hours per week, provided it is in keeping with the Department's service objectives and placement goals; and it is further ordered that the respondents, pursuant to Social Services Law § 409-e(3), shall be notified of any and all planning conferences, of their right to attend the conference(s), and of their right to have counsel or another representative or companion with them; and it is further ordered that the court specifically prohibits any trial discharge without court leave; and it is further ordered that, subject to future petitions or hearings, return to parents is the permanency goal, provided that the child obtains and maintains a healthy weight and lifestyle before returning home and further provided that one or both parents can actually demonstrate an ability to provide appropriate home, school and community supports so as to so maintain the child, including indicia of consistently affording an environment conducive to healthy eating habits, exercise regimens and to meeting educational attendance requirements; and it is further ordered that . . . the prior disposition is revoked, but the same terms and conditions of supervision are hereby reimposed on this violation, for a period of 12 months.

NOTE:

In *In re Brittany T.*, 852 N.Y.S.2d 475 (App. Div. 2008), the appeals court reversed the trial court's finding that the County had established by clear and convincing evidence that Brittany's parents had willfully violated the terms of the supervision order.

With respect to Terms 22 and 27, the court found that Brittany had attended a local gym at least one day per week for 27 of the 31 weeks in question, despite the fact that her parents claimed that they could not afford the membership fees. This record, said the court, "while not perfect, did represent a recognition by [the parents] of their obligations" under the order, and constituted a good faith effort to satisfy them.

With respect to Term 23 relating to regular school attendance, the court noted that school officials confirmed that each of the child's 18 absences were excused, and that the majority of them were for appointments for court-ordered services. The court also observed that Brittany had received passing grades in all her subjects during the relevant period, and for part of the year qualified for the honor roll.

Finally, the court found that the parents had not willfully violated the requirement under Term 26 that they participate with Brittany in a nutrition program. It noted that the parents had regularly traveled 130 miles with the child to meet with a nutritionist, and that she had continued to participate in programs at the nutrition clinic; that her cholesterol and liver functions were normal and showed improvement; and that the parents had maintained food logs for Brittany. The court rejected the County's claim that the increase in Brittany's weight established that her parents had continued to allow her to consume inappropriate foods. It suggested that factors outside of their control may have accounted for this increase, such as her food consumption at school.

As the trial court found, Brittany suffers from morbid obesity and associated co-morbities. The latter include gallstones, sleep apnea, intermittent high blood pressure, pain in her joints, insulin resistance indicating an increased risk of diabetes, and depression. She has lost weight every time she has been removed from the care of her parents and has gained weight every time she has been returned to them. The appeals court found that Brittany must remain with her parents because the County did not prove that they willfully violated the conditions of the order.

Under these circumstances, should the danger to Brittany or the good faith of her parents be the determining factor in whether she remains in their custody? Suppose that she had lost close to 100 pounds when removed from her parents and regularly gained it back when she was returned to them. Should that trigger a focus on the effect of parental custody rather than on the willfulness of the parents?

C. FOSTER CARE
4. Liability

Page 1303. Add after *Nichol v. Stass*:

Gomes v. Wood

U.S. Court of Appeals for the Tenth Circuit, 2006.
451 F.3d 1122.

■ HENRY, CIRCUIT JUDGE.

On April 30, 2000, Megan Annes, a child protection caseworker with the Utah Division of Child and Family Services, removed nine-month-old Rebekah Gomes from Rebekah's home and placed her in protective custody. Ms. Annes's decision was based on a four-inch linear skull fracture that Rebekah's treating physician had reported to Child and Family Services four days earlier. In September 2000, the Division of Child and Family Services found that protective custody was no longer warranted and returned Rebekah to her family.

Rebekah and her parents, Shauna and Domingo Gomes, then filed this 42 U.S.C. § 1983 action against Ms. Annes, Kerri Ketterer and Tess

Blackmer (Ms. Annes's supervisors), and Assistant Attorney General Deborah Wood. The Gomeses alleged that the removal of Rebekah from their home without prior notice and a hearing violated their due process rights under the Fourteenth Amendment.

The district court granted summary judgment to all the defendants. Relying on *Carey v. Piphus*, 435 U.S. 247, 98 S. Ct. 1042 (1978), the court reasoned that the state's affording the Gomeses a post-removal hearing on May 3, 2000[,] foreclosed their claims for damages for failing to provide a pre-removal hearing. The court also indicated that "it likely would have reached the same result" on alternative grounds—that emergency circumstances justified removal without a hearing and that the defendants were entitled to qualified immunity. Aplts' App. at 941 (Dist. Ct. Order, filed July 16, 2004).

We disagree with the district court's application of Carey to these facts, but we affirm its decision for a different reason: we hold that because Ms. Annes did not violate clearly established law of which a reasonable official would have known, she and the other defendants are entitled to qualified immunity.

I. BACKGROUND

A. The Removal of Rebekah

On April 26, 2000, Shauna Gomes took Rebekah to her pediatrician, Dr. Brent Knorr. She told Dr. Knorr that Rebekah had injured her head on the previous day when she fell off the bed. She reported that Rebekah had slept a lot since the fall and was "cranky" and "clingy." Aplts' App. at 585.

Dr. Knorr examined Rebekah and found a large amount of swelling. An x-ray revealed a four-inch parietal fracture on Rebekah's skull. However, there was no depressed fracture—a significant finding because such fractures are more likely to injure the brain. The fracture was linear, not star-shaped, which suggested to Dr. Knorr that it had been caused by a blunt trauma.

Dr. Knorr found Ms. Gomes's explanation of the injury "possible but suspicious." *Id.* at 930. He stated that the shape of Rebekah's fracture was "consistent with a fall on a flat object." *Id.* at 929. However, in deposition testimony, he explained that he had seen many children who had fallen from beds, or objects of similar heights, but had not suffered the kind of fracture that he had seen on Rebekah. Dr. Knorr was also concerned that Ms. Gomes had waited until the day after Rebekah's injury to seek medical attention. To Dr. Knorr, the delay in seeking care was "one of the warning signs that maybe something—wasn't on par with what I was told." *Id.* at 596.

Dr. Knorr prescribed Motrin. He told Ms. Gomes that he was required to report the fracture (and Ms. Gomes's explanation of it) to the Division of Child and Family Services. Nevertheless, he sent Rebekah home and told Ms. Gomes that he was comfortable doing so.

Dr. Knorr then reported the incident to Child and Family Services by telephone. The intake caseworker responded that, because the matter did not appear to be an emergency, an investigator would call him back on the following day.

On April 27, 2000, Ms. Gomes returned to the doctor's office with Rebekah. She was concerned that Rebekah had been vomiting. Dr. Knorr was out of the office, but his partner examined Rebekah and concluded that the vomiting was caused by the stomach flu and not by the head injury.

On April 28, 2000, Ms. Gomes again returned to Dr. Knorr's office for a follow-up visit. She asked him if he had contacted Child and Family Services, noting that no one had contacted her. Evidently, no one had contacted Dr. Knorr either, as he responded that he would follow up with the agency. He concluded that Rebekah was doing well, and he again "felt comfortable leaving the child in her mother's care." *Id.* at 930-31.

On the same day, Dr. Knorr spoke by telephone with the defendant Megan Annes, a caseworker in the Division of Child and Family Services. He told her that "the mother's explanation was possible but suspicious" but that he "felt comfortable leaving [Rebekah] in her mother's care." *Id.* at 930.

After speaking with Dr. Knorr, Ms. Annes met with her supervisors, Tess Blackmer and Kerri Ketterer (who are also named as defendants in this case). They advised Ms. Annes that it might be necessary to take Rebekah into protective custody immediately—without first conducting a hearing. Ms. Blackmer indicated that "there were substantial reasons to believe that there was a substantial danger to Rebekah's physical health and safety." *Id.* at 550. Ms. Blackmer based that conclusion on the severity of Rebekah's skull fracture, Dr. Knorr's suspicions regarding Ms. Gomes's explanation of the fracture, the Gomeses' apparent delay in seeking medical treatment for the fracture, Rebekah's young age, and the possibility that further medical treatment for the skull fracture might be delayed. *Id.* Ms. Ketterer added that she did not find Ms. Gomes's explanation of Rebekah's injury to be credible. See *id.* at 556 (stating that "[b]ased on my training and experience . . . I did not believe it was possible for a nine-month-old child to receive a four-inch skull fracture from a two-foot fall off a bed because of the softness of a baby's skull bones"). Both supervisors advised Ms. Annes to investigate further and to seek legal advice.

Ms. Annes then telephoned the defendant Deborah Wood, an Assistant Attorney General for the State of Utah in the child services division (and the fourth defendant in this case). Ms. Wood also concluded that Rebekah's "physical health and safety were in substantial danger." *Id.* at 563. Ms. Wood and Ms. Annes agreed that Ms. Annes should conduct a home visit. Ms. Wood advised Ms. Annes that "if [Ms. Annes] concluded there was substantial cause to believe that placing Rebekah Gomes into protective custody was necessary to protect her from a substantial danger to her physical health and safety, the decision would comply with the applicable state statutes." *Id.* at 564. Ms. Wood added that she would support the removal by filing a petition in the juvenile court seeking an out-of-home placement. Id.

On the following day, April 29, 2000, Ms. Annes contacted a police detective and proceeded with him to the Gomeses' home. They arrived at 12:30 p.m. but discovered that no one was there.

On April 30, 2000, Ms. Annes and another police officer returned to the Gomeses' home and interviewed them there. Ms. Annes asked how Rebekah had been injured. After Ms. Gomes offered the same explanation that she had given to Dr. Knorr, Ms. Annes inspected the bed and the floor where Ms. Gomes maintained that Rebekah had fallen. Her inspection confirmed her view that Ms. Gomes's explanation was not plausible. Ms. Annes was also concerned because Ms. Gomes told her that she had not noticed the fracture until the day after the fall. Accordingly, Ms. Annes decided to take Rebekah into protective custody and removed her from the Gomeses' home.

On May 3, 2000, Assistant Attorney General Wood filed a petition for custody in the Utah County Fourth District Juvenile Court. The petition recited the facts surrounding Rebekah's skull fracture, alleged that there was a substantial danger to Rebekah's health and safety, and requested the court to award custody to the Division of Child and Family Services for out-of-home care and placement. The court conducted a hearing on the same day. The Gomeses were represented by counsel, and they agreed that Rebekah could be placed in the temporary custody of the Division of Child and Family Services. Rebekah remained in state custody until September 2000, when the Division of Child and Family Services determined that the circumstances warranted returning her to her family.

B. The Gomeses' Section 1983 Action

In September 2001, the Gomeses filed this 42 U.S.C. § 1983 action against Ms. Annes, Ms. Ketterer, Ms. Blackmer, and Ms. Wood. They asserted that taking Rebekah into state custody without prior notice and a hearing violated their due process rights under the Fourteenth Amendment, and they sought actual damages for this alleged constitutional violation.

The Gomeses and the defendant state officials each moved for summary judgment, and the district court granted summary judgment to all the defendants. The court reasoned that the state court's finding after a post-removal hearing that Rebekah should remain in state custody foreclosed the Gomeses' claim for damages arising out of failure to provide a pre-removal rehearing. According to the district court, "[t]he

Supreme Court had made clear that where an adverse action would have nevertheless been taken had the plaintiff received adequate due process, the plaintiff would not be entitled to recover damages to compensate her for the adverse action." Aplts' App. at 939 (discussing *Carey v. Piphus*, 435 U.S. 247, 98 S. Ct. 1042, 55 L. Ed. 2d 252 (1978)). "In such circumstances, 'the failure to accord procedural due process could not properly be viewed as the cause of the [adverse action]' and to 'award damages for injuries caused by [such action] would constitute a windfall, rather than compensation.'" *Id.* at 939-40 (quoting Carey, 435 U.S. at 260).

The district court also concluded that it would likely reach the same result on two alternative grounds. First, the court stated, there were emergency circumstances posing an immediate threat to Rebekah's safety. As a result, the Due Process Clause of the Fourteenth Amendment did not require a pre-removal hearing. Second, the court suggested that the defendants might be entitled to qualified immunity because they had relied on (a) a state statute, Utah Code Ann. § 64A-4a-202.1 (1998), that authorized removal without a hearing if there was a substantial danger to the physical health or safety of the child; and (b) the advice of Assistant Attorney General Wood.

II. DISCUSSION

. . . .

We begin by reviewing the requirements of the Due Process Clause when the state seeks to remove children from the home. Then, we proceed to the parties' arguments regarding the significance of the post-removal hearing and the defense of qualified immunity.

A. Removing Children from the Home in Emergency Circumstances

. . . .

[W]hen a state agency seeks to remove children from the home, due process requires that the parents receive prior notice and a hearing, except in "extraordinary situations where some valid governmental interest is at stake that justifies postponing the hearing until after the event." *Spielman v. Hildebrand*, 873 F.2d 1377, 1385 (10th Cir. 1989) (quoting *Smith v. Org. of Foster Families for Equal. & Reform*, 431 U.S. 816, 848 (1977)). These "extraordinary situations" include "[e]mergency circumstances which pose an immediate threat to the safety of a child." *Hollingsworth v. Hill*, 110 F.3d 733, 739 (10th Cir. 1997). However, "the 'mere possibility' of danger is not enough to justify a removal without appropriate process."

Importantly, even when such a pre-hearing removal is justified, the state must act promptly to provide a post-removal hearing.

Our cases have not offered a precise definition of "emergency circumstances which pose an immediate threat to the safety of a child." *Hollingsworth*, 110 F.3d at 739. . . .

. . . The First Circuit has concluded that a majority of circuits addressing this issue have held that "a case worker . . . may place a child in temporary custody when he has evidence giving rise to a reasonable and articulable suspicion that the child has been abused or is in imminent peril of abuse." *Hatch v. Dep't for Children, Youth, & Their Families*, 274 F.3d 12, 20 (1st Cir. 2001).

. . . .

In our view, the reasonable suspicion standard appropriately balances the interests of the parents, the child, and the state. The failure to act when a child is in danger may have "unthinkable consequence[s]." *Jordan v. Jackson*, 15 F.3d 333, 350 (4th Cir. 1994). As a result, social workers should be afforded some discretion when they seek to protect a child whose safety may be at risk. Following the majority approach, we conclude that state officials may remove a child from the home without prior notice and a hearing when they have a reasonable suspicion of an immediate threat to the safety of the child if he or she is allowed to remain there. We emphasize again that even in these instances in which emergency removal is justified, the state must afford the parents a prompt post-removal hearing.

As to whether state officials have time to seek judicial authorization for the removal, we agree with the Eleventh Circuit that this consideration should not be "the single focus" of the inquiry. *Kearney*, 329 F.3d at 1295. In many instances, it may not be entirely clear either how long it would take to obtain judicial approval or whether this period of delay would jeopardize the safety of the child. Nevertheless, we also agree with the Second Circuit's observation that, if we do not give any consideration to whether state officials might obtain judicial authorization of the removal without additional risk to the child, then the definition of an emergency may be broadened to such an extent that due process rights are eroded. *Tenenbaum*, 193 F.3d at 584.

Accordingly, we conclude that in determining whether state officials have a reasonable suspicion of an immediate threat to the safety of the child, we must consider "*all relevant circumstances*, including the state's reasonableness in responding to a perceived danger, as well as the objective nature, likelihood, and immediacy of danger to the child." [*Doe v.*] *Kearney*, 329 F.3d [1286,] 1295 [(11th Cir. 2003)] (emphasis added). Ordinarily, the question of whether state officials had time to seek and obtain judicial authorization for the removal without jeopardizing the safety of the child will be an important consideration, and the failure to establish that judicial authorization was impracticable will undermine the contention that emergency circumstances existed. However, neither this factor, nor any other single factor, is necessarily dispositive.

We now turn to the particular arguments raised by the parties in this appeal.

B. The Effect of the Post-Removal Hearing on the Gomeses' Claim for Damages

As we have noted, the district court concluded that it was not required to fully decide the issue of whether emergency circumstances existed to justify Rebekah's removal. Aplts' App. at 942. The court did state that it believed "that the defendants have adequately established that Rebekah faced an immediate threat, especially in light of the state court's conclusion that she did." *Id.* at 941-42. However, the court concluded that the defendants were entitled to summary judgment on an alternative ground.

In particular, the court observed that the state had provided an adequate post-removal hearing and that the Gomeses did not challenge the state judge's decision that Rebekah remain in state custody. As a result, it concluded, the Gomeses could not prevail on their due process challenge to the pre-hearing removal. We agree with the Gomeses that the district court erred in relying on *Carey v. Piphus*, 435 U.S. 247, 98 S. Ct. 1042, 55 L. Ed. 2d 252 (1978), for this conclusion.

In *Carey*, the Supreme Court held that when a procedural due process violation occurs and adverse action results, damages for injuries caused by the adverse action may not be recovered if the defendant can prove the action would have been taken even absent the violation. See *id.* at 260 (stating that "in such a case, the failure to accord procedural due process could not properly be viewed as the cause of the [adverse action]"). Significantly, however, the Court also concluded that a plaintiff may recover nominal damages and actual damages arising *not* from the deprivation of liberty or property but from the denial of procedural due process itself. As to the latter category of damages, the Court emphasized that the plaintiff is still required to prove causation:

> In sum, then, although mental and emotional distress caused by the denial of procedural due process itself is compensable under § 1983, we hold that neither the likelihood of such injury nor the difficulty of proving it is so great as to justify awarding compensatory damages without proof that such injury actually was caused.

Here, the Gomeses have not contested the state judge's finding that the removal of Rebekah was justified. Moreover, they have not sought nominal damages. Accordingly, they may only recover damages arising from the denial of due process itself. On this issue, the district court stated that "the only damage [the Gomeses] claim to have suffered is the emotional damage that resulted from [Rebekah's] removal."

In our view, the district court read the Gomeses' allegations too narrowly. We acknowledge that the line drawn by the Supreme Court in *Carey*—between (a) damages arising from the deprivation of liberty or property and (b) damages arising from the denial of procedural due process itself—may be a fine one. Moreover, in many instances, plaintiffs may offer the same evidence to support both classes of damages claims.

Nevertheless, the Gomeses have alleged that they have suffered damages from the denial of procedural due process itself (and thus recoverable under *Carey*). In particular, Rebekah Gomes's mother, Shauna Gomes, answered a deposition question about the damages that she had suffered as follows:

> Q: Could you describe those [damages] for me, please. I understand you've talked about pain and anguish earlier, so is there anything in addition . . . that you've suffered?
>
> A: Yes. It's—I compare it to being attacked by a terrorist. I mean they come in and take something that is of most value to you, and I was able to get that thing back.
>
> However, it's always there. . . . I wonder when they're going to strike again. I wonder what could happen. I have no control over it, they could come at any time. It doesn't depend upon my actions.
>
> I've had dreams . . . from the trauma I went through, . . . when my child gets hurt with an accident or something, it just makes me sick to my stomach to have to take him in to the doctor. Who knows what might happen?

Aplts' App. at 783-84.

Viewing the record in the light most favorable to the Gomeses, this testimony concerns, in part, *the manner* in which Rebekah was removed (i.e., without prior notice and a hearing), and not merely *the fact* that she was removed. Ms. Gomes's statement that "they could come at any time" and her analogy to "being attacked by a terrorist" concern damages for the violation of procedural due process itself; her testimony addresses both the lack of notice and the randomness with which the Gomeses experienced the removal.

Accordingly, we conclude that the district court erred in ruling that the post-removal hearing and the findings by the state-court judge precluded the Gomeses from seeking damages for their due process claim.

C. Qualified Immunity

In light of its conclusion that *Carey* forecloses the Gomeses' claims for damages, the district court did not definitively resolve the merits of their due process claim. However, in the district court proceedings and in this appeal, the defendant state officials have argued that they are entitled to summary judgment on the grounds of qualified immunity. They focus on the removal decision made by Ms. Annes, but they argue that because Ms. Annes is entitled to qualified immunity, the other defendants (who advised her regarding the removal decision) are also entitled to the same immunity. Upon de novo review of this legal question, we agree.

1. General Principles

Qualified immunity generally shields from liability for civil damages "government officials performing discretionary functions . . . insofar as their conduct does not violate clearly established statutory or constitutional rights of which a reasonable person would have known." *Harlow v. Fitzgerald*, 457 U.S. 800, 818 (1982).

. . . .

In analyzing the qualified immunity defense, this court has adopted a three-part inquiry. First, we ask whether the plaintiffs' allegations, if true, establish a constitutional violation. If the allegations do not meet that standard, we must dismiss the claim.

Second, if the plaintiffs have alleged a constitutional violation, we examine "whether the law was clearly established at the time the alleged violations occurred." The law is clearly established if a reasonable official in the defendant's circumstances would understand that her conduct violated the plaintiff's constitutional right. *Moore v. Guthrie*, 438 F.3d 1036, 1042 (10th Cir. 2006). . . .

Finally, if the law was clearly established, we proceed to the third part of the inquiry. We ask whether, in spite of the fact that the law was clearly established, "extraordinary circumstances"—such as reliance on the advice of counsel or on a statute—"so prevented [the official] from knowing that [her] actions were unconstitutional that [she] should not be imputed with knowledge of a clearly established right." "[W]here the right is clearly established, a defendant should only rarely be able to succeed with a qualified immunity defense."

2. Application

a. [E]xistence of a constitutional violation

We begin with the threshold inquiry of whether the Gomeses' allegations, if true, state a constitutional violation. Under the due process principles we have outlined, we must determine whether Ms Annes had a reasonable suspicion of "emergency circumstances which pose an immediate threat to the safety of a child," when she removed Rebekah from the home. Because the defendant state officials raised the qualified immunity defense in their motion for summary judgment, we must view the evidence in the light most favorable to the Gomeses.

Viewing the evidence in the light most favorable to them, genuine issues of material fact exist as to whether the defendants had reasonable suspicion to remove Rebekah before holding a hearing. First, although it was Rebekah's pediatrician, Dr. Knorr, who reported her injury to the Division of Child and Family Services, his testimony may be plausibly read to conclude that there was not an immediate threat to Rebekah's safety. In particular, Dr. Knorr stated that the shape of Rebekah's fracture was "consistent with a fall on a flat object," Aplts' App. at 929, and thus supported the Gomeses' statements that she had fallen onto the floor from a bed. Moreover, in his initial telephone call to the Division of Child and Family Services on April 26, 2000, and again in his second call to the agency on April 28, 2000, Dr. Knorr reported that he was "comfortable" allowing Ms. Gomes to take Rebekah home. *Id.* at 930-31. Dr. Knorr added that "I never was highly suspicious that Rebekah had been the victim of child abuse, and I never told anyone at DCFS, or anyone else, that I was highly suspicious that the child had been abused." That testimony is supported by the statement of the intake worker who answered Dr. Knorr's initial call and who told him that the circumstances did not sound like an emergency.

The Gomeses' own conduct also offers some support for their allegations. Ms. Gomes took Rebekah to the doctor on three successive days, and she now contends that these visits demonstrate that she was quite concerned about Rebekah's welfare. That behavior is at least arguably inconsistent with that of a neglectful or abusive parent. Moreover, during the appointment with Dr. Knorr on April 28, 2000, it was Ms. Gomes herself who informed him that she had not yet been contacted by the Division of Child and Family Services, thus leading him to call the agency a second time.

Thus, viewed in the light most favorable to the Gomeses, the record supports their contention that the defendant officials removed Rebekah without "reasonable and articulable suspicion that the child ha[d] been abused or [was] in imminent peril of abuse." We therefore proceed to the second part of the qualified immunity inquiry.

b. Whether the defendants violated clearly established law

We consider whether a reasonable official in the defendants' circumstances would understand that his or her conduct violated the Gomeses' due process rights. "[T]he salient question . . . is whether the state of the law [at the time of the incident] gave the [defendants] fair warning that their conduct was unconstitutional." Officials who are mistaken about the lawfulness of their conduct may still be entitled to qualified immunity if the mistake is reasonable in light of the applicable law and the facts known to them at the time.

. . . .

"[I]f officers of reasonable competence could disagree" about the lawfulness of the challenged conduct, then "[qualified] immunity should be recognized." In those instances, the fact that the uncontroverted evidence supports opposite legal conclusions as to the reasonableness of an official's conduct demonstrates that the official has not violated clearly established law.

Here, in light of those principles, we must determine whether a reasonable official, presented with the relevant information regarding Rebekah's skull fracture in April 2000, would have understood that there were no "[e]mergency circumstances which pose an immediate threat to [her] safety," and that, as a result, removing her from home without prior notice and a hearing violated the Gomeses' due process rights. Resolution of that question requires consideration of the case law in existence at that time.

As of April 2000, we had announced the emergency circumstances exception to the notice and hearing requirement, see *Hollingsworth*, 110 F.3d at 739, and we had had two occasions to apply that standard: in *Hollingsworth* itself and in *Malik* [*v. Araphoe County Dep't of Social Servs.*], 191 F.3d [1306,] 1315 [(10th Cir. 1999)]. However, in neither case was there any evidence whatsoever of an immediate threat. Moreover, as of April 2000, we had not yet identified as an important consideration the time available to state officials to seek and obtain judicial authorization for the removal without jeopardizing the safety of the child. Nor had we held that the reasonable suspicion standard applies to the determination of whether emergency circumstances exist. Additionally, we had stated that "considerable deference should be given to the judgment of responsible government officials in acting to protect children from perceived imminent danger or abuse."

In applying that case law to the circumstances confronted by the defendants, we conclude that "officers of reasonable competence could disagree" as to whether there were emergency circumstances justifying the removal of Rebekah without a hearing. In conducting the first step in the qualified immunity analysis (whether the Gomeses have alleged the violation of a constitutional right), we have set forth the evidence that supports their contention that emergency circumstances did not exist. However, other evidence supports the opposite conclusion.

In particular, Dr. Knorr informed Ms. Annes that Ms. Gomes's explanation of Rebekah's injury was "possible, but suspicious." He added that he had seen many children who had fallen from beds or objects of similar heights but who had not suffered such a fracture. Dr. Knorr's suspicion was supported by Ms. Annes's inspection of the bed at the Gomeses' residence. Based on her inspection, she too thought it unlikely that Rebekah could have sustained her head injury from the reported fall. Dr. Knorr also expressed concern about the Gomeses' delay in seeking medical treatment. He explained that Rebekah's skull would have shown swelling and bruising within hours of the reported fall from the bed but that Ms. Gomes did not seek treatment until the following day. Confronted with evidence of a significant head injury to an infant, a questionable explanation from the parents, and a delay in seeking medical treatment, a reasonable official could have believed that there was an immediate threat to Rebekah's safety.

. . . .

Our holding is also supported by the policies underlying the qualified immunity doctrine. Here, as we have noted in discussing the grounds supporting the reasonable suspicion standard, "[s]ocial workers face extreme difficulties in trying simultaneously to help preserve families and to serve the child's best interests." When confronted with evidence of child abuse, they may be required to make "on-the-spot judgments on the basis of limited and often conflicting information," with limited resources to assist them. They must balance the parents' interest in the care, custody and control of their children with the state's interest in protecting the children's welfare. Additionally, social workers must consider "the vital importance of curbing overzealous suspicion and intervention on the part of health care professional and government officials, particularly when such overzealousness may have the effect of discouraging parents or caretakers from communicating with doctors or seeking appropriate medical attention for children with real or potentially life-threatening conditions." In the circumstances of this case, imposing the added burden of potential liability for damages under § 1983 would interfere unnecessarily with the performance of a difficult and essential job.

Accordingly, we conclude that the defendants Megan Annes, Kerri Ketterer, Tess Blackmer, and Deborah Wood are entitled to qualified immunity from the Gomeses' claim for damages under § 1983.

III. CONCLUSION

We therefore AFFIRM the district court's grant of summary judgment to the defendants.

CHAPTER 11: ADOPTION

C. Standards
3. Sexual Orientation

Page 1384. Add after *In re M.M.D.*:

Finstuen v. Crutcher

U.S. Court of Appeals for the Tenth Circuit, 2007.
496 F.3d 1139.

■ EBEL, CIRCUIT JUDGE.

Defendant-Appellant Dr. Mike Crutcher, sued in his official capacity as the Commissioner of Health (hereinafter referred to as "Oklahoma State Department of Health ('OSDH')") appeals a district court judgment that a state law barring recognition of adoptions by same-sex couples already finalized in another state is unconstitutional. . . . We hold that final adoption orders by a state court of competent jurisdiction are judgments that must be given full faith and credit under the Constitution by every other state in the nation. Because the Oklahoma statute at issue categorically rejects a class of out-of-state adoption decrees, it violates the Full Faith and Credit Clause. We therefore affirm the order and judgment of the district court declaring the statute unconstitutional and directing the issuance of a new birth certificate for E.D.

I.

Three same-sex couples and their adopted children have challenged the following amendment to Oklahoma's statute governing the recognition of parent-child relationships that are created by out-of-state adoptions.

§ 7502-1.4. Foreign adoptions

A. The courts of this state shall recognize a decree, judgment, or final order creating the relationship of parent and child by adoption, issued by a court or other governmental authority with appropriate jurisdiction in a foreign country or in another state or territory of the United States. The rights and obligations of the parties as to matters within the jurisdiction of this state shall be determined as though the decree, judgment, or final order were issued by a court of this state. Except that, this state, any of its agencies, or any court of this state shall not recognize an adoption by more than one individual of the same sex from any other state or foreign jurisdiction.

Okla. Stat. tit. 10, § 7502-1.4(A) (the "adoption amendment").

Each of the three families has a different set of circumstances. Mr. Greg Hampel and Mr. Ed Swaya are residents of Washington, where they jointly adopted child V in 2002. V was born in Oklahoma, and pursuant to an "open" adoption agreement with V's biological mother, the men agreed to bring V to Oklahoma to visit her mother "from time to time." However, they do not state any plans to move to Oklahoma or have any ongoing interactions with the state of Oklahoma. After V's adoption, Mr. Hampel and Mr. Swaya requested that OSDH issue a new birth certificate for V. OSDH did so on July 7, 2003, but named only Mr. Hampel as V's parent. Mr. Hampel and Mr. Swaya contested that action, prompting OSDH to seek an opinion from the Oklahoma attorney general as to whether it must fulfill the request to list both fathers on the birth certificate. The attorney general opined that the U.S. Constitution's Full Faith and Credit Clause required Oklahoma to recognize any validly issued out-of-state adoption decree. OSDH subsequently issued V a new birth certificate naming both men as parents. The state legislature responded one month later by enacting the adoption amendment.

Lucy Doel and Jennifer Doel live with their adopted child E in Oklahoma. E was born in Oklahoma. Lucy Doel adopted E in California in January 2002. Jennifer Doel adopted E in California six months later in a second parent adoption, a process used by step-parents to adopt the biological child of a spouse without terminating the parental rights of that spouse. OSDH issued E a supplemental birth certificate naming only Lucy Doel as her mother. The Doels have requested a revised birth certificate from OSDH that would acknowledge Jennifer Doel as E's parent, but OSDH denied the request.

Anne Magro and Heather Finstuen reside in Oklahoma with their two children. Ms. Magro gave birth to S and K in New Jersey in 1998. In

2000, Ms. Finstuen adopted S and K in New Jersey as a second parent, and New Jersey subsequently issued new birth certificates for S and K naming both women as their parents.

These three families brought suit against the state of Oklahoma seeking to enjoin enforcement of the adoption amendment, naming the governor, attorney general and commissioner of health in their official capacities. The Doels also requested a revised birth certificate naming both Lucy Doel and Jennifer Doel as E's parents.

. . . .

II.

. . . .

B. Full Faith and Credit Clause

. . . The district court concluded that the adoption amendment was unconstitutional because the Full Faith and Credit Clause requires Oklahoma to recognize adoptions—including same-sex couples' adoptions—that are validly decreed in other states. . . .

The Constitution states that "Full Faith and Credit shall be given in each State to the public Acts, Records, and judicial Proceedings of every other State." U.S. Const. art. 4, § 1. The Supreme Court has often explained the purpose and policies behind the Full Faith and Credit Clause.

> The very purpose of the full faith and credit clause was to alter the status of the several states as independent foreign sovereignties, each free to ignore obligations created under the laws or by the judicial proceedings of the others, and to make them integral parts of a single nation throughout which a remedy upon a just obligation might be demanded as of right, irrespective of the state of its origin.

Milwaukee County v. M. E. White Co., 296 U.S. 268, 276-77 (1935). . . .

In applying the Full Faith and Credit Clause, the Supreme Court has drawn a distinction between statutes and judgments. Specifically, the

Court has been clear that although the Full Faith and Credit Clause applies unequivocally to the judgments[12] of sister states, it applies with less force to their statutory laws.

However, with respect to final judgments entered in a sister state, it is clear there is no "public policy" exception to the Full Faith and Credit Clause:

> Regarding judgments . . . the full faith and credit obligation is exacting. A final judgment in one State, if rendered by a court with adjudicatory authority over the subject matter and persons governed by the judgment, qualifies for recognition throughout the land. For claim and issue preclusion (res judicata) purposes, in other words, the judgment of the rendering State gains nationwide force. . . .
>
> A court may be guided by the forum State's 'public policy' in determining the law applicable to a controversy. But our decisions support no roving 'public policy exception' to the full faith and credit due judgments.

Baker [*ex rel. Thomas v. Gen. Motors Corp.*], 522 U.S. [222,] 232-33 [(1998)]. . . .

OSDH stops short of arguing that the Full Faith and Credit Clause permits states to invoke a "policy exception," but contends that requiring Oklahoma to recognize an out-of-state adoption judgment would be tantamount to giving the sister state control over the effect of its judgment in Oklahoma. Specifically, OSDH argues that the recognition of adoptive status in Oklahoma would extend the gamut of rights and responsibilities to the parents and child of the adoption order, including the right of a child to inherit from his parents, and therefore would constitute an impermissible, extra-territorial application of California law

---

[12] Despite the fact that courts may use different words, such as "decree" or "order," to refer to final adoption decisions, it is clear that all such decisions are "judgments" under the common definition of the term as a "court's final determination of the rights and obligations of the parties in a case. The term judgment includes an equitable decree and any order from which an appeal lies." Black's Law Dictionary (8th ed. 2004) (citing Fed. R. Civ. P. 54).

in Oklahoma. OSDH argues that inheritance is an Oklahoma property right which California courts lack the power to confer.

OSDH's argument improperly conflates Oklahoma's obligation to give full faith and credit to a sister state's judgment with its authority to apply its own state laws in deciding what state-specific rights and responsibilities flow from that judgment. In *Baker*, the Supreme Court drew the distinction between the mandate to give full faith and credit to another state's equity decree and the forum state's options for enforcing that decree:

> The Court has never placed equity decrees outside the full faith and credit domain. . . .
>
> Full faith and credit, however, does not mean that States must adopt the practices of other States regarding the time, manner, and mechanisms for enforcing judgments. Enforcement measures do not travel with the sister state judgment as preclusive effects do; such measures remain subject to the even-handed control of forum law. See *McElmoyle ex rel. Bailey v. Cohen*, 13 Peters 312, 325, 10 L.Ed. 177 (1839) (judgment may be enforced only as "laws [of enforcing forum] may permit"); see also Restatement (Second) of Conflict of Laws § 99 (1969) ("The local law of the forum determines the methods by which a judgment of another state is enforced.").

Baker, 522 U.S. at 234-35. . . .

A California court made the decision, in its own state and under its own laws, as to whether Jennifer Doel could adopt child E. That decision is final. If Oklahoma had no statute providing for the issuance of supplementary birth certificates for adopted children, the Doels could not invoke the Full Faith and Credit Clause in asking Oklahoma for a new birth certificate. However, Oklahoma has such a statute—i.e., already has the necessary "mechanism[] for enforcing [adoption] judgments." The Doels merely ask Oklahoma to apply its own law to "enforce" their adoption order in an "even-handed" manner.

Oklahoma continues to exercise authority over the manner in which adoptive relationships should be enforced in Oklahoma and the rights and obligations in Oklahoma flowing from an adoptive relationship. And Oklahoma has spoken on that subject:

> After the final decree of adoption is entered, the relation of parent and child and all the rights, duties, and other legal consequences of the natural relation of child and parent shall thereafter exist between the adopted child and the adoptive parents of the child and the kindred of the adoptive parents. From the date of the final decree of adoption, the child shall be entitled to inherit real and personal property from and through the adoptive parents in accordance with the statutes of descent and distribution. The adoptive parents shall be entitled to inherit real and personal property from and through the child in accordance with said statutes.
>
> After a final decree of adoption is entered, the biological parents of the adopted child, unless they are the adoptive parents or the spouse of an adoptive parent, shall be relieved of all parental responsibilities for said child and shall have no rights over the adopted child or to the property of the child by descent and distribution.

Okla. Stat. tit. 10, § 7505-6.5(A) and (B). By way of illustration, the right of a parent in Oklahoma to authorize medical treatment for her minor child, *id.*, § 170.1, extends by virtue of § 7505-6.5 to adoptive parents as well. Whatever rights may be afforded to the Doels based on their status as parent and child, those rights flow from an application of Oklahoma law, not California law.

. . . .

We hold today that final adoption orders and decrees are judgments that are entitled to recognition by all other states under the Full Faith and Credit Clause. Therefore, Oklahoma's adoption amendment is unconstitutional in its refusal to recognize final adoption orders of other states that permit adoption by same-sex couples. Because we affirm the district court on this basis, we do not reach the issues of whether the adoption amendment infringes on the Due Process or Equal Protection Clauses.

We REVERSE the district court's order in this matter to the extent it held that the Magro-Finstuen plaintiffs had standing and directed OSDH to issue new birth certificates for the Magro-Finstuen plaintiffs. The order and judgment of the district court in all other respects is AFFIRMED.

INDEX

References are to pages.

ABORTION
Constitutional limits on, 50,
  123-142
Health exception, and, 123-142

ADOPTION
Standards for adoptive parents,
  Sexual Orientation, 199-204

ALIMONY
  Generally, 89-95
Modification of, 117-122
Separation agreements, and,
  117-122

**ARTIFICIAL
REPRODUCTIVE
THERAPIES**
See In Vitro Fertilization

**BEST INTERESTS OF THE
CHILD STANDARD**
See Custody

BIRTH CONTROL
Constitution, and, 50, 123-142

CHILD ABDUCTION, 82-88,
  156-163

CHILD ABUSE
Claims of abuse, 1-10, 51-62,
  156-163, 184-198
Obesity as a form of, 171-184
Perpetrated by minors, 164-170
Religion, and, 1-10, 51-62

CHILD ABUSE (cont'd)
State authority to deal with,
  including constitutional
  limitations on, 184-198

CHILD SUPPORT
Guidelines, 102-109
Modification of, 102-109
Paternity, and 110-116
Standards for awarding, 102-109
Unmarried partners, 102-116

CHILDREN
  See also Child Abduction;
  Child Abuse; Child Support;
  Custody
Criminal law, and, 164-170
Religion, and, 1-10, 51-62
Sexuality, and, 9-74, 164-170
Unwanted, 110-116

**CONSTITUTION AND
CONSTITUTIONAL
RIGHTS**
Abortion, and, 50, 123-142
Adoption, and, 199-204
Child abuse accusations, and,
  184-198
Fathers of illegitimate children,
  and, 110-116
Privacy, and, 50, 123-42
Sex-based discrimination, and,
  110-116

CONTRACEPTION
See Abortion

CUSTODY
Hague Convention on Child
  Abduction, 82-88
Homosexuality, and, 74-82
Joint, 63-69
Jurisdiction, 82-88
Modification, 63-69
Polygamy, and, 1-10, 51-62
Religion, and, 1-10, 51-62
Relocation, and, 63-69
Unmarried parents, and, 74-82
State (emergency) authority to
  take, 1-10, 184-198

"DEFENSE OF MARRIAGE"
AMENDMENT, 30-42

DIVORCE
See Alimony; Child Support;
Custody; Property

DOCTRINE OF FAMILY
PRIVACY
See Privacy

DOMESTIC VIOLENCE
Legal Responses to, 50
Same-sex marriage, and, 41

FAMILY
Conceptions of, 43-49
Limit on Women's Equality, as,
43-49

FAMILY AND MEDICAL
LEAVE ACT, 43

FAMILY PRIVACY
See Privacy

FATHERS
Rights of, 69-74, 110-116

GENDER
DISCRIMINATION
  See also Abortion;
  Homosexuality
Family structure, and, 43-49
FMLA, and, 43
Forced pregnancy, and, 69-74
Men's claims of, 110-116
Same-sex marriage, and, 10-29
Private Limitations on, 43-49,
  142-155

HEALTH CARE
Abortion, and, 123-142
Domestic partnership benefits,
  and, 30-41
Parents' duty to provide, and,
  171-198
Right of physicians not to
  provide, and, 142-155
Right to receive, free from
  discrimination, 142-155

HOMOSEXUALITY
Adoption, 199-204
Child custody, and, 74-82
Civil Unions, and, 41
Domestic partnership benefits,
  and, 30-41
In Vitro Fertilization, and,
  142-155

HOMOSEXUALITY (cont'd)
Parenthood, and, 74-82, 142-155
Religious Discrimination, and,
   142-55
Reproduction, and, 142-155
Right to marry, and, 10-29
Right to privacy, 10-29
Same-sex marriage, and, 10-42
Suspect Classification, as 10-
   29, 154 n.*

HUSBAND AND WIFE
See also Family; Marriage;
Parents; Property

IN VITRO FERTILIZATION
   Generally, 142-155
Discrimination, and, 142-155
Religious belief, and, 142-155

JURISDCTION
International child custody, and,
   82-88

**LESBIAN AND GAY
RIGHTS**
See Homosexuality

MARITAL PROPERTY
See Property

MARRIAGE
Challenges to the traditional
   model of, 43-49
Restrictions on who may marry,
   Polygamy, 1-10
   Same-Sex, 10-42
State constitutions, and, 10-42

MINORS
See Children

MOTHERS
See Parents

NEGLECT
   See also Child Abuse
Health, and, 171-198
Intermediate dispositions,
   State liability, 184-198

PARENTS
By estoppel, 74-82
De facto, 74-82
Homosexuals, as, 74-82
Parental duties,
   Child support, 102-116
   Health care, 156-63, 171-198
Rape and Parenthood, 69-74

POLYGAMY
   See also Marriage; Religion
Custody, and, 1-10, 51-62

PREGNANCY
   See also Abortion; Sexual
   Injury
Children, and, 69-74
Forced (by rape), 69-74

PRIVACY
Abortion, and, 50, 123-142
Marriage, and, 10-29
State Constitutional right to,
   10-29

PROPERTY
Dissipation, and, 96-102
Equitable Distribution of, 89-95
Financial Misconduct, and,
  96-102
Marital and separate property
  distinguished, 89-95

RAPE
See Sexual Injury; see also
Child Abuse

RELIGION
Children, and, 1-10, 51-62
Homosexuality, and, 142-155
In Vitro Fertilization, and,
  142-155
Procreation, 142-155
Sexuality, and, 142-155

**REPRODUCTIVE
TECHNOLOGY**
See In Vitro Fertilization

SAME-SEX MARRIAGE, 10-
42

**SEPARATION
AGREEMENTS**
Enforceability, 117-122
Modification, 117-122

**SEPARATION
AGREEMENTS** (cont'd)
Murder-for-hire, and, 117-122

SEXUAL INJURY
Children, 69-74, 164-170
Claims of possible, 1-10, 51-62,
  164-170
Rights of perpetrators of, 69-74

**SEX-BASED
DISCRIMINATION**
See Gender Discrimination;
Homosexuality; Sexual Injury

SUPPORT
See Alimony; Child Support

**TERMINATION OF
PARENTAL RIGHTS**
See Neglect; Sexual Injury

VISITATION, 63-74

WOMEN
  See also Gender
  Discrimination; Pregnancy
Abortion, and, 123-142
Economic position, and, 43-49
Family as glass ceiling, 43-49
Reproduction, and, 142-155

WORK
Mothers and wives, 43-49